45.95
6PC

CACHE AND MEMORY HIERARCHY DESIGN:

A Performance-Directed Approach

Steven A. Przybylski

MORGAN KAUFMANN PUBLISHERS, INC.
SAN MATEO, CALIFORNIA

Editor	Bruce Spatz
Production Editor	Sharon Montooth
Cover Designer	Gary Head
Copy Editor	Robert Klinginsmith
Proofreader	Martha Ghent

Library of Congress Cataloging-in-Publication Data

Przybylski, Steven A.
  Cache and memory hierarchy design: a performance-directed
approach / Steven A. Przybylski.
    p.   cm.
  ISBN 1-55860-136-8
  1. Cache memory. 2. Memory hierarchy (Computer science)
I. Title
TK7895.M4P79   1990   90-6007
621.39 73--dc20   CIP

Morgan Kaufmann Publishers, Inc.

Editorial Office:
    2929 Campus Drive
    San Mateo, CA 94403

Order from:
    P.O. Box 50490
    Palo Alto, CA 94303-9953

94   93   92   91   90   5   4   3   2   1

To Michelle,

who so quickly changed my life so completely.

Preface

Over the past several years caches have become commonplace across a wide range of computer systems. Fundamentally, this book is designed to help engineers and computer scientists appreciate the significance of memory hierarchies to computer performance. I assume only a basic understanding of cache and computer system design. However, this is an advanced book on cache design in the sense that I take the reader through a thorough analysis of each of the major memory hierarchy design variables and their interdependencies. This book was written for scholars as well as those with more pragmatic interests: not only does it present concrete data on the relative performance of a wide spectrum of machines, but it also offers analytical evaluations of the underlying phenomena. I have also kept the primary results accessible to computer professionals who are not necessarily interested in the gory details, by including separate summaries of the major points together with their broad implications for trends in computer organization.

My theme is maximizing computer system performance. In the past, cache design has frequently taken a back seat to CPU design: the cache subsystem is often designed to fit the constraints imposed by the CPU implementation. The execution time of a program is fundamentally dependent on how well the two units work together to execute instructions. The execution time is most effectively minimized when the realities of cache design influence the CPU design and vice versa. Furthermore, caches have traditionally been evaluated solely on the basis of miss ratios – a metric that can often be deceiving. In this book I shift the focus of cache design from time-independent miss ratios to the true goal of computer design: maximizing system-level performance. This shift in perspective reveals many important tradeoffs that are commonly ignored in computer architecture texts as well as in practise. In addition, as multi-level cache hierarchies become more common, this book will help engineers and academics encountering them for the first time to understand the circumstances under which multi-level hierarchies can dramatically improve execution times.

The first three chapters lay the foundation on which the rest of the book rests. The introduction examines in detail the motivation for shifting the metric for the comparison of memory hierarchies from cache miss ratios to system-level performance. Chapter 2 defines the terminology and summarizes the relevant recent literature on caches. The third chapter formally presents the cache design problem as a minimization problem with four design variables – the cache size, the set-associativity, the block size and the system cycle time – and two given parameters – the main memory's latency and peak bandwidth. Given a memory system, the cache design problem is to find the cache organization and matching cycle time that together minimize the execution time of programs. Chapter 3 concludes by presenting the simulation environment and analytical models that are used throughout Chapters 4 and 5 to explore the tradeoffs inherent in single- and multi-level hierarchy design.

The focus of Chapter 4 is performance-directed cache design: the design of single-level cache hierarchies that maximize performance. The performance tradeoffs between each of the major organizational variables – size, associativity, and block size – and the appropriate temporal variables – cycle time and memory characteristics – are examined in turn. In addition, the performance attained through the use of aggressive fetch strategies is contrasted to that obtained with a common, simple strategy. Finally, the disparate effects of all these design variables are brought together in a single graph. Figure 4-35 presents the system-level performance as a function of all of the main design variables across a very large portion of the four-dimensional design space. Furthermore, by equating changes in the memory characteristics to equivalent changes in the cache size, the graph can be used to compare the performances of vastly different machines with different memory systems.

Chapter 5 deals with multi-level cache hierarchies. It begins by describing the motivation for the use of multi-level hierarchies from the perspective of the opportunities they present to increase the maximum attainable performance by decreasing the performance-optimal cycle time and reducing the memory's component of the mean cycles per instruction. Next, the characteristics of caches within performance-optimal cache hierarchies are contrasted with those of an optimal single-level cache. For instance, caches in a multi-level hierarchy are more likely to be set-associative than those in a single-level environment. Given a set of implementable caches, there is a straightforward algorithm for finding the multi-level hierarchy that achieves the maximum possible performance. The chapter concludes by discussing future trends in cache hierarchy design.

Finally, Section 6.1 summarizes the major results of the previous two chapters without the encumbering detail and analysis, and Section 6.2 discusses the realities of real-world cache design and some of the practical implications of performance-directed memory hierarchy design.

Fundamentally, this book is about what happens to cache and memory hierarchy design when the design problem is viewed from the perspective of minimizing execution times instead of miss rates. By systematically approaching each of the major design variables from this perspective, the characteristics of performance-optimal single- and multi-level cache hierarchies are exposed.

Much of the research presented in this book was carried out at Stanford University with Professors John Hennessy and Mark Horowitz in 1987 and 1988 [Przybylski 88]. I am indebted to them for their support and guidance while I was at Stanford. I would also like to thank my many friends who helped make my tenure there fun as well as rewarding: Helen Davis, Jonathan and Barbara Rose, Mark Horowitz, Jun Nogami, Arturo Salz, Rich Simoni, John Vlissides, Michael Levine, Eric Linder, Ed Hudson, Chris Rowen, Thomas Gross, Norm Jouppi, and the accompanying cast of thousands. I would also like to acknowledge the love and support of my brother, Martin, his wife Susanne, Elizabeth and Hans Wolf, and especially my parents, for enduring through what must have seemed an interminable graduate career.

While at Stanford, I was funded by a Postgraduate Scholarship from the Natural Sciences and Engineering Research Council of Canada and by Defense Advanced Research Projects Agency contracts #MDA903-79-C-0680, #MDA903-83-C-0335 and #N00014-87-K-0828. I am indebted to Ray Kunita, Allen Roberts and Jake Vigil of MIPS Computer Systems for their encouragement and the resources needed for this book to come to fruition.

Above all though, I am eternally grateful to my wife, Michelle Deatrick Przybylski, who has so dramatically changed the course of my life. In addition to being a scholar of international education, she is an exceptional writer and copy editor. After 28 years, it was finally she that taught me the proper use of the English language. That this book and the dissertation from which it is derived are readable is primarily her doing.

Steven Przybylski
April, 1990

Contents

Preface   **v**

Symbols   **xi**

1. Introduction   **1**

2. Background Material   **9**

    2.1. Terminology   9
    2.2. Previous Cache Studies   13
    2.3. Analytical Modelling   14
    2.4. Temporal Analysis in Cache Design   16
    2.5. Multi-Level Cache Hierarchies   18

3. The Cache Design Problem and Its Solution   **21**

    3.1. Problem Description   21
    3.2. Two Complementary Approaches   26
    3.3. Experimental Method   27
        3.3.1. The Simulator and Related Infrastructure   27
        3.3.2. The System Models   29
        3.3.3. The Input Traces   33
        3.3.4. Observations, Lessons and Summary   35
    3.4. Analytical Approach   36

4. Performance-Directed Cache Design   **45**

    4.1. Speed – Size Tradeoffs   46
    4.2. Speed – Set Size Tradeoffs   57
    4.3. Block Size – Memory Speed Tradeoffs   67
        4.3.1. Optimal Block Size with Cycle Time Degradation   78
        4.3.2. Independent Block and Fetch Sizes   85
        4.3.3. Optimal Block Size with Alternate Fetch Strategies   90
    4.4. Globally Optimum Cache Design   101

5. Multi-Level Cache Hierarchies 111

5.1. Introduction 111
5.2. Motivation 112
5.3. Intermediate Cache Design 115
    5.3.1. Decomposition of the Hierarchy 115
    5.3.2. Speed – Size Tradeoffs 118
    5.3.3. Set Size Tradeoffs 127
    5.3.4. Block Size and Fetch Size Tradeoffs 130
    5.3.5. Summary 133
5.4. Optimal Memory Hierarchy Design 134
5.5. A Detailed Example 144
5.6. Fundamental Limits to Performance 149
5.7. Summary 156

6. Summary, Implications and Conclusions 159

6.1. Summary 159
6.2. The Implications of Performance-Directed Cache Design 168
    6.2.1. Real-Life Cache Design 168
    6.2.2. Rules of Thumb for Cache Designers 172
6.3. Suggestions for Further Research 175

Appendix A. Validation of the Empirical Results 177

A.1. The VAX Traces 177
A.2. The R2000 Traces 181
A.3. Combining the R2000 and the VAX Results 186

Appendix B. Modelling Write Strategy Effects 201

References 207

Index 221

Symbols

Problem Statement:

$\mathbf{C}(C,S,A,B)$ A specific cache organization.

C Cache size in words.[1]

S Number of sets.

A Degree of associativity.

B Block size, in words. *Block size* is frequently used to mean *equal block and fetch sizes.*

F Fetch size, in words.

m (Local) miss ratio.[2]

M Global or solo miss ratio.

$L_1, L_2, \ldots, L_i, \ldots, L_n$

     The first, second, through n^{th} levels of a multi-level cache hierarchy. Main memory is level L_{n+1}.

T_{Total} The total execution time in seconds of a program or trace.

$m(\mathbf{C}) = f(S,C,A,B)$

     The function relating the miss ratio and the organizational parameters.

$N_{Total} = g(m(\mathbf{C}),B,LA,TR,t_{CPU})$

     The function relating the total CPU cycle count to the miss rate, memory characteristics and the cycle time.

$t_{CPU} = h(C,S,A,B)$

     The function relating the CPU cycle time to the cache parameters.

---

[1] One word is defined as four bytes.

[2] "Miss rate" and "miss ratio" are used interchangeably.

Execution Time Model; Section 3.4:

N	A cycle count over a whole trace or program.
N_{Total}	Total cycle count over a whole trace or program.
$N_{Execute}$	Number of cycles not doing memory references.
N_{MM}	Number of cycles waiting for main memory.
N_{Ifetch}	Number of instruction fetches in the program.
N_{Load}	Number of loads in the program.
N_{Store}	Number of stores in the program.
N_{Read}	Number of read references reaching a cache.
N_{Write}	Number of write references reaching a cache.
n_{Write}	Number of cycles needed to perform a write to a cache.
$\overline{n}_{Write}$	Average number of cycles needed to complete a write operation, including write-back and write-buffer delays.
$\overline{n}_{MMread}$	Average number of cycles needed to do a main memory read.
n_{MMread}	Number of cycles needed to do a main memory read in the absence of any delays. $n_{MMread} = la + \frac{B}{tr}$.
$\overline{n}_{ReadDelay}$	Average number of cycles per memory fetch spent waiting for main memory to be free.
n_{Li}	The read access time of L_i in CPU cycles.
t_{Li}	The read access time of L_i in nanoseconds. $t_{Li} = t_{CPU} \times n_{Li} = t'_{Li} \times n'_{Li} = t_{Li-1} \times K_{Li} \times n'_{Li}$.
LA	Main memory latency in seconds.
la	Main memory latency in (CPU) cycles.
TR	Main memory to cache transfer rate in words per second.
tr	Main memory to cache transfer rate in words per cycle.
$\frac{B}{tr}$	Transfer period: the number of cycles needed to transfer a block from main memory into a cache.
$N_{Transfer}, N_{Tr}$	Number of cycles spent transferring in data from main memory.
$N_{Latency}, N_{La}$	Number of cycles spent waiting for transfers from main memory to begin.

Associativity Modelling; Section 4.2:

$r(A,B)$

The ratios of miss ratios when the associativity is doubled. $r(A{=}a,B) = \frac{m(A=2a,B)}{m(A=a,B)}$.

Δt_{IBE}

The incremental set-associative break-even time. The incremental set-associative break-even time for a set associativity of $A{=}a$ is the change in the cycle time that is equivalent to a change in associativity from $A{=}\frac{a}{2}$ to $A{=}a$. A cycle time degradation greater than this amount results in a net decrease in performance.

Δt_{CBE}

The cumulative break-even time for associativity $A{=}a$ is cycle time change equivalent to a change from a direct-mapped cache ($A{=}1$) to a set-associaitve cache of associativity $A{=}a$. It is the sum of the incremental break-even times of all associativities less than A.

Block Size Modelling; Section 4.3:

$g(B)$

The ratio of the fully associative miss rate to the direct-mapped miss rate for the same sized cache. $g(B) = \frac{m(S=1,B)}{m(A=1,B)}$.

$R(B)$

The ratios of miss ratios when the block size is doubled. $R(B{=}b) = \frac{m(B=2b)}{m(B=b)}$.

k

Fractional cycle time degradation accompanying a doubling of the block size.

$K(B)$

Aggregate cycle time degradation across a change in block size. $K(B) = \frac{k-1}{k^{\log_2 B} - 1}$.

Optimal Hierarchy Specification; Section 5.4:

t'_{Li}

The internal operating cycle of L_i.

t'_{min}

The minimum internal operating cycle time of a cache.

$n'_{Li}(W)$

The number of internal cycles to satisfy a read request as a function of the read request width.

n'_{la}

The number of internal cycles of latency before data begins to be passed upstream.

$n'_{tr}(W)$	The number of internal cycles needed to transfer W words upstream.
K_{Li}	The internal cycle time of L_{i+1} in L_i internal cycles.
P	A probability.

Agarwal's Miss Ratio Model:

τ	The chunk size: the number of references over which u is measured.
$u(B)$	The number of unique blocks touched in a chunk.
T	The total trace length, in references.
U	The total number of unique blocks touched in the trace.
$c(S,A)$	The number of collisions to a single set within a chuck.
$P(a)$	The probability that a blocks map onto one set over the course of a chunk.
t_s	Duration of a time slice, in chunks.
$f(t)$	The fraction of blocks belonging to a given process that are purged by other processes between time slices.
$u'(B)$	The sum of $u(B)$ for all the other processes sharing the cache a multiprogramming system.

Chapter 1

Introduction

Computer systems are, in general, composed of three basic units: a CPU, which
does the work; a memory, which stores instructions and data; and an I/O system,
which moves information into and out of the system. The process of executing a
program involves repeatedly retrieving an instruction from memory to the CPU,
fetching any operands that it specifies, performing an operation and possibly
writing a result to that same memory. The time that it takes to execute a program
is thus critically dependent on the speed with which instructions and data can be
fetched and written to main memory. Main memory is burdened with the need
to store all the information that a processor needs over significant periods of
time. Unfortunately, like bureaucracies, memories get slower as they get larger.
Main memories are typically much slower than the CPU: the CPU's ability to
execute instructions and process data far outstrips the main memory's ability to
provide them. To rectify this mismatch, most computers today include caches:
small, fast memories that are conceptually and physically close to the CPU and
that, with high probability, provide the instructions and data needed by the CPU
at a rate more in line with the CPU's demands. Only when the cache does not
contain the necessary information is the much slower main memory queried.
Caches dramatically reduce the average time that it takes for the CPU to access
desired information. Caching is by far the simplest and most effective

mechanism for dramatically improving the execution time of programs and thus system-level performance.

Caches work by automatically retaining information that the CPU has used or generated recently. Their success in reducing the mean time that it takes for the CPU to fetch an instruction or datum relies on a high probability that a requested datum is contained in the cache – that is, that it was used or generated recently. The expectation that instructions and data that are currently in use will be referenced again soon is called temporal locality. Spatial locality refers to the likelihood that two items adjacent in main memory will be needed within a short span of time of each other. Caches are successful because programs generally exhibit good spatial and temporal locality – high probabilities of data use and reuse based on current and recent activity. The frequency with which the cache does not hold the piece of information demanded of it by the CPU is called the miss ratio. The consequence of a cache miss is that the item must be fetched from the slower main memory. While this is taking place, the CPU generally sits idle, since it does not have the item that it needs to proceed with the sequential execution of instructions. The higher the miss ratio, the more frequently the CPU idly waits for instructions and data to be fetched from main memory, and the longer it takes programs to execute. Since the execution time is thus dependent on the cache's miss ratio, miss ratios have traditionally been the metric by which caches are evaluated and judged.

A program's execution time on a computer with a cache is dependent on three factors:

1. The number of instructions needed to perform the desired task.
2. The average number of CPU cycles needed to execute an instruction.
3. The CPU's cycle time.

Figure 1-1 illustrates that the middle factor, the mean cycles per instruction, is easily broken down into three separate factors: the base number of cycles per instruction independent of cache miss effects, the number of references per instruction, and the mean number of additional cycles spent satisfying a memory reference. The four circles in Future 1-1 represent four points of leverage that computer systems designers have in their constant search for faster machines. By applying technology, resources or creativity to one of these aspects of the system design, the designer can influence one or more of the factors that together determine the overall performance level.

The first factor, the number of instructions needed to perform a function, is commonly referred to as the path length. The minimum path length is a function

$$\begin{array}{l} \text{Execution} \\ \text{Time} \end{array} = \begin{array}{l} \text{Instruction} \\ \text{Count} \end{array} \times \begin{array}{l} \text{Cycles per} \\ \text{Instruction} \end{array} \times \begin{array}{l} \text{Cycle} \\ \text{Time} \end{array}$$

$$= \begin{array}{l} \text{Instruction} \\ \text{Count} \end{array} \times \left(\begin{array}{l} \text{CPU Cycles} \\ \text{per Instr.} \end{array} + \begin{array}{l} \text{Memory Cycles} \\ \text{per Instr.} \end{array} \right) \times \begin{array}{l} \text{Cycle} \\ \text{Time} \end{array}$$

$$= \begin{array}{l} \text{Instruction} \\ \text{Count} \end{array} \times \left[\begin{array}{l} \text{CPU Cycles} \\ \text{per Instr.} \end{array} + \left(\begin{array}{l} \text{References} \\ \text{per Instr.} \end{array} \times \begin{array}{l} \text{Cycles per} \\ \text{Reference} \end{array} \right) \right] \times \begin{array}{l} \text{Cycle} \\ \text{Time} \end{array}$$

Instruction Set Architecture · Compiler Technology · CPU Implementation · Cache and Memory Hierarchy

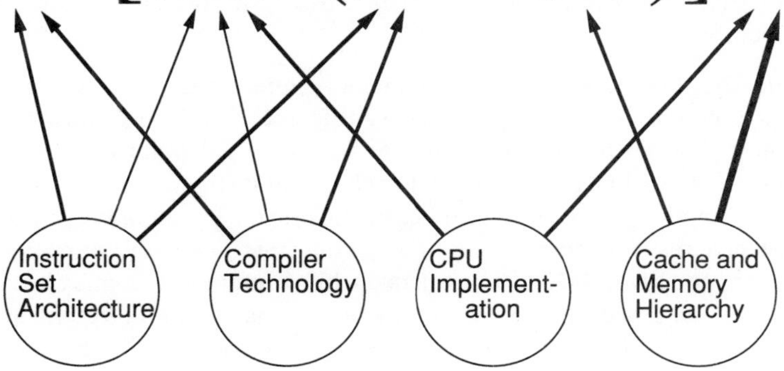

Influences on Performance

Figure 1-1

of the instruction set architecture and is common across all implementations of an architecture. The actual path length of a compiled program is also a function of the compiler's use of the instruction set architecture and its ability to generate efficient code. The main way that optimizing compilers improve execution times is by producing programs with fewer executed instructions – that is, whose path length is closer to the minimum path length for that program and instruction set.[3]

The mean cycles per instruction (CPI)– being the combination of the CPU cycles per instruction, the mean references per instruction and the mean cycles

---

[3] More precisely, optimizing compilers properly strive to minimize the sum of the expected execution times of the instructions needed to implement a function.

per reference – is primarily determined by a computer's organization. The number of CPU cycles needed to execute an instruction in the absence of any cache misses will vary significantly from one implementation of an architecture to another: the base CPU cycles per instruction is chiefly dependent on the degree of pipelining in the implementation, the hardware resources available for the execution of the instructions, and the complexity of the instruction set architecture. Greater parallelism in the hardware, either temporally or spatially, overlaps the execution of more instructions, thereby reducing each instruction's contribution to the overall execution time. The compiler can affect this factor by preferentially selecting instructions with shorter execution times or by reordering instructions so that they share the hardware resources more efficiently.

Finally, the average number of memory references per instruction and the average number of cycles per memory reference combine to form the average number of cycles per instruction due to the memory hierarchy. The first of these two factors is a function of the architecture and instruction selection algorithms of the compilers. Though it need not be, this factor is generally considered to be constant across implementations of an architecture. All implementations have to execute the same object files generated by a common compiler because local area networks and file servers promote the sharing of object files by many machines. In a sense, by mandating object code compatibility across machines, the system designer and compiler writer have together lost a degree of freedom with which to tune the performance of each implementation of an architecture.

The average number of cycles needed to satisfy a memory reference is dependent on the organization and speed of the memory hierarchy of the machine. More specifically, it is dependent on the frequency with which the requested data is in the cache (the cache miss rate), the number of cycles needed to fetch the data from the cache if it is there, and the number of cycles needed to fetch the data from main memory in the case of a cache miss. Clearly, decreasing the cache miss rate decreases the number of cycles needed to execute an instruction and improves overall performance. When a cache is being designed in isolation from the rest of the system, minimizing its miss ratio simultaneously maximizes the system performance. This straightforward decomposition of the overall design task into the seemingly distinct cache and CPU design problems, combined with the monotonic relationship between miss rate and performance, has led to the strong focus on miss ratios in the design and analysis of cache subsystems.

Unfortunately, an exclusive focus on miss rates is misleading because the important dimension of time is ignored. Miss ratios are independent of time in that a cache exhibits the same miss ratio regardless of the speed of the main memory or of the CPU. All but a few of the many papers about uniprocessor cache design fail to discuss any of the ways that caches affect performance through temporal dependencies. Decisions about the cache's organization influence both the total cycle count and the cycle time of the resulting computer system – the last of the factors that determine the execution time of programs. By concentrating on miss ratios as an indicator of performance, students of cache design have ignored the ways in which the memory hierarchy affects performance through the cycle time. The thick arrow in Figure 1-1 represents the cache hierarchy's influence on the cycle time: it is the focus of much of this book.

Since the overall cycle count of a program depends on both the miss ratio and the miss penalty, the impact of the cache organization on overall performance needs to be analyzed in light of the main memory's characteristics. Changes in the miss ratio can cause either dramatic or negligible changes in the performance of a machine, depending on the speed of main memory. In addition, there are aspects of a cache's organization – the write policy and fetch strategy – that directly affect the cycle count in other ways than through the miss ratio and miss penalty. Focusing solely on the time-independent miss ratios is dangerous because the designer can be easily distracted from his or her goal of producing the fastest, most cost-effective computer.

The cache's cycle time and the CPU's cycle time are interdependent in that, for the most part, they cannot be set individually. Since they are forced to be equal, the larger of the two determines the smaller. The key to this link between a cache's organization and the CPU cycle time is the observation that smaller memories can generally be made to cycle faster. More generally, the maximum rate at which a cache can cycle is dependent on many factors, including its size, associativity and block size.[4] Ignoring the temporal implications of these organizational decisions removes from consideration any tradeoffs that involve the cycle time, and failure to choose a cycle time that accommodates the needs of both the CPU and the cache leads to less than optimal performance. It is crucial to realize that short cycle times and low miss rates are at odds with each other: large caches have low miss rates but long cycle times; small caches have short cycle times but high miss rates. Engineering is the art of finding the appropriate balance or tradeoff between such opposing forces.

In recent years there has been a growing interest in multi-level cache hierarchies. High performance systems commonly have more than one level of caching between the CPU and main memory. Each successive cache is larger and slower than its predecessor. If a desired instruction or datum is not in the first-level cache (the one conceptually closest to the CPU) then the second level cache is queried. If it is not there, then the subsequent level is checked, and

---

[4] These terms are defined in Section 2.1.

so on all the way to the main memory if necessary. This recent introduction of multi-level cache hierarchies stems from the realization that there is a temporal link between a cache organization and cycle time. In the absence of any such link, single-level caches would get larger and larger, with ever-diminishing miss ratios and improving performance. However, since larger caches are slower, there comes a point when it is no longer advantageous to increase the cache size. Any further increases in the cache size would increase the system cycle time sufficiently to overcome any reduction in the miss rate. The net result would be a reduction in the overall performance. Simply put, for any given set of circumstances, there is a maximum performance level that can be obtained with a single level of caching. By employing multi-level cache hierarchies, designers can transcend this single-level performance limit and get shorter execution times out of the same main memory system.

This book is divided into two main parts. The first three chapters lay the foundation on which the final three rest. In addition to presenting the necessary background material and terminology, Chapters 1 through 3 introduce the empirical and analytical methods used to generate the results presented in the second half. The final three chapters in turn present the single-level and multi-level cache design problems and discuss the implications for cache design as it is practiced in industry.

Given that caches are such a simple and effective way of increasing computer performance, it is not surprising that they have been extensively studied since their introduction in the late 1960s [Wilkes 65]. After describing the terminology used throughout this book, Chapter 2 presents a summary of the previous cache studies on which the substantive chapters build. In particular, it pays special attention to those works which have concentrated on analytical modelling of caches, the temporal dependencies in cache design and multi-level cache hierarchies. Chapter 3 formally states the cache optimization problem in terms of minimizing overall execution time and briefly illustrates the nature of some of the tradeoffs examined in depth in subsequent chapters. It also discusses the techniques and tools used to investigate this optimization problem: trace-driven simulation is used to expose the essence of several tradeoffs for a particular set of conditions, and analytical modelling is used to generalize those specific empirical results to a wider portion of the overall cache design space. In the first half of the chapter, the simulator, the system models and input traces are each described in turn. Appendix A presents the input traces in more detail and discusses the credibility and limitations of the analyses based on this simulation study. It also compares the cache miss rates of the RISC and CISC processors used to generate the traces.

Chapters 4 and 5 form the bulk of the substantive half of the book. Chapter 4 considers the single-level cache design problem. It examines four key design decisions from the perspective of maximizing system performance. The cache size, set associativity, block size and the fetch strategy all affect the overall performance through both the cycle time and the cycle count. The analysis of the influence of the block size is extended to include the effects of two other very important elements: the fetch size and the fetch strategy. After the tradeoffs involving the individual organizational parameters are examined, the results are combined into a unified mechanism for directly evaluating widely varying implementations. An equivalency or mapping between all four design variables is established by determining the changes in each that have the same impact on performance. Figure 4-35 makes use of this equivalency to simultaneously display the relative performance as a function of the cache size, the set associativity, the block size and the cycle time. The figure thus permits the direct comparison of the performance obtained by an extremely wide range of systems.

Chapter 5 draws on the results of Chapter 4 to illustrate that there is a limit to the performance that can be achieved with a single cache. Specifically, the primary path to higher performance implementations of an architecture is through reduced cycle times. Performance-directed cache analysis reveals two dilemmas facing machine designers: short cycle times coupled with small fast caches are not optimal, and there is a definite upper bound to the performance that a single-level cache can deliver. If the cycle time is too short, it is beneficial to performance to increase the cycle time to facilitate a larger cache size.

Chapter 5 shows that implementing a multi-level cache hierarchy can dramatically improve the overall performance over the single-level case by reducing the total cycle count and the performance-optimal cycle time. Unfortunately, the problem of optimal cache design becomes more impenetrable when there are several layers to the memory hierarchy. The complexity of the design problem is increased more than linearly over the single-level case in that there are many more parameters to be specified and they depend on each other in new, non-trivial ways. The first and most important step in dealing with this design problem is illustrating how it can be decomposed into individual pieces. Chapter 5 demonstrates how to view the design problem from the correct perspective so that all the knowledge and intuition that we have gained about the single-level caches can be applied to the multi-level case. Chapter 5 then examines the problem of designing a layer at an arbitrary depth in a multi-level memory hierarchy and comments specifically on how the design problem and its solution differ from the normal, single-level case. In the process, it again treats each of the major organizational variables – cache size, set size and block size – in turn before dealing with the problem as a whole. It presents a straightforward dynamic programming algorithm for selecting the performance-optimal memory hierarchy from a given set of implementable caches. An example of the use of the algorithm illustrates many of the important characteristics of multi-level hierarchies discussed in the earlier sections. Finally, an analytical model of the relationship between a cache's access time and its miss ratio is used to speculate about the characteristics of performance-optimal memory hierarchies in general and about future trends in memory hierarchy design.

Chapter 6 brings together the empirical and analytical results of Chapters 4 and 5. After summarizing and distilling the main observations of those two chapters, it places them in perspective by relating them to the problems of "real world" cache design. After discussing the important differences between cache design for a real machine and cache design for an academic study, it presents a set of "rules of thumb" designed to help designers quickly zero in on the best design for their specific set of circumstances.

Fundamentally, this book is about the changes that occur to the cache design process when system-level performance is used as the metric for evaluation of uniprocessor cache and memory subsystems. Performance-directed cache design is the result: the systematic treatment of each of the major cache organizational variables from the perspective of maximizing system-level performance. It is also about the consequences of this design style – that is, performance-optimal caches and memory hierarchies.

Chapter 2

Background Material

Not by silence does one become a sage if one be
foolish and untaught. But the wise man who, as if
holding a pair of scales, takes what is good and
leaves out what is evil, is indeed a sage. . . . He who
understands both sides in this world is called a sage.

– Buddha

This chapter and the next provide the foundation on which this book rests. The
first two layers of this foundation are a set of definitions and a brief discussion
of the most relevant previous works on caches. The results of Chapters 4 and 5
rely on three specific concepts: the temporal effects in cache design, analytical
models of caches, and multi-level cache hierarchies. Sections 2.3 through 2.5
explore these topics in a bit more depth.

2.1. Terminology

One difficulty with the existing literature on caches is inconsistent and
conflicting terminology. Generally speaking, this book adopts the terminology
that A.J. Smith uses in his detailed survey of cache design [Smith 82]. In the list
of definitions that follows, the bold-faced terms are those that a reader familiar
with uniprocessor cache design should review. They include non-standard
definitions and expressions referring to multi-level hierarchies. The final
paragraphs note and rationalize the few deviations from Smith's usage.

9

Cache: A cache is a small, hopefully fast, memory that at any one
                    time can hold the contents of a fraction of the overall
                    memory of the machine. Its organization is specified by its
                    size, number of sets, associativity, block size, sub-block
                    size, fetch strategy and write strategy. The total size is given
                    as the product of the other three primary organizational
                    parameters: degree of associativity, number of sets and
                    block size. Any layer in a hierarchy of caches can contain
                    either one unified cache for both instructions and data or two
                    separate caches, one specifically for each reference stream.
                    These two alternatives are referred to as the basic
                    organizations.[5] The reader is referred to any introductory
                    computer organization text for a description of the basic
                    theory and practise of cache design, and the fundamentals of
                    their operation [Hennessy 90, Hamacher 78].

First-Level Cache:
                    The cache closest to the CPU is denoted L1. If the cache
                    level is split, the instruction and data caches are individually
                    referred to as L1I and L1D. The first-level cache is also
                    commonly know as the primary cache.

Second-Level Cache:
                    In a multi-level cache hierarchy, the one beyond L1 from the
                    CPU is called L2. Cache at an arbitrary level in the
                    hierarchy is denoted Li. The second-level cache is also
                    frequently called the secondary cache.

Main Memory: The main memory, being the last level in any memory
                    hierarchy, is designated as MM.

Multi-Level Cache or Memory Hierarchy:
                    These terms are almost synonymous. The only difference is
                    whether or not the main memory is counted as a layer. If
                    there is a single level of caching, the memory hierarchy has
                    two levels, but the cache hierarchy has only one level, and
                    so the term multi-level cache hierarchy is not applicable.
                    When referring to caches in a multi-level cache hierarchy,
                    caches closer to the CPU (if any) are called predecessor or
                    upstream caches, while those closer to main memory are
                    referred to as successor or downstream caches.

Block: The unit of data for which there is an address tag is a block.
                    It is also commonly called a Line [Smith 87a]. The tag
                    indicates which portion of main memory, called a memory
                    block, is currently occupying this block in the cache. Since

---

[5] A split instruction/data cache is said to have a Harvard organization.

the block size and the fetch size are most frequently the same size, much of the time *block size* is used to refer to the pair of equal variables.

Set:

A set is the collection of blocks, the tags for which are checked in parallel. It is also the collection of blocks any one of which can hold a particular memory block. If the number of sets is one, the cache is called fully associative, because all the tags must be checked to determine that a reference missed. Typically, a contiguous set of address bits selects which set a memory block can reside in.

(Degree of) Associativity:

The number of blocks in a set is called the set size or the degree of associativity. If the number is one, the cache is said to be direct-mapped. If a cache is neither direct-mapped nor fully associative, it is called set-associative.

Sub-block:

A sub-block is the unit of data with which a valid bit is associated. In the case of write-back caches, it can also be the quantity that has a unique dirty bit. Its size can vary from one byte to many words. The sub-block size must be less than or equal to the block size.

Fetch Size:

The amount of memory that is fetched from the next level in the hierarchy as a unit is the fetch size. It must be a multiple of the sub-block size, but it can be smaller or larger than the block size. Smith calls this the transfer size [Smith 87a], while Hill calls it the sub-block size [Hill 87]. The most common situation is equal block and fetch sizes. In this case, *block size* is frequently used to refer to the pair of variables.

Read:

A read request to a cache is a request to present a consecutive collection of words of a predefined length at a given address. The CPU generates instruction fetch and load references, both of which are reads. Read requests can sometimes cross block boundaries, in which case they are generally treated as two or more distinct requests.

Write:

A write request consists of an address, a predefined number of sub-blocks, and a mask indicating which words in the collection are actually to be written because they are dirty. The CPU generates stores, which are write requests to the first-level cache.

Read Miss:

A miss is a read request for data not completely contained in the cache. A miss occurs either when none of the tags in the appropriate set matches the high-order address bits of the request, or when one or more of the requested sub-blocks in a matching block are invalid.

Local (Read) Miss Ratio:

The local read miss ratio is defined as the number read misses in a cache divided by the number of **read** requests presented to that cache. Miss ratio and miss rate are synonymous.

Global (Read) Miss Ratio:

The global read miss ratio is defined as the number of read misses in a cache divided by the number of **read** requests generated by the CPU. It is a measure of the performance of the overall cache hierarchy from the cache in question up to the processor.

Solo (Read) Miss Ratio:

The solo miss ratio is the miss ratio of a cache when it is the only cache in the memory hierarchy. When a cache is part of a deeper memory hierarchy, its global miss ratio can be less than its solo miss ratio, depending on the influences of upstream caches.

(Local) Read Traffic Ratio:

The local read traffic ratio of a cache is the number of words fetched from the next level in the hierarchy divided by the number of words fetched from the cache. The global read traffic ratio is the same numerator divided by the number of words fetched by the CPU.

(Local) Write Traffic Ratio:

This is the ratio of the number of words written out by a cache to the number of words written out to the previous level. It is calculated by counting either the dirty blocks in their entirety or just the dirty words.

Fetch Strategy: The fetch strategy or policy is the algorithm for deciding when a fetch of some data from the next level in the hierarchy is going to be initiated, which address is to be fetched, and which word or group of words is to be returned first.

Write Strategy: The write policy is all the details of how writes are handled in a cache. The basic choices are write-through and write-back [Smith 82], but they must be accompanied by a selection of write buffering (width and depth) and a strategy for dealing with a write miss.

Replacement Strategy:

The algorithm for choosing which block of a set will receive a newly fetched block of data is the replacement policy. The most common choices are Random and Least Recently Used

	(LRU). For a direct-mapped cache, there is only one block per set, so there is no choice.

Word: A word is defined to be 32 bits.

The major deviations from common terminology are *sub-block*, *miss ratio*, and *fetch size*. Sub-block is used to denote the unit associated with a valid bit because this quantity can be smaller than a block [Agarwal 87a, Smith 87a]. In contrast, Hill uses sub-block to mean the fetch size [Hill 84, Hill 87], and Liptay uses block for sub-block and sector for block [Liptay 68]. This book adopts *fetch size* instead of sub-block [Hill 87], or transfer size [Smith 87a] in order to associate it more with just fetches, as opposed to all bus transactions. The number of words in a write transaction is frequently different from the number of words in a read [Freitas 88].

For conceptual and analytical simplicity, the miss ratio is defined solely in terms of read operations, as opposed to read and write operations. Writes are generally handled differently from reads, so their impact on performance is related to different effects. One of the main goals of the write strategy is to hide writes as much as possible, and consequently the importance of a write miss depends strongly on the write strategy. The contributions to the overall execution time of reads and writes and their misses are dependent on different things, and lumping them together into a single metric is counter productive. Algebraically, equations that accurately attribute cycles to operations are significantly burdened with unnecessary terms if the miss ratios are combined.

2.2. Previous Cache Studies

Caches are currently found in all classes of computers from personal computers to supercomputers. Their prominence stems from the fact that they are among the simplest and most effective ways of improving performance. It is not surprising then that cache design has been extensively studied over the years. A recent bibliography listed over 400 papers, books and notes published since 1968 [Smith 86], and numerous new papers appear each year in various forums. Each of the major design decisions (for example, size [Agarwal 87b, Smith 85a], associativity [Hill 88, Hill 89, Puzak 85, Singh 88, Smith 78a, So 88], basic organization [Mulder 87, Smith 83, Smith 85b], block size [Smith 87a] and fetch strategy [Rau 77a, Smith 78b]) has been the focus of many papers. A survey paper by A.J. Smith gives the most complete summary of these issues [Smith 82]. CPU caches memories have also been presented in varying degrees of detail in a number of books on computer architecture and memory system design [Hamacher 78, Hennessy 90, Matick 77, Pohm 83, Sieworek 82, Stone

90]. With a few exceptions [Agarwal 87b, Hill 87, Smith 87a], the metrics used to evaluate and compare caches consistently have been miss rates and transfer ratios [Goodman 85, Hill 84].

Over the years, the analysis of caches has become more sophisticated in that researchers have been more aware of the processes underlying cache behaviour. Consequently, they have taken more care that their results are reliable and applicable to real design situations. Several researchers have taken accurate measurements of real computer systems [Agarwal 86, Clark 83] and generated address traces that exhibit proper operating system and multiprogramming characteristics [Agarwal 86, Alexander 86]. Individual aspects of reference streams have been studied, including stores [Smith 79], working set behaviour [Kobayashi 89, Strecker 83, Thiebaut 87a, Thiebaut 89], variations in miss rates with workload [Smith 85a, Wong 88], programming environment and architecture [Alpert 84, Mitchell 86, Peng 89]. More recently, the development of commercial multiprocessors has sparked a great deal of research into cache coherence protocols and cache design for shared memory multiprocessors in general [Archibald 86, Atkinson 87, Hill 86, Jog 88, Miya 85, Thacker 86, Thacker 87, Vernon 89].

The primary tools for the study of caches are analytical models and simulations. There are several important new techniques for speeding up cache simulations which use either inclusion properties to facilitate simultaneous simulations of several cache organizations [Hill 87, Mattson 70] or redundancy in the reference stream to reduce the trace size [Puzak 85]. Modelling methods have improved through the application of more insight into the processes that determine a cache's behaviour [Agarwal 89].

Integrated circuit technologies have improved to the extent that a single chip can contain a complete processor and at least a small cache. Consequently, interest in studying small caches has increased. Even though the goal has explicitly been to get the most performance out of a limited silicon area, most of the studies have not ventured beyond a consideration of hit rates [Alpert 83, Alpert 88, Agarwal 87a, Hill 84, Katz 85, MacGregor 84].

2.3. Analytical Modelling

Analytical models and algebraic analysis of program and cache behaviour have been used since caches first appeared [Agarwal 89, Chow 76, Denning 68, Haikala 84a, McCrosky 86, Rao 78, Rau 77b, Singh 88, Smith 78a, Smith 79, Smith 87a, Strecker 83, Thiebaut 87b]. For the most part, the stated purposes for development of analytical models include one or more of the following:

- Allow for quick and moderately accurate estimation of a performance metric, be it miss ratio, total cycle count or execution time.

- Provide some intuitive insight into the underlying processes, with the intent that through understanding come better and more robust designs.

- Corroborate simulation results and vice versa. Agreement between an analytical model and some simulation results allows for limited generalization of any conclusions based on the empirical results beyond the portion of the design space that was simulated.

In all cases where the first benefit is cited, the reader's enthusiasm is moderated by a statement to the effect that the model is a simplification of reality and that though it may be good for general performance estimates or comparative analyses, detailed simulations are needed to pinpoint the value of the metric for any given design and workload. A common philosophy is that models are fine for making course design decisions but that a simulation study is needed to "fine tune" the result of this first phase of the design process.

The models found in the literature vary immensely in their complexity and applicability. The range is from the straightforward, probabilistic model of just a few terms and parameters [Smith 78a] to more sophisticated models involving measured and derived input parameters [Agarwal 89]. Generally, the greater the need for accuracy, reliability and a large range of applicability, the more complex the equations and the reasoning behind them.

An elegant exception to the rule is the power law model developed by Singh, Stone and Thiebaut [Singh 88, Thiebaut 87b]. They begin by analyzing the number of unique lines referenced as a function of time. This rate is independent of the cache size. The miss ratio is just the time derivative of this function, evaluated at the appropriate point. This yields a surprisingly accurate model for medium to large fully associative caches for a variety of block sizes. The model only contains four parameters, which are measures of the working set size, the temporal and spatial localities of reference, and the interaction between the two localities of reference. Most significantly, it clearly shows a power relationship between the cache size and the miss rate – a result that is illustrated in Section 4.1.

In addition to the models that predict a given cache's performance, several researchers have attempted to develop an algorithm that finds the "best" cache or memory hierarchy [Chow 75, Chow 76, MacDonald 75, Welch 78]. The object of minimization has consistently been the average access time subject to some cost constraints, though the notion of cost varies among the studies. The researchers have all been forced to make gross assumptions about various relationships between cycle times, miss rates and costs as needed to make the minimization problem algebraically tractable. In spite of these simplifications, they have made an important contribution in demonstrating that given a set of available memory technologies and a fixed overall cost, there is a minimum average access time that can be obtained, regardless of the number of levels in the storage hierarchy. It is unfortunate, however, that these procedures lack practicality because of the assumptions made as well as the impenetrable and unintuitive forms of the results.

2.4. Temporal Analysis in Cache Design

The papers that have specifically considered temporal issues have appeared only recently. One of the first was Smith's analysis of the choice of block size for a cache and the influence of that choice on the cycle count [Smith 87a]. He assumed that the memory access time consists of a latency portion and a transfer time, the latter of which is dependent on the block size and the transfer rate. Given this model, Smith goes on to investigate the interdependencies between these parameters with the goal of minimizing the mean memory delay per reference. This average memory access time is the average time spent waiting on main memory, averaged over all references. It is the product of the miss rate and the cache miss penalty, or memory access time. In most computer systems, the mean memory delay constitutes a significant portion of the cycles per instruction. As such, it is a much closer measure of performance than the miss rate alone. Smith's paper makes several important contributions:

1. He shows that given the model of the mean memory access time described above, the optimum block size, being the choice that minimizes this time, is a function of the product of the latency and transfer rates, and not of either independently.[6] He presents design targets for the miss ratio, bus traffic and mean delay per reference based on an empirical model derived from simulations of a wide variety of benchmarks. The idea of a design target, like that of an EPA mileage estimate, is to provide a means for quick and coarse comparison among a large number of alternatives. Actual performance may vary depending on workload.

2. He uses these design targets to illustrate the optimum block size as a function of cache size for three radically different memory

---

[6] Smith uses a bus cycle time instead of a transfer rate, so the optimum block size is said to be dependent on the ratio of the latency and the bus cycle times.

systems: a (P896) IEEE Future Bus-based system, the same bus but with a much lower memory latency, and a synchronous bus system with block transfer.

Agarwal also adopted the mean access time metric in his discussion of block size in relation to multiprogramming [Agarwal 87b]. His results were of the same general flavour as Smith's. In another paper [Agarwal 87a], he discusses the implementation tradeoffs that went into the design of the MIPS-X microprocessor at Stanford University. Most notably, he exposes the tradeoffs that existed between the machine's pipeline structure and the cache's organization.

In their 1988 paper on a simulation study of two-level caches, Short and Levy present results obtained from a simulator which attempts to accurately measure the cycles spent in the memory hierarchy during normal program execution [Short 88]. This contrasts with previous simulation studies [Eggers 88, Haikala 86, Smith 85b] and with Smith's. In these earlier studies, simulations provide miss ratio numbers, which are then applied to analytical models to obtain cycle counts or performance estimates. Their simulator allows for variation of the number of cycles spent at each level of a two-level cache hierarchy. Unfortunately, their simulator does not appear to deal with write buffering, nor do they relate total cycle counts and overall performance.

More significantly, Hill devotes a large portion of his thesis [Hill 87] to the analysis of temporal tradeoffs involving set-associativity. The first portion of his third chapter deals with the effects of associativity on miss ratios and concludes that the relative improvement in the miss ratio that results from an increase in the set size is largely independent of the cache size. Once he quantifies these increments in the miss ratio, Hill equates the change in the effective access time due to a change in associativity with a change in the cache cycle time. The effective access time, as he defines it, is directly related to the overall performance of the machine if the CPU cycle time and the cache cycle time are the same. Equating temporal effects with organizational changes is precisely the tradeoff that legitimately determines the viability of an organizational decision. He proceeds from this simple equation to a discussion of the circumstances under which a set-associative cache is better than a direct-mapped one. After examining the general case, he presents detailed designs for TTL, ECL and custom CMOS caches that include temporal as well as organizational values. His overall conclusion is that for larger caches, direct-mapped wins consistently and that even for smaller custom CMOS caches, where set-associative caches have a slight edge in effective access time, the difference may not make the implementation of a set-associative organization worthwhile.

In the final chapter of his thesis, Hill contrasts on-chip instruction buffers (caches) with instruction target buffers. Though he occasionally translates various aspects of the comparison into equivalent changes in cycle time, for the most part he contrasts the two using the equivalent of total cycle counts. The reader is left with the impression that the large number of organizational and temporal (memory access) parameters made impractical the consistent use of cycle time as a basis for comparison. As the first published instance of the consistent application of the simultaneous consideration of temporal and organizational effects, this thesis is an important landmark in the annals of cache design.

An important prerequisite to a proper balance of organizational effects and changes in cycle time is an understanding of how the access times of RAM arrays change with their characteristics. Though little of this sort of analysis is available, Duncombe's description of the SPUR [Hill 85] instruction cache is a good example [Duncombe 86]. Part of his analysis of various design alternatives involves simulating several RAM arrays with different sizes and aspect ratios. Circuit simulation predicts the speed of each of the resulting caches. Combining the predicted cycle times with the appropriate cache miss ratios yields an accurate metric for choosing one alternative over another. The aspect ratio of the RAM array had a significant impact on the RAM's access time, so that cache organizations that facilitated square arrays were favoured.

In these and other papers we see a number of important themes appearing:

1. Consideration of the total cycle count instead of the miss ratio alone as the metric of performance affected by organizational decisions [Agarwal 87b, Hill 87, Short 88, Smith 87a].

2. Detailed simulation of all aspects of a memory hierarchy so that cycle counts are credible [Hill 87, Short 88].

3. Analysis and incorporation of cycle time effects into the cache design process [Hill 87].

In Chapters 4 and 5, these three concepts are applied to the analysis of various aspects of single- and multi-level cache hierarchies.

2.5. Multi-Level Cache Hierarchies

With the exception of a few analytical studies [Chow 76, MacDonald 75, Welch 78], almost all papers until recently have focused only on two-level memory hierarchies[7]: a main memory and a single level of caching. Recently, though, there is growing interest in the idea of reducing the impact of a cache miss by placing a second cache between the first level of caching and main memory [Baer 87a, Baer 87b, Bennett 82, Cohen 89, Colglazier 84, Gecsei 74, Hattori 83, Rau 77a, Short 87, Short 88, Smith 85c, Sohi 87, Sparacio 78, Wang 88, Wilson 87]. The intuitive argument for augmenting the cache hierarchy is that the difference in cycle times between the main memory and the CPU is increasing, so that there is a need to bridge that larger gap in several smaller steps.

There are three types of machines that currently have more than a single-level cache. Multiprocessor machines that have make use of the cache hierarchy to assist in the sharing of data constitute the first class. An example of this class of machine is the FACOM M-380/382 built by Hitachi [Hattori 83]. In this high-speed system, two CPUs, each with a 64KB local cache share, share a 128KB to 256KB second-level cache. Another example of this class of machine is the 4D series of multiprocessor graphics workstations built by Silicon Graphics, Inc. In these machines the 64KB split instruction/data primary caches are backed by a 256KB coherent unified cache [Akeley 89]. The second-level cache, being of approximately the same speed as the primary caches, is used chiefly to isolate the L1 caches from the coherency activity on the backplane.

The second and most common class combines a small on-chip cache with a larger external cache made of discrete static RAMs (SRAMs). Although constantly improving integrated circuit technologies provide ever more area for caches, the on-chip caches of many of the microprocessors existing prior to about 1989 are restricted to instructions only. Since then, both instructions and data caches have begun to appear on chip [Edenfield 90, Kohn 89]. The most common system organizations are a small unified or split first-level cache or branch target buffer on chip, optionally backed up by a larger second-level cache off chip [AMD 87, Archer 87, Berenbaum 87, Hill 86, Horowitz 87]. Papers describing these machines have generally ignored the multi-level nature of the memory hierarchy to the extent that none considers any interactions between the levels of caching.

Recently there have appeared a few uniprocessor machines to use a multi-level hierarchy strictly as a mechanism for achieving high performance. An example of this class is the RS6280 built by MIPS Computer Systems. This machine also has a split first-level cache, with 64KB of single-cycle instruction cache and 16KB of data cache. The two-cycle two-way set-associative, unified, L2 cache contains 512KB [Roberts 90].

---

[7] "Two-level memory hierarchy" is synonymous with "single-level cache hierarchy." The only distinction is whether or not the main memory is counted as a layer.

One significant simulation study of two-level cache hierarchies is presented in Short's master's thesis [Short 87]. He described a series of simulation experiments of a few two-level cache organizations. Among the parameters varied in the simulations were the main memory speed, the first- and second-level cache sizes, the block size, the basic cache organization and the write policy at both levels. His most significant conclusions were that a second level of caching is clearly beneficial when the memory access times are long or when the first-level cache is sufficiently small that it has a large miss rate. However, the study is incomplete in that it does not vary the access time of the second-level cache, so that the crucial tradeoff between the L2 cache size and speed is left unexplored.

There is a growing belief that multi-level cache hierarchies will assume increasing importance in the years to come [Smith 85c]. Some researchers hold the counter view that since cache sizes have continually increased as cycle times have fallen, the cost of a multi-level hierarchy will continue to override the performance benefit, if any, over a large single-level cache. The answer, as discussed in Chapter 5, depends on the particular characteristics of the relationship between cache size and cycle time. This relationship, combined with the constraints imposed by the marketplace will determine the future prevalence of deep cache hierarchies. Finally, several groups of researchers have been looking at the problem of multi-level cache hierarchies for multiprocessors before properly understanding the design space for uniprocessors.

Chapter 3

The Cache Design Problem
and Its Solution

Behold, I send an angel before thee, to keep thee in the way,
and to bring thee to the place I have prepared.

– Exodus 23:20

Though this be madness, yet there be method in 't.

– Hamlet II(2):208

This chapter completes the foundation necessary for the understanding of the empirical and analytical results that follow. The first section of this chapter formally presents the cache design problem from the perspective of optimizing the execution time. In doing so, it exposes the primary tradeoffs explored and quantified in Chapters 4 and 5. The remainder of this chapter familiarizes the reader with the empirical and analytical methods used to probe those tradeoffs.

3.1. Problem Description

As the introductory chapter points out, the execution time of a program is the product of the total number of CPU cycles needed to execute a program, N_{Total}, and the CPU's cycle time, t_{CPU}. One way to compare the significance of various apparently independent parameters is to relate them to a cache's minimum cycle time, t_{L1}, and thus to the execution time. In reality, these tradeoffs between organizational variables are complicated by the link between the cache cycle time and the CPU cycle time. A change in the cache's organization may or may not affect the processor's cycle time, depending on the critical paths in the design. Clearly, if the cache is not determining the CPU cycle time, then any change in its organization that improves the total cycle count will be beneficial, providing the new cache cycle time is still less than or equal to the unchanged CPU cycle time. Since the tradeoffs in the cache are clear and uninteresting when the cache's cycle time is less than the CPU's, we can consistently assume that the system cycle time is determined by the cache. The CPU and system cycle times are therefore set to minimum cache cycle time, and the terms are all used synonymously.

For a memory system with a single level of caching, total cycle count is, to first order, a function of the memory speed and the cache miss ratio. The cache miss ratio for a cache $\mathbf{C}$ is denoted $m(\mathbf{C})$. The primary organizational characteristics that determine the miss ratio are a cache's size, C, its associativity, A, the number of sets, S, and the block size, B. The choices of the fetch and write strategies introduce other factors into the miss ratio equation, but these will be ignored temporarily for the sake of conceptual clarity. Thus, the miss ratio is given as a function of these four parameters:[8]

$$m(\mathbf{C}) = f(S, C, A, B) \qquad [3.1]$$

It is generally accepted that as any of these parameters increases, the miss rate decreases, but that after a certain point, further increases do little good (See Figure 3-1). The block size is unique among them in that there is a block size which minimizes the miss rate. For large block sizes, increasing the block size further actually worsens the miss rate.[9]

---

[8] The four main cache parameters are related: the product of the block size, degree of associativity and number of sets is equal to the total size. Thus, only three need be given to fully specify these primary cache characteristics. Most commonly, either the total size or the number of sets is left out. These cases are symbolically denoted as $\mathbf{C}(S, A, B)$ and $\mathbf{C}(C, A, B)$, respectively. This relationship can be a source of confusion. In general, an experiment which ostensibly varies only one parameter is actually keeping two of the four fixed and varying the other two. When only one variable is mentioned, care must be taken to understand which other parameter is also changing.

[9] As discussed in Section 4.3.2, most of the block size's effect on the miss ratio and performance is actually due to the change in the fetch size that typically accompanies a change in the block size.

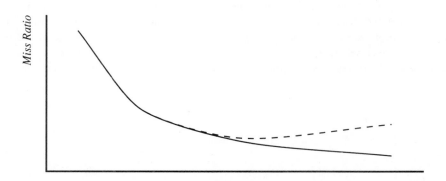

Cache Size, Number of Sets, Associativity or Block Size

Miss Ratio versus Cache Parameters

Figure 3-1

The portion of the total cycle count attributable to main memory, N_{MM}, depends on the memory's characteristics, the block size, and, surprisingly, on the CPU cycle time. This latter link results from the fact that some of the memory attributes are typically specified in seconds. The most significant of these is the latency (LA) between the start of a memory fetch and the start of the transfer of the requested data. The number of cycles spent waiting on main memory is dependent on the latency expressed in cycles, denoted by la, which is given by the ceiling of the ratio of the latency expressed in seconds and the cycle time. The other dominant memory characteristic is the rate at which data can be transferred to and from main memory. The transfer rate, tr in words per cycle and TR in words per second, is actually the smallest of the three different rates: the rate at which memory can present data, the speed at which the cache can accept it, and the maximum bus transfer rate as determined by the backplane's physical and electrical properties. The time spent transferring the data of a single fetch is called the transfer period. It is equal to the ratio of the fetch size in words and the transfer rate.

The function that relates the memory and cache parameters to the total cycle count, to first order, is linear in the miss rate, latency and transfer period (See Figure 3-2):

$$N_{Total} \;=\; g(\, m(\mathbf{C})\,, B\,, LA\,, TR\,, t_{CPU}\,) \tag{3.2}$$

Figure 3-3 illustrates the consequence of the linear relationship between the miss rate and the total cycle count: as the organizational parameters increase in value, the miss rate declines asymptotically. This in turn causes the total cycle count to decline. However, for a fixed relative change in any of the cache size, associativity or block size, the incremental improvement declines as their values increase.

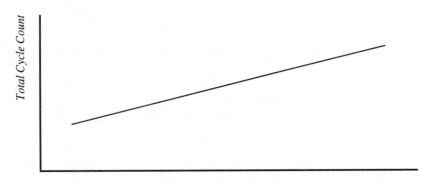

Latency (LA) or Transfer Period (1/TR)

Total Cycle Count versus Memory Parameters

Figure 3-2

The relationship between the cycle time and the cache parameters is the most difficult to quantify, primarily because it is extremely dependent on the lowest-level details of the implementation. The strongest statement that can be made is that the cycle time is monotonic, though not strictly so, in each of the four basic parameters: size, associativity, number of sets and block size:

$$t_{CPU} = h(C, S, A, B) \hspace{4cm} [3.3]$$

The minimum cycle time is also influenced by the complexity of the control logic mandated by the fetch, write and replacement policies. The unpredictability of this function, h, makes it difficult to determine the optimal cache configuration without doing a number of individual designs to a fair degree of detail. Figure 3-4 illustrates that there are usually regions of each of the domains over which the cycle time changes dramatically, and others where it is quite constant.

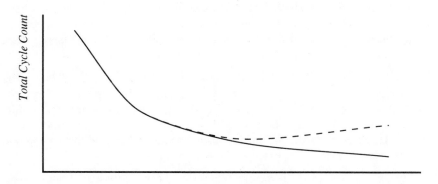

Cache Size, Number of Sets, Associativity, or Block Size

Total Cycle Count versus Cache Parameters

Figure 3-3

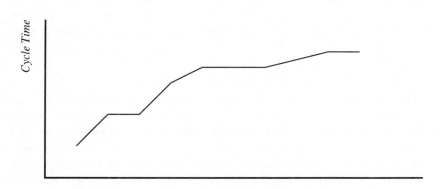

Cache Size, Number of Sets, Associativity or Block Size

Cycle Time versus Cache Parameters

Figure 3-4

This book is about the minimization of the total execution time, T_{Total}, through the appropriate choice of the cache parameters. The choice of parameters determines the cycle time and miss rate, which when combined with a given set of memory parameters yields the metric being minimized. Since the memory parameters affect the total cycle count, it is reasonable to expect that the optimum cache organization will change, depending on the memory system, along with the various other factors that affect the functions f, g and h.

Figures 3-3 and 3-4 illustrate the existence of the tradeoff. If the cache parameters are too small, then a high cycle count dominates the performance equation. Conversely, if they are too large, then the large cycle time that results overwhelms the advantage of a lower miss rate, and so performance again suffers. The need to reconcile such opposing trends and to find the appropriate balance between them is the essence of engineering.

Thus far, only a single level of caching has been discussed. When several layers are considered, the problem becomes dramatically more complicated. Not only are there three more free variables for each additional level in the hierarchy, but the functions that relate the various cache parameters to the execution time transcend levels in the hierarchy: the miss penalty at one level of the cache is dependent on the speed and mean access time of the downstream cache, and conversely the local miss ratio at one level is dependent on the miss rate of the upstream cache. Despite the additional complexity, multi-level hierarchies are important because frequently execution times can be substantially lowered by increasing the depth of the hierarchy [Chow 76, Short 87]. The ultimate step is to make the number of levels in the hierarchy a free variable and to investigate the maximum performance obtainable as a function of the depth.

On the surface, the optimization problem in all its detail appears intractable. To make it somewhat more manageable, Chapter 4 first examines each of the variables individually. Once the variables' individual effects on performance are understood, their interdependencies can be folded into the understanding of the problem so that a mechanism for finding the global optimum can be developed. Unfortunately, the individual functions described above are not necessarily smooth or well behaved, so that we must use caution in generalizing the individual tradeoff results to the overall cache design problem.

3.2. Two Complementary Approaches

Trace-driven simulations and analytical modelling are two separate yet complementary techniques used to investigate the relationship between the execution time and each of the cache parameters. Each of these approaches has strengths and weaknesses. Just as theoretical physicists and experimentalists constantly keep one another honest and on track towards the truth, these two techniques together strengthen the other's results.

Simulation studies frequently suffer from a microscopic perspective; presentations of simulation results in the form of graphs and tables frequently give little insight into the reasons for the observed behaviour. Without an understanding of the underlying phenomena, it is impossible to reliably extrapolate any trends beyond the simulated domain. Caution must also be exercised when using finite sized address traces to draw any conclusions whatsoever about very large caches.

Analytical efforts, on the other hand, tend to have a tenuous link with reality. It is often unclear whether simplifications made for the purposes of conceptual elegance and algebraic expediency cause the resulting model to deviate too far from reality. Nevertheless, both types of simplifications are necessary: both help expose the primary underlying trends through the elimination of secondary and tertiary terms that clutter the equations. This need for approachable results must be tempered by the realization that a model that does not accurately reflect reality is of limited utility.

When used together, simulation results and analytical models are complementary. The simulation results can be used to quantify the error in the analytical equations, and a good fit between the two permits extrapolation of the simulation results to a wider range of parameters. Above all, the use of both techniques adds confidence through redundancy. When used in tandem, they can corroborate each other, facilitating much stronger statements about the accuracy and applicability of the results than either could justify individually.

Both these techniques are used in Chapters 4 and 5 in the analysis of the tradeoffs that are part of the cache design process. The following two sections describe in detail the particular simulation environment and analytical models used to generate the results presented throughout those chapters.

3.3. Experimental Method

Three things are needed to investigate experimentally the tradeoffs in memory hierarchy design: a trace-driven simulator, a set of points in the design space to be simulated and a set of traces used to stimulate those memory hierarchies.

3.3.1. The Simulator and Related Infrastructure

The primary goals in the design of the memory hierarchy simulator were accuracy, flexibility and efficiency. Most cache simulators only report miss rates and other non-temporal statistics. In this case though, there were additional requirements to accumulate accurate cycle counts and to precisely attribute execution time to specific components and operations within the simulated system.

"Flexibility" refers to the ability of a single simulator and associated analysis programs to emulate a wide variety of target systems. Again, most cache simulators need only change a cache's size, associativity and block size, but this simulator needed to model an arbitrarily deep memory hierarchy, with variation of all the temporal parameters throughout the system.

Efficiency is important because cache simulation is CPU intensive. Believable results rely on running a variety of large traces for each cache organization. The variety of different scenarios that have to be simulated per experiment can be quite large. Though the computing resources available to researchers have increased dramatically over the last few years, so has the amount of work necessary per data point. A less efficient simulator necessitates running fewer references past fewer scenarios, thereby restricting both the quality and range of the experimental results.

The inputs to the simulator are a detailed description of a memory hierarchy, a CPU model and an input trace consisting of a sequence of pairs of addresses and memory operations. The set of operations defined in the trace format used are load, store, instruction fetch, and context switch. The trace is conceptually split into two parts by a warm-start boundary [Easton 78]. Statistics are gathered on the whole trace and the second segment separately. The description of the memory hierarchy includes the number of levels, the basic organization of each layer (split I/D versus unified, size, associativity and block size) and temporal parameters, as well as the fetch and write strategies at each level. Several fetch strategies, spanning a wide range of complexity, and virtually every conceivable write strategy are available to the experimenter.

Time is implemented in the simulator by keeping track of the cycle number at which every operation is started and completed at each level of the memory hierarchy. As a reference trickles down from one level to the next, the start time at the new level is determined from the time the previous level forwarded the reference, the completion time of the last event at this level and any pending events, such as writes waiting in write buffers or prefetch operations in progress. Part of the specification of the memory hierarchy is the separation between, and duration of, the various types of operations (for example, read, write and replace) for each level, as well as any communication delays between layers in the memory hierarchy.

An interesting aspect of this simulator is that the penalty for flexibility is divided between compile time and run time. Specifically, a simulation run consists of three phases: preprocessing, compilation and execution. The preprocessing phase starts with a pointer to a base system description file and up to three variation files. The base system specification fully defines a memory hierarchy in all its detail. About 130 parameters are needed to fully specify a two-level cache system. Each of the variation files changes one or more characteristics: for example, set size, number of sets, cycle time or memory latency. A change typically involves altering several parameters to maintain consistency in the modelled system. In this preprocessing phase, macro-expansion produces a C program in which all expressions of fixed model parameters are resolved into constants and as much as possible of the complexity of the full cache model is removed. A different C program is generated for each unique system simulated. The second phase is compilation, which takes this program and generates an executable binary that is subsequently run with an appropriate trace file as input.

The result of running the simulator is an output file containing 300 to 400 statistics, depending on the complexity of the system simulated. An experiment consists of picking a base system and the variables to be modified. A variety of shell scripts spawn numerous simulations to the available computers around the network. For example, in the speed – size tradeoff experiment of Section 4.1, the cycle time and cache size are varied (16 and 11 values, respectively), and each of the 176 resulting systems is simulated with all eight of the traces, resulting in 1408 files. Separate programs, one per investigated tradeoff, then read these result files and compile the graphs and tables scattered throughout this book.

3.3.2. The System Models

The entire cache design space is incredibly diverse. At any one time, cache researchers must restrict themselves to a portion of the overall design space. With the simulation environment described above, the design space explored in each experiment centers on a single base scenario. By consistently using a smaller number of base scenarios, we can more thoroughly examine a small region of the overall design space. Selecting the base systems so that they are representative of a common or interesting class of machines makes the results valuable despite their limited domain. Only two base scenarios are used in the simulation experiments that follow: one with a single split I/D cache and a second with a two-level hierarchy.

The first base model has a Harvard organization. The split I and D virtual caches are 64 kilobytes (KB) each, organized as 4K blocks of four words (W), direct-mapped. Entire blocks are fetched on a miss. The data cache is write-back, with no fetch done on a write miss. All read hits take one CPU cycle, while write hits take two – one to access the tags, followed by one to write the data. A four block write buffer between the cache and the memory is deep enough that it essentially never fills up. In the case of a dirty miss, the memory read starts immediately, and the dirty block is transferred into the write buffer during the memory latency period. If the latency is sufficiently long, then the write-back is completely hidden. However, since all the data paths are set to be one word wide, this is not always the case for long block sizes. The base CPU cycle time is 40ns and the CPU and cache cycle times are assumed to be identical. Each experiment in Chapter 4 varies one or more of the following: the cycle time, cache size, associativity, block size, fetch strategy, main memory latency or transfer rate.

Main memory is modelled as a single, non-interleaved functional unit. Read access times consist of a latency portion, followed by a transfer period. The default latency is one cycle to get the block address to the memory, plus 180ns. Since the memory is synchronous, the latency becomes $1 + \lceil 180ns/40ns \rceil$, or six cycles. The transfer rate is one word per cycle, or four cycles for a block. Once a read is completed, at least 120ns (three cycles in the default case) must elapse before the start of the next operation. This delay is based on the difference between DRAM access and cycle times. Writes take one cycle for the address, followed by one word per cycle transfer. At this point the write buffer is emptied of that operation, and if it was full, a new write can be then be entered. The actual memory write occurs in the 100ns following the data transfer, and it is followed by the same 120ns of recovery time. On write-backs, the entire block is transferred, regardless of which words were dirty.

The CPU model consistently used emulates a highly pipelined machine capable of issuing both an instruction and data reference on every cycle. If there are separate instruction and data caches, adjacent instruction and data references in the trace are paired up and issued simultaneously. Both references must be completed before the CPU can proceed to the next reference or reference pair.

These parameters were chosen to be representative of a machine built around a 25 MIPS peak CMOS RISC processor. In particular, the memory system is moderately aggressive by today's standards. The backplane has more than double the transfer rate of VME or MULTIBUS II, and memory latency is roughly half that of commercially available boards for these buses. The values used are more representative of a single master private memory bus.

The second base model has two levels of caching. The first level has a split I/D cache, both caches being 2KB, direct-mapped. The L1 block size is still four words. The unified second-level cache is 512KB, with a block size of eight words. It too is direct-mapped, virtually addressed and write-back with the same fetch and write strategies, including four blocks of write buffer. The CPU model is unchanged, but the CPU and L1 cycle time is now 10ns, and the default L2

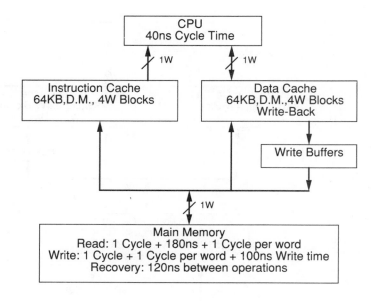

Single-Level Base System

Figure 3-5

cycle time is 30ns. The memory characteristics are also unchanged from the single-level model.

Many of these characteristics remain unchanged in the experiments that follow. As was mentioned earlier, they have been selected to be generally representative of an interesting pair of machines. Some of the characteristics, such as the virtual addressability, are the result of practical limitations: the traces were virtual traces, and there is no way of reconstructing the memory map to find the actual physical addresses. It is also important to choose parameters that do not distract from the tradeoffs under investigation. An early decision was to not investigate the effects of changing write policy. A reasonably aggressive implementation with a generous amount of buffering wherever possible minimizes the influence of the writes on the execution time. Furthermore, as many parameters as possible were kept consistent between the base scenarios: both used the same memory system, write strategy and fetch policy. The motivation was to maximize the coupling between the two sets of results to help with both the debugging process and the investigation of the tradeoffs.

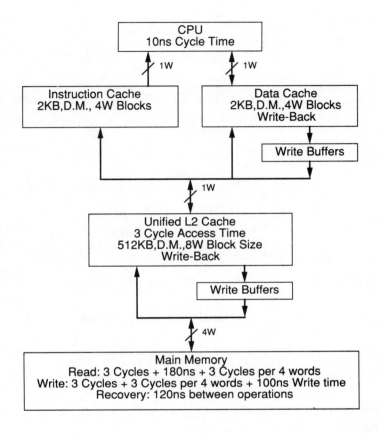

Two-Level Base System

Figure 3-6

Failure to vary these important design decisions inevitably limits the domain of applicability of any conclusions based on the simulations. In particular, since only one especially aggressive write strategy was used, we must be cautious when applying the results to machines with substantially different base assumptions.

3.3.3. The Input Traces

Two sets of four traces each are used to generate the empirical results in the following chapters. Table 3-1 lists some of trace's main characteristics. The first four are concatenations of several 400,000 reference snapshots taken on a VAX 8200 running with microcode modifications to catch generated virtual addresses [Agarwal 86]. They include operating system references and exhibit real multiprogramming behaviour. Rather than deal with the variety of VAX data types, the traces were preprocessed to contain only word references. Specifically, sequences of instruction fetches from the same word were collapsed into a single word reference, and quad references were split into several sequential accesses. The warm-start boundary for these was consistently 450,000 references.

Agarwal [Agarwal 87b] discusses the applicability of concatenations of snapshots into larger traces; he concludes that if the individual snapshots contain a similar proportion of new (non-stationary) references, then, as in this case, the concatenation is valid.

It is somewhat unrealistic to expect an implementation of the VAX architecture to issue memory references at the rate of the CPU model used in the simulations. However, the use of such an aggressive CPU model is justifiable on two counts. First, this book is about memory hierarchies. Higher performance, pipelined machines depend more heavily on the effectiveness of the cache and memory subsystems. If the CPU model stresses those functional units more than might be realizable, then the results will be biased in favour of the memory hierarchy. If a CISC CPU model were used instead, the results of Chapters 4 and 5 would show a bias towards short cycle times over low miss ratios.

Second, an aggressive implementation of a rationalized subset of the VAX architecture could duplicate the temporal characteristics of the CPU model. The modest code size penalty that accompanies the substitution of the dense byte stream instruction encoding of the VAX with a fixed width format would not substantially affect the tradeoffs for the instruction cache. The insensitivity of the tradeoffs to the code density is shown in Appendix A by the similarity between the results of these traces and the RISC machine traces described below. To introduce a less demanding CPU model for these traces would unnecessarily complicate the interpretation of the results by introducing a factor that is unrelated to the memory hierarchy. The traces are valuable regardless of the CPU model because of their multiprogramming and operating system characteristics.

The second four traces were generated by interleaving several uniprocess virtual address traces of optimized C programs compiled for the MIPS

Name	Size (K Refs)	Unique Addresses (K)	OS	Programs (Number of Processes)
mu3	1439	33.1	VMS	FORTRAN compile, microcode allocator, directory search. (7)
mu6	1543	49.6	VMS	mu3 + Pascal compile, 4x1x5, spice. (11)
mu10	1094	49.4	VMS	mu6 + jacobian, string search, assembler, octal dump, linker. (14)
savec	1162	25.2	Ultrix	C compile with miscellaneous other activity. (6)
rd1n3	1489	299	none	emacs, rsim, C compiler front end (ccom). (3)
rd2n4	1314	241	none	emacs, troff, a trace analyzer program, ccom. (4)
rd1n5	1314	248	none	rd2n4 + egrep searching 400KB in 27 files. (5)
rd2n7	1678	448	none	rd2n4 + rsim, emacs, grep doing a constant search. (7)

Description of the Traces

Table 3-1

Computer System's R2000 architecture. The programs are randomly interleaved to duplicate the distribution of context switch intervals seen in the VAX traces. Each trace begins with references to all the locations that the programs have touched up to the point in their execution at which tracing begins. This technique guarantees that the cache occupancy at the warm-start boundary is realistic regardless of the cache size. Appendix A discusses the generation of these traces in greater length.

Though various specific differences between the two groups of traces are addressed as relevant, the two behaved similarly both qualitatively and quantitatively in all the experiments presented in Chapters 4 and 5. Appendix A describes the two sets of traces and how they were generated in more detail. It discusses the variation in the miss rates that derives from the different code densities of the RISC R2000 and CISC VAX architectures, and then explicitly validates the use of the geometric mean of the warm-start statistics of all eight traces as the basis for all the numerical and graphical results of Chapters 4 and 5.

3.3.4. Observations, Lessons and Summary

The main idea behind the decomposition of the simulator into three phases was to remove as much overhead as possible from the simulator's run time. The drawback of this decision was that the macro-expansion and compilation phases accompanied each simulation run. Though the simulation rates achieved are adequately high – up to 2000 references per second per MicroVAX-II workstation – the time penalty for the preparation and compilation of the simulator is quite large: for a one million-reference trace, close to half of the total time is spent in the first two phases. Unfortunately, the size of the traces (60MB in total) prevents more effective amortization of this compilation time: disk space restrictions force iteration over all traces to be the outermost loop, instead of the innermost. If the cache models were structured so that the preprocessing produced a simulator for a moderately sized class of machines instead of a single specific one, then the compilation overhead per simulation could be even further reduced, though at the expense of a modest increase in run time. These efforts, combined with judicious performance tuning of the simulator itself, would double to triple the simulation rates.

Further increments in the simulation rate could only be obtained by using techniques that facilitate multiple simultaneous simulations [Hill 87, Laha 88, Mattson 70, Smith 77, Thompson 87, Thompson 89]. These techniques were not used for two reasons: initial trials showed the simulation rates to be adequate given the computing resources available;[10] also, the implementation of any such technique would be complicated by the reordering of events caused by write buffers, and by the need to keep accurate track of the cycles spent in each level of the hierarchy. It was important to minimize the amount of novelty in the simulator. Appendix B illustrates that the the write buffers have a significant effect on the contributions of writes to the execution time, so that modelling them accurately is crucial to the credibility of the empirical results.

In summary, the credibility of the trace-driven simulation results presented in Chapters 4 and 5 stem from the strength of all three important components: an accurate simulator, realistic system models and representative input traces.

---

[10] The bulk of the simulations were done on an MIPS Computer System's M/1000, a DEC Western Research Lab Titan and about 20 MicroVax IIs scattered around the Center for Integrated Systems at Stanford.

Together, they reliably duplicate the behaviour of real systems running real programs.

3.4. Analytical Approach

The motivation behind the following analytical efforts is to examine the nature of Equations 3.1, 3.2, and 3.3, and thereby to relate system-level performance to the various cache and memory parameters. This section introduces the nomenclature, fundamental assumptions and basic algebraic models that are used in subsequent chapters.

The total execution time is the product of the cycle time and the total cycle count:

$$T_{Total} = t_{CPU} \times N_{Total} = t_{L1}(\mathbf{C}) \times N_{Total} \qquad [3.4]$$

Recall that the CPU cycle time is determined by the cache's cycle time, which is a function of its organizational parameters.

Since the execution time is a convex function of the organizational and temporal variables, the minimum execution time is obtained when the partial derivative with respect to some variable is equal to zero. For example, if the cache size is the focus of attention, the optimum organization is one that equates the magnitudes of the relative change in the cycle time and cycle count:

$$\frac{1}{t_{L1}} \times \frac{\partial t_{L1}}{\partial C} = -\frac{1}{N_{Total}} \times \frac{\partial N_{Total}}{\partial C}$$

Most of the cache parameters are not continuous: they are restricted to either integer or binary[11] values. For these discrete variables, the balancing equation above has a difference form – one that equates the relative change in the cycle time and cycle counts across the change from one cache organization to an "adjacent" one:[12]

---

[11] A binary value is any integral power of two.

[12] This discrete form was used by Hill to look at set-associativity tradeoffs [Hill 87].

$$\frac{1}{t_{L1}} \times \frac{\Delta t_{L1}}{\Delta C} = -\frac{1}{N_{Total}} \times \frac{\Delta N_{Total}}{\Delta C}$$ [3.5]

Given a particular change from one organization to another, if the left- and right-hand sides are equal, then the change is performance neutral. If, however, the left-hand size is greater (closer to $+\infty$), then the change increases overall execution time, and if the right-hand side is more positive, there is a net gain in performance.

A commonly used estimate for the total cycle count, $g(m(\mathbf{C}), B, LA, TR, t_{CPU})$, is the sum of the cycles spent waiting on each level of the memory hierarchy. For a single level of caching, the total number of cycles is given by the number of cycles spent not performing memory references; plus the number of cycles spent doing instruction fetches, loads and stores; plus the time spent waiting on main memory.

$$N_{Total} = N_{Execute} + N_{Ifetch} + N_{Ifetch} \times m(\mathbf{C}) \times \overline{n}_{MMread}$$

$$+ \quad N_{Load} + N_{Load} \times m(\mathbf{C}) \times \overline{n}_{MMread}$$

$$+ \quad N_{Store} \times \overline{n}_{L1write} \qquad [3.6]$$

where

$N_{Execute}$	Number of cycles spent not performing a memory reference.
N_{Ifetch}	Number of instruction fetches in the program or trace
N_{Load}	Number of loads.
N_{Store}	Number of stores.
$\overline{n}_{MMread}$	Average number of cycles spent satisfying a read cache miss.
$\overline{n}_{L1write}$	Average number of cycles spent dealing with a write to the cache.

We can apply a few simplifying assumptions without a loss of generality. For RISC machines with single-cycle execution, the number of cycles in which neither reference stream is active, $N_{Execute}$, is zero. The CPU model used in the simulations exhibits this behaviour. As written, the above equation assumes that read references (instruction fetches and loads) take one cycle when they hit in the cache. It also assumes that there is a single port into a single cache, so that loads and instruction fetches are serialized. By noting that the cache's read miss ratio is the weighted average of the cache's instruction and data read miss ratios, we can collapse all the parallel instruction fetch and load terms together. This leaves us with a simpler form, in which the total cycle count is the sum of cycles spent doing reads and writes. Then for each read, there is a single cycle of overhead, plus the cache miss penalty per reference.

$$N_{Total} = N_{Read}\left(1 + m_{Read}(C) \times \bar{n}_{MMread}\right) + N_{Store} \times \bar{n}_{L1write} \qquad [3.7]$$

The mean time to retrieve a block[13] from main memory, $\bar{n}_{MMread}$, has two components: the time to actually fetch the block and, occasionally, some delay due to the memory being busy at the time of the request. If there is no prefetching or I/O bus traffic, the only possible source of such a delay is a write in progress. The average amount of delay per memory reference is denoted by $\bar{n}_{ReadDelay}$. The number of cycles spent fetching the block is the sum of a latency period, la, and a transfer period, $\frac{B}{tr}$. When dealing with tradeoffs involving the block size, it is frequently necessary to assume that the average delay to memory fetches due to writes in progress, $\bar{n}_{ReadDelay}$, is small with respect to the sum of the transfer and latency periods. In practice, this is generally the case if the write strategy is effective and the cycles spent waiting on main memory do not dominate the execution time.

$$N_{Total} = N_{Read}\left[1 + m_{Read}(C) \times \left(la + \frac{B}{tr} + \bar{n}_{ReadDelay}\right)\right]$$

$$+ N_{Store} \times \bar{n}_{L1write}$$

$$\approx N_{Read}\left[1 + m_{Read}(C) \times \left(la + \frac{B}{tr}\right)\right]$$

$$+ N_{Store} \times \bar{n}_{L1write}$$

Similarly, the number of cycles to complete a write, $\bar{n}_{L1write}$, includes the time to do the write and any additional cycles needed to put data in the write

---

[13] In this analytic model of the execution time, the fetch size is assumed to be one block.

buffer. This latter component also includes any time waiting for the write buffer to become not full. For a write-through cache, the written data always needs to be placed in the buffer, while for a write-back cache, this potential penalty occurs only when a dirty block is being replaced. If a read caused the replacement of a dirty block, it is assumed that the time needed to place the dirty data into the buffer is hidden by the necessary memory fetch, accounted for in read cycles. So, for write-back caches the mean number of cycles to do a write, $\bar{n}_{L1write}$, can be approximated by the number of cycles needed to do the write into the cache, $n_{L1write}$, when the frequency of write-backs caused by writes is low. Appendix B deals explicitly with the validity of this treatment of writes in single- and multi-level hierarchies.

Equation 3.6 assumes a single unified cache and the serial issuance of instruction and data references; both streams contribute symmetrically to the execution time. For a machine with single-cycle execution and a Harvard organization, capable of parallel instruction and data reference generation, loads contribute to the cycle count only if they miss in the data cache. Furthermore, writes only add to the execution time if they take longer than one cycle, or if they incur write buffer or write-back delays. The base total cycle count is the number of instruction fetches.

$$N_{Total} = N_{Ifetch} + N_{Ifetch} \times m(\mathbf{C}_{L1I}) \times \bar{n}_{MMread}$$

$$+ N_{Load} \times m(\mathbf{C}_{L1D}) \times \bar{n}_{MMread}$$

$$+ N_{Store} \times (n_{L1write} - 1) \qquad [3.8]$$

Equation 3.7 can be used instead of Equation 3.8 for this class of systems if the number of reads, N_{Read}, the read miss ratio, $m_{Read}(\mathbf{C})$, and the mean number of cycles per write, $\bar{n}_{L1write}$, are defined appropriately. The number of reads is defined to be the number of instruction fetches, the read miss ratio is the instruction cache miss ratio plus the data cache miss ratio weighted by the ratio of the number of instruction fetches and loads, and the mean write time is one less than the time to perform the write.

$$N_{Read} = N_{Ifetch}$$

$$m_{Read} = m(\mathbf{C}_{L1I}) + \frac{N_{Load}}{N_{Ifetch}} \times m(\mathbf{C}_{L1D})$$

Similarly, if the number of free cycles of any memory system activity, $N_{Execute}$, is non-zero, as in a CISC machine, the model represented by Equation 3.7 can still be used without modification if the number of reads and the read miss ratio are suitably defined.

To find the execution time, the total cycle count must be multiplied by the cycle time. The execution time becomes a function of the cycle time, t_{L1}, the miss ratio, $m(\mathbf{C})$, the mean main memory read access time, $\bar{t}_{MMread}$, the average number of cycles to retire a write, $\bar{n}_{L1write}$, and the numbers of reads and writes:

$$T_{Total} = N_{Read} \times t_{L1} + N_{Read} \times m(\mathbf{C}) \times \bar{t}_{MMread}$$

$$+ N_{Store} \times \bar{n}_{L1write} \times t_{L1} \qquad [3.9]$$

When dealing with a multi-level cache hierarchy, the average time to satisfy a read request at each level of caching is a function of the cache's read access time, miss rate and miss penalty. Each cache's miss penalty is exactly the mean time to satisfy a read at the next level in the hierarchy. This recursion extends all the way to the last level of caching, where the cache miss penalty is again the mean main memory access time. All of these read access times, n_{Li}, are expressed in CPU cycles.

$$N_{Total} = N_{Read}\left(n_{L1} + m_{L1}(\mathbf{C}) \times \left(n_{L2} + m_{L2}(\mathbf{C}) \times \left(n_{L3} \right.\right.\right.$$

$$+ \cdots + m_{Ln}(\mathbf{C}) \times \bar{n}_{MMread} \left)\cdots\right)\right) + N_{Store} \times \bar{n}_{L1write}$$

The global miss ratio, M_{Li}, is defined as the number of read misses at level i divided by the number of read references generated by the CPU. Expressed in these terms, the total cycle count becomes dependent on the sum of the products of a cache's global miss rate and the next cache's cycle time.

$$N_{Total} = N_{Read} \left(n_{L1} + M_{L1}(\mathbf{C}_{L1}) \times \overline{n}_{L2} + M_{L2}(\mathbf{C}_{L2}) \times \overline{n}_{L3} \right.$$

$$\left. + \cdots + M_{Ln}(\mathbf{C}_{Ln}) \times \overline{n}_{MMread} \right)$$

$$+ N_{Store} \times \overline{n}_{L1write} \qquad [3.10]$$

These equations relate the cache miss ratios to the total cycle count and, consequently, to the execution time. However, to properly investigate the link between the organizational parameters and the execution time, we need to investigate the miss rate as a function of cache parameters, expressed in Section 3.1 as $f(S,C,A,B)$. Section 2.3 illustrates that other researchers have already extensively studied this function. Rather than duplicate their efforts, we will use these previous results as a starting point. The remainder of this section presents in some detail a model developed by Agarwal that is used in Chapter 4 to probe the tradeoff between a cache's size and its cycle time [Agarwal 89].

Agarwal's model is based on the decomposition of misses into different classes. A non-stationary miss is the inevitable warm-start miss caused by the initial reference to an address if it is first used after the program's initial start-up phase. Intrinsic misses result from multiple addresses within a single address space mapping onto the same set. If the number of distinct addresses mapped onto a given set is greater than the set size, then they compete for the available blocks, knocking each other out of the cache in the process. Extrinsic misses are caused by multiprogramming effects: between time slices, a program will have some of its working set knocked out of the cache by the other programs that were executed in the interim. Agarwal's thesis describes the development, rationale and validation of this model [Agarwal 87b]. In its full form, the miss ratio over the t chunks of τ references is given as the sum of three terms, one for each type of miss:

$$m(\mathbf{C}(S,A,B),t) = \frac{u(B)}{\tau t} \left[1 + \frac{(U - u(B)) \times (t-1)}{T u(B)} \right] \quad \begin{matrix} \text{Non-stationary} \\ \text{misses} \end{matrix}$$

$$+ \frac{c(A)}{\tau} \left[u(B) - \sum_{a=0}^{A} S a P(a) \right] \quad \begin{matrix} \text{Intrinsic} \\ \text{misses} \end{matrix}$$

$$+ \frac{f}{\tau t} \left\lfloor \frac{t-1}{t_s} \right\rfloor \sum_{a=0}^{A} S a P(a) \quad \begin{matrix} \text{Extrinsic} \\ \text{misses} \end{matrix} \qquad [3.11]$$

The miss ratio is defined in terms of the number of unique blocks touched in the fragment of references, $u(B)$, the total trace length, T, the total number of unique blocks touched in the trace, U, the collision rate within this chunk of the trace, $c(A)$, and the probability that a blocks of the $u(B)$ unique ones map onto the same set, $P(a)$. The collision rate is bounded below by 0 and above by $\frac{\tau}{u}$.

Assuming a random replacement, the probability, $P(a)$, is given by a binomial distribution, which can be approximated by a Poisson distribution for large caches (a large S) and large numbers of unique references per chunk (a large u). Finally, the miss ratio also depends on the fraction of blocks, $f(t)$, belonging to a given process, that are purged by other processes between time slices consisting of t_s chunks of τ references. For a direct-mapped cache, the fraction can be approximated by a simple exponential form of the number of unique blocks per chunk, $u(B)$, and the number of unique blocks touched by all other processes sharing the cache in the multiprogramming system, $u'(B)$:

$$f(S,B,t) \; = \; 1 - e^{-\frac{u(B)}{S}}\left(1 + \frac{u'(B)}{S}\right)$$

For a direct-mapped cache ($A = 1$), all the summations can be eliminated, leaving each of the three terms easily differentiable:

$$m(\; \mathrm{C}(S,A{=}1,B),t) \; = \; \frac{u(B)}{\tau t}\left[1 + \frac{(U - u(B)) \times (t - 1)}{T u(B)}\right]$$

$$+ \frac{c\,u(B)}{\tau}\left[1 - e^{-\frac{u(B)}{S}}\right]$$

$$+ \; \frac{1}{\tau t}\left\lfloor \frac{t-1}{t_s}\right\rfloor u(B)\, e^{-\frac{u(B)}{S}}\left[1 - e^{-\frac{u(B)}{S}}\left(1 + \frac{u'(B)}{S}\right)\right] \qquad [3.12]$$

This form is on the verge of being too complicated for practical use. In particular, its dependence on the block size is obscured by the number of unique blocks per fragment, $u(B)$. Though Agarwal presents an elaborate formula for estimating its value, he generally treats it as a measured input to the model. Despite this complication and the complexity of the form, the accuracy and intuitive basis of this model make it useful in investigating the tradeoffs between a cache's size and its cycle time.

This concludes the introductory portion of the book. We now have all the tools at our disposal to proceed with the problem of understanding the dependencies between organizational and temporal parameters with cache hierarchies and solving them to maximize system-level performance. The previous chapter presented the necessary terminology and discussed the existing work relevant to this task. This chapter has presented that problem in formal terms and discussed the plan of attack: trace-driven simulation is used to find how the execution time varies with each of the organizational parameters, and analytical reasoning is used to verify those findings and to provide some insight into the important phenomena at work.

Chapter 4

Performance-Directed Cache Design

Time and space are fragments of the great infinite for
the use of finite creatures.

– Henri Frederick Amiel

Those who make the worst use of ... time are the first
to complain of its brevity.

– La Bruyere

The cache design problem is often constrained by limiting the cache cycle time
to a given CPU cycle time. However, this is a biased perspective, in that it treats
as secondary the cache's large impact on overall performance. A better strategy
is to choose a system cycle time that accommodates the needs of both the CPU
and cache and also optimizes program execution time. This chapter explores that
choice through the presentation of simulation results and an analytical analysis
using the models presented in Section 3.4. Since the cache size is the most
significant of the organizational design parameters, we begin by examining the
important tradeoff between the system cycle time and the cache size.

4.1. Speed – Size Tradeoffs

As noted in Chapter 2, the usual cache metrics are miss rates and transfer ratios. Figure 4-1 confirms the widely held belief that larger caches are better in that the miss ratio declines with increasing cache size, but that beyond a certain size the incremental improvements are small [Agarwal 87b, Haikala 84b, Smith 85a]. It plots the miss rates[14] for the single-level base system of Figure 3-5 as a function of the combined size of the instruction and data caches. The sizes of the two caches are varied simultaneously from 2KB through 2MB, so that the total cache size ranges from 4KB to 4MB. The block size and other cache parameters are kept constant as the number of sets is increased.

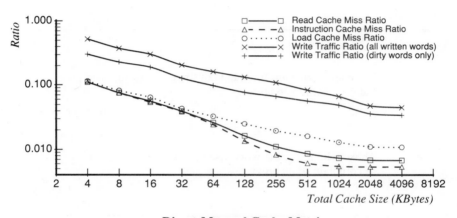

Direct-Mapped Cache Metrics

Figure 4-1

The larger of the two write traffic ratios counts all words in replaced blocks that have at least one dirty word, while the smaller counts only the dirty words themselves. Since only a small proportion of words in a dirty block are actually modified, the two write traffic ratios are quite different. In the system modelled, no fetching occurs on a write miss, so the write miss ratio is not interesting.

---

[14]Recall that the miss ratios are calculated as read misses per read requests, as opposed to being relative to the total number of references, and that read is defined as either a load or an instruction fetch.

Since the block size is fixed, and all references are assumed to be word references, the read traffic ratio is simply four times the miss ratio.

There are two parts to the speed – size tradeoff: cache size and cycle time. As the cycle time is varied over the range of 20ns through 80ns, the total cycle count for the traces decreases, creating the illusion of improved performance. In Figure 4-2, the cycle counts are normalized to the smallest count in the experiment, that being for two 2MB caches operating at 80ns. The decrease in cycle count with increasing cycle time stems from the reduced number of cycles per main memory reference at the slower clock rates. The total number of cycles to execute a program varies quite dramatically – by a factor of 3.2 across the entire experiment, and by a factor of 1.5 alone when each cache is 2KB. As the cache size increases, the number of misses drops, causing the main memory component of the total cycle count to decrease as well. Table 4-1 shows that the cost in cycles of each type of memory operation changes with the cycle time. Though the transfer rate is assumed to be one word per cycle, regardless of the cycle time, the latency parameters are kept constant, independent of the cycle time.

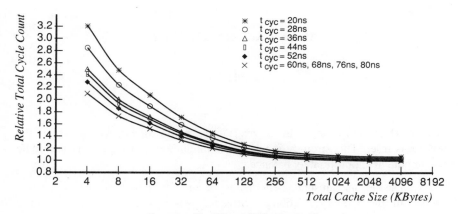

Speed - Size Tradeoff: Cycle Count

Figure 4-2

Total execution time is the product of cycle time and cycle count. Figure 4-3 shows that the overall performance is strongly dependent on both the cache size and cycle time. For small caches, incremental changes in the cache size have a

Cycle Time (ns)	Read Time (cycles)	Write Time (cycles)	Recovery Time (cycles)
20	14	10	6
24	13	10	5
28	12	9	5
32	11	9	4
36	10	8	4
40	10	8	3
48	9	8	3
52	9	7	3
60	8	7	2

Read Operation Time: 180 ns
Write Operation Time: 100 ns
MM Recovery Time: 120 ns

Memory Access Cycle Counts

Table 4-1

greater effect than changes in the cycle time, while for larger cache sizes the reverse is true. This strongly indicates the likelihood of a region in the middle where both are appropriately balanced.

As an aside, an unusual phenomenon occurs for these systems with small caches in the vicinity of 60ns. Strangely enough, performance is not a monotonic function of cycle time. Decreasing the cycle time from 60ns to 56ns slows the machine down nearly 3%. Since the memory access time is quantized to a discrete number of cycles, the cache miss penalty increases from eight to nine cycles at this boundary. Because of the poor miss rate for small caches, the total cycle count increase that results easily overwhelms the decrease in cycle time to increase the total execution time. The 56ns design is a poor one in that a significant fraction of the read access time is wasted in synchronizing the asynchronous DRAM access with the synchronous backplane and cache.

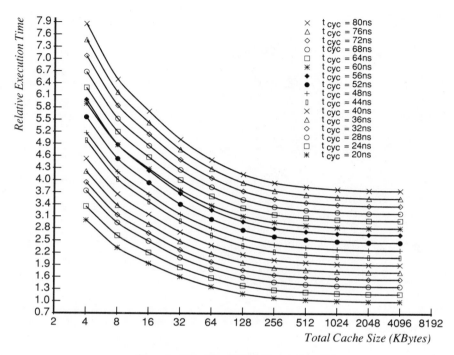

Speed - Size Tradeoff: Execution Time

Figure 4-3

Horizontal slices through Figure 4-3 expose groups of machines with equal performance. By vertically interpolating between the results for simulations with the same cache size, we can estimate the cycle time required for each cache organization to attain any given performance level. This interpolation process smoothes the quantization effects to the point that they are inconsequential. The results of the interpolation, shown in Figure 4-4, follow lines of equal performance across the design space. The best performance level displayed is 1.1 times slower than the best case: the scenario with 4MB of cache cycling at 20ns. The increment between the lines is an increase in execution time equal to 0.3 times this base value. The uppermost line depicts a class of machines that run 5.9 times slower[15] than the best case for this experiment.

---

[15] Being the 16th line from the bottom, its performance level is $1.1 + (16 - 1) \times 0.3 = 5.9$.

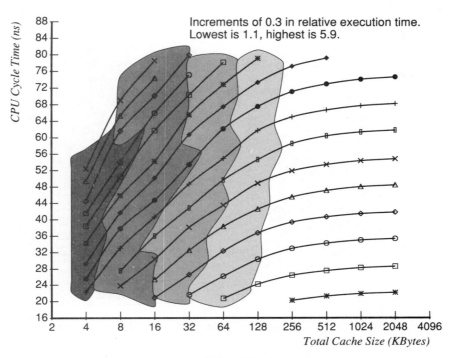

Lines of Equal Performance

Figure 4-4

The slope of the lines indicates how much cycle time can be exchanged for a doubling in cache size without changing the overall performance. A slope of 5ns per doubling in size means that a straight swap of cache RAMs for chips four times as large (typically the next size up) but 10ns slower is performance-neutral. For this slope, less than a 10ns degradation in cycle time improves performance, while more than 10ns of additional cycle time moves the machine to a design point on a poorer performance curve. The number of lines crossed in the transition from one design point to another indicates the difference in execution time between the two machines. The shaded areas indicate regions of the design space in which the slope of the curves falls into specific ranges. In the unshaded region at the right, the slopes are less than 2.5ns per doubling, while in the leftmost shaded zone, the slopes are consistently greater than 10ns per doubling. The four boundaries between the five regions are the contours at slopes of 2.5ns, 5ns, 7.5ns and 10ns per doubling.

The shaded regions are the portions of the design space in which the exchange of discrete static RAMs for the next size up is beneficial if the speed difference is less than twice the minimum slope of the zone; in the rightmost region, a swap is called for if the access time difference is 5ns or less, while in the leftmost region, the substitution is advantageous even with an access time difference as large as 20ns. Conversely, the delineated zones are the parts of the design space in which exchanging the RAMs for smaller yet faster ones is beneficial. In the unshaded area, such an exchange is warranted if the cycle time of the machine drops by only 5ns, again assuming a change in the cache size by a factor of four. With each region farther to the left, the cycle time improvement needed to justify the reduction in the cache size increases by 5ns.

For example, consider a system being built around a 40ns CPU, requiring 15ns RAMs to attain that cycle time. If the best available 16Kb and 64Kb RAMs run at 15 and 25ns, respectively, then two comparable design alternatives are 8KB per cache with the 2K by 8b chips or 32KB per cache with the 8K by 8b chips. Both contain the same number of chips in the same physical configuration; the only changes are the number of tag bits, the width of the cache index and the system clock frequency. The slope of constant performance curve at the (16KB,40ns) design point is 16ns per quadrupling, which is greater than the 10ns difference in the RAM speeds. As a result, running the CPU at 50ns with a larger cache improves the overall performance by 7.3%.[16] Performance is maximized when the CPU is running at less than its maximum frequency. This makes sense from the perspective of mean time per reference – a critical parameter for all architectures, but especially RISC machines, which generally rely more heavily on an effective memory hierarchy. If a small cache has a miss rate of 10% and a 10 cycle miss penalty, then the average time per read is two cycles. A reduction in the miss rate to 9% reduces the average time per reference to 1.9 cycles. Thus, the cycle time can degrade by 5% without affecting the mean execution time per reference.

The main memory access time has two components: the latency and the transfer time. In the simulation model, the latency is a fixed number of nanoseconds. Therefore, as the cycle time decreases, the number of cycles per miss penalty increases. As the miss penalty increases, a fixed change in the miss rate has a greater impact on performance. Alternatively, as the miss penalty increases, a fixed change in the miss rate is equivalent to an increasing proportion of the cycle time. So, as the cycle time decreases, an increasing fraction of a cycle that is equivalent to a change in cache size is offset by the

---

[16] With the smaller cache, the execution time is 3.15 times the best case for the experiment, while with the 64KB total cache, the mean execution time is only 2.92 times the normalization point, yielding a 7.3% improvement.

decreasing cycle time, causing the tradeoffs between the cycle time and miss rate to be relatively constant. This explains why the regions of Figure 4-4 are nearly vertical: the cycle time – cache size tradeoff is independent of the cycle time.

If a less aggressive memory model were used in the simulated system, the smaller caches would perform even worse in relation to the larger caches. The higher miss rates increase the sensitivity of systems with smaller caches to the memory access time; slowing down the memory system would have the effect of bending the lines of constant performance down for small cache sizes and increasing their slope across the entire range of sizes. This in turn increases the desirability of larger caches at the expense of cycle time.

An inevitable consequence of the asymptotic shape of the lines of constant performance is a strong tendency to increase the total cache size to the 32KB to 128KB range. Beyond that region, the curves are flat enough that there is little motivation for further increases in cache size, regardless of how infinitesimal the cycle time penalty. If the cache size is within this range, any additional hardware is more effectively used improving the cycle time of the cache/CPU pair.

Analytically, it is quite straightforward to perceive the nature of the tradeoff. If the general functions, described in Section 3.1, relating the size of a cache to its minimum cycle time were known (Equation 3.3), it would be possible to solve for the optimal design problem exactly. Unfortunately, these functions, especially the relationship between the size and cycle time, are not known in the general case, and at best can be approximated over a limited portion of the overall design space.

Recall Equation 3.5, which balanced the cycle time and cycle count effects of a change in the organizational parameter at the optimal design point:

$$\frac{1}{t_{L1}} \times \frac{\partial t_{L1}}{\partial C} = -\frac{1}{N_{Total}} \times \frac{\partial N_{Total}}{\partial C}$$

Since Agarwal's model of the miss ratio, given in Equation 3.11, is relatively complex, it is more convenient to pretend that the cache size is a continuous variable and to use the differential form. When this model is folded into the assumed relationship between the miss rate and the cycle count, then the terms relating to the miss rate become manageable for direct-mapped caches. Specifically, with minor rearrangement and some simplification, Equation 3.5 yields an optimum configuration when the derivative of the miss rate with respect to the size, modified by the proportion of reads in the reference stream, is the negative inverse of the derivative of the size with respect to the cycle time, modified by the memory access time:

$$\frac{N_{Read}}{N_{Read}+N_{Store}\,\overline{n}_{L1write}}\times\frac{\partial m(\mathbf{C})}{\partial C} = \frac{-1}{\overline{t}_{MMread}}\times\frac{\partial t_{L1}}{\partial C}\qquad [4.1]$$

Alternatively, this equation indicates that the optimum is characterized by a change in the cache size causing an equal sized decrease in the time spent fetching from main memory, $N_{Read}\times\overline{t}_{MMread}\times\frac{\partial m(\mathbf{C})}{\partial C}$, and increase in the time spent fetching from the cache, $(N_{Read}+N_{Store}\,\overline{n}_{L1write})\frac{\partial t_{L1}}{\partial C}$. Equation 4.1 is useful though because it equates organizational parameters on the one side with temporal ones on the other: a form in which the two can be considered independently. We are interested in the optimal cache size – being the size that satisfies this equation – as a function of the other design variables. We will first consider the left-hand side, then the right.

For Agarwal's miss ratio model, the general form of the derivative of the miss ratio with respect to cache size is rather obscure. However, for medium and large caches, the number of sets, S, is large with respect to the total of the working set sizes of all programs, $u'(B)$. This allows some dramatic simplification. For these caches, the miss ratio is proportional to the inverse square of the number of sets, and exponential in the ratio of the number of unique blocks, $u(B)$, and the number of sets:

$$\frac{\partial m(\mathbf{C})}{\partial C} = \frac{u(B)^2}{B\,\tau\,S^2}e^{-\frac{u(B)}{S}}\left(a - \frac{1}{t}\left\lfloor\frac{t-1}{t_s}\right\rfloor e^{-\frac{u'(B)}{S}}\right) \text{ for } S \gg u'(B)$$

where

$$a = \frac{1}{t}\left\lfloor\frac{t-1}{t_s}\right\rfloor - c$$

Since the cache size is directly related to the number of sets, the rate of change of the miss rate with respect to the cache size, $\frac{\partial m(\mathbf{C})}{\partial C}$, varies as the inverse square of the cache size ($\frac{1}{C^2}$). This relationship corresponds to a linear relationship between the log of the miss rate, $\log m$, and the log base two of the cache size, $\log_2 C$, with the slope dependent on the constant of proportionality. Figure 4-1 shows just such a linear correspondence over a fairly wide range of cache sizes. This linear plot on a log-log graph is precisely what is predicted by Singh's power law model [Singh 88]. The slope of the line in Figure 4-1 indicates an exponent of approximately -1.54 for the derivative of the miss rate, instead of the predicted -2. For his single, six million reference trace, Singh measured a value of -1.49 for this same derivative.

The slope of the lines of constant performance in Figure 4-4 is the derivative of the cycle time with respect to the cache size for a constant execution time. This derivative is related to the partial derivatives of performance with respect to the two design variables. Starting from the basic execution time model of Equation 3.9, we find that these slopes are directly proportional to the partial derivative of the miss ratio with respect to the cache size that was part of the balancing equation, Equation 4.1. The inverse square relationship between this derivative and the cache size carries over to the slope of the lines of constant performance that determine the strength of the tradeoff:

$$
\frac{dt}{dC} = \frac{\dfrac{\partial T_{Total}}{\partial C}}{\dfrac{\partial T_{Total}}{\partial t}} = \frac{-N_{Read}\,\overline{t}_{MMread}}{N_{Read}+N_{Store}\,\overline{n}_{L1write}}\,\frac{\partial m(\mathbf{C})}{\partial C} \quad \propto \quad \frac{1}{C^2} \qquad [4.2]
$$

Furthermore, the slope is dependent on the cache size, C, and the mean main memory access time, $\overline{t}_{MMread}$, but not on the cycle time. Intuitively, the slope is the ratio of the change in the cycle time to the balancing change in the cache size. However, a change in cache size is performance-neutral when the change in total main memory fetch time exactly balances the change in the time spent using the cache. Since the first of these two times is independent of the cycle time, so must be the second. The change in the time spent using the cache is proportional to the change in the cycle time: the balancing change in cycle time must therefore also be independent of its magnitude. It follows then that the slope is also independent of the cycle time. The regions of slope in Figure 4-4 have a slight lean to them because in the simulation model the main memory transfer time is a fixed number of cycles. Therefore, as the cycle time increases, the mean main memory access time, $\overline{t}_{MMread}$, also increases somewhat.

This independence of the tradeoff on the CPU cycle time is critical. Given the same cache miss penalty, expressed in nanoseconds, to first order, the slope of the lines of constant performance are the same number of nanoseconds per doubling regardless of whether the CPU cycle time is 5ns or 500ns. For the memory system and block size simulated, the cache miss penalty was between 300 and 500ns depending on the cycle time. With these values of $\overline{t}_{MMread}$, 4KB and 8KB total caches experience slopes in excess of 10ns per doubling in cache size. For a 5ns system, that represents a 200% increase in the cycle time for a single doubling. That percentage of the cycle time is directly proportional to the main memory access time. If the slopes are expressed in terms of the CPU cycle time, then the slopes increase as the cycle time decreases, unless the cache miss penalty decreases proportionately with the cycle time. Fundamentally, the tradeoff for each cache size is independent of the unit of time, be it a nanosecond or a cycle time.

Equation 4.2 indicates that the slope of the lines of constant performance is related to the rate of change of the miss rate with respect to the cache size, which in turn is related to the locality of workload through the number of blocks touched per quantum ($u(B)$ in Equation 4.2). In the most comprehensive published study of workload characteristics, Smith provides the miss rates for a wide variety of single-process and multiprogramming traces [Smith 85a]. For the non-trivial traces, the ratio of the maximum to minimum change in miss ratio across six cache sizes[17] was 6.4. Across a single doubling of the cache size, the ratio of maximum to minimum change is much higher – between 15 and 20. Superficially, it might seem that the optimum cache size would also depend dramatically on the workload. However, the inverse square relationship between the cache size and the slope means that a factor of six change in the slope due to variations in the workload can be compensated for by a change of slightly more than a factor of two cache size. Thus, one can expect the regions of Figure 4-4 to move relatively little from left to right across a wide variety of workloads: the optimum cache size is quite workload independent.

The relationship between the cache size and cycle time determines the right-hand side of the balancing equation (Equation 4.1). Unfortunately, this link is difficult to quantify, essentially because of the myriad factors affecting it. In lieu of an exact form for this function, we will use a crude approximation which loosely characterizes all such functions. Using the proportionality and general shape of the estimate, the temporal half of the tradeoff equation is compared with the organizational half.

Conceptually, a cache's minimum cycle time has three main components: data access, tag access and comparison overhead, and data selection.

$$t_{L1} = t_{DataAccess}(C , S) + t_{TagOverhead}(A , C) + t_{Select}(C , A , B)$$

---

[17] Between 2KB total and 64KB total.

The first term is related to the RAM technology and the size and physical organization of the data array. It includes any buffering from the address input of the cache to the RAM array, address selection and decoding, and data-out drive back to the CPU. The tag access portion is non-zero only if the critical path includes the tag access and comparison, which constitutes the amount of time the data access could slow down before the two paths were equally critical. The data selection overhead is related to the set associativity and the block size of the cache. This overhead is the time along the critical path through any multiplexors or an alignment network so that just the requested data is presented to the CPU. All three components are related to cache size in that as the size decreases, more aggressive technologies can be used (assuming a fixed board area and power allocation to the entire memory system), thus allowing reduction in the basic wire and gate delays. This technology dependence unfortunately complicates the model, since it is neither continuous nor related to only one or two parameters.

We are interested in the change in cycle time that accompanies a change in the cache size, $\frac{\Delta t_{L1}}{\Delta C}$. In practice, the change in the data access time dominates the increment in cycle time. Given that only the number of sets is changing, the variation in size probably will be implemented by a doubling in the depth of the RAM array. Thus, the movement in the minimum cycle time is most strongly related to the change in the access time as a result of that doubling in depth.

The denominator of $\frac{\Delta t_{L1}}{\Delta C}$ is proportional to the cache size, C. The numerator is approximately the change in access time as the RAM size doubles, which, in practice, does not follow any particular trend. It is safe to say, though, that any proportionality based on the cache size is bounded by $O(\sqrt{C})$ above and one below. The rationale for the upper bound stems from the physical organization of RAM arrays. The access time is minimized when the array is divided into approximately square chunks [Duncombe 86]. This corresponds to bit and word lines that grow in length at most as the square root of the number of bits. The lower limit comes simply from the realization that access times do not decrease as the size increases. Clearly, if the cycle time is constant over a range of cache sizes, the optimal size within that range will be at its maximum where the miss ratio is lowest.

The distinctiveness and consistency of the speed – size tradeoff as seen in Figure 4-4 is the result of the difference in proportionalities between the left- and right-hand sides of the balancing equation:

$$\frac{N_{Read}}{N_{Read}+N_{Store}\,n_{L1write}} \times \frac{\partial m(\mathbf{C})}{\partial C} \ \propto\ C^{-2}$$

$$\frac{-1}{\overline{t}_{MMread}} \times \frac{\Delta t_{L1}}{\Delta C} \ \propto\ \frac{1}{\overline{t}_{MMread}}\,C^{-\frac{1}{2}}$$

Given these proportionalities, the immobility of the optimal design point is demonstrated by noting the effect of a change in the cache size. A doubling or halving of the size, C, multiplies one side of the crucial inequality by a factor of between 2 and 2.8 relative to the other side. Any linearly dependent factor, such as the main memory access time, t_{MMread}, must change by that same amount to compensate or to substantially affect the optimal operating point.

Despite several points of consistency between this analytical analysis and previous simulation results, it is important to recognize that this analysis makes many assumptions and simplifications. Most significantly, the assumption that the number of sets, S, is larger than the working set is not true for small caches. When intrinsic misses become a significant fraction of the total, the relative change in the miss ratio becomes less strongly dependent on the size, C. In addition, the dependency between the cycle time and the mean memory access time changes the tradeoff if the changes in cycle time become large. It is difficult to generalize the dependence between the cache size and the cycle time because the relationship between the two is extremely dependent on the implementation. However, these and other factors are not sufficiently strong to override the basic conclusion supported by the simulation results: the optimum total cache size is typically in the 32KB to 128KB range, and this range is relatively insensitive to variations in the workload and memory system.

4.2. Speed – Set Size Tradeoffs

The primary motivation for set associativity is twofold. First, there is a reduction in the miss rate over that of a direct-mapped cache of the same size [Smith 78a]. Second, the virtual memory constraints often indirectly impose a large set size. Unrestricted aliasing of multiple virtual pages to a single physical page is effectively handled in hardware by doing the virtual to physical translation before or in conjunction with the cache access. Completing the address translation before starting the cache access frequently incurs a substantial performance penalty, due to either an increased cycle time or greater cache access latencies. If the performance goals then require simultaneous access of the cache and address translation hardware, only the virtual address is available when access of the physically addressed cache begins. If more than the page offset bits[18] are used in the cache access, the data may reside in any of several sets [Tucker 86]. Beyond a certain point, the number of sets cannot be increased without introducing this ambiguity in the location of the desired data: the only easy way to make the cache larger is to increase the set size. For example, the IBM 3033 has a 16-way set-associative 64KB cache for this reason [Smith 87b]. Restricting the virtual to physical map [Mahon 86] and increasing the page size postpone this problem by increasing the maximum number of sets. Alternatively, any of several cache sets can be allowed to hold each piece of data. This strategy is more complex, and it suffers from a degraded mean cache hit time because the sets which may hold a piece of data must be searched serially [Goodman 87].

An additional advantage of set-associative caches over direct-mapped caches is that they are much less likely to encounter pathological situations. If two frequently referenced objects happen to collide in a direct-mapped cache, then the miss rate for the program can be many times the expected value. For physically addressed caches, the performance may unexpectedly and dramatically fall if, on a particular run, the virtual to physical address map happens to cause some unfortunate collisions. For instance, if the inner loop of a program collides with the library routine it calls, both will consistently miss on instruction fetches. Set-associative caches endure a greater number of coincidental collisions before performance noticeably degrades. The probability of a random drop in performance due to contention within individual sets drops dramatically with each increase in set size. As a result of the growing prominence of direct-mapped caches [Clark 87, Fu 87, Jouppi 88, Moussouris 86], compiler and operating system techniques that minimize the number of avoidable collisions have been evaluated and introduced [Karlovsky 89, McFarling 89].

The cost of set associativity is difficult to assess in absolute terms. If the total cache size remains the same, the number of tags is not affected by a change in the associativity. However, such a change does affect the number of tags and blocks that must be accessed simultaneously. Thus, data path widths are directly related to the set size. If the cache is distributed across several integrated circuits, increasing the number of bits that must be read in parallel can dramatically affect the area and cost of the cache.

The largest temporal impact of set associativity stems from the need to complete the tag access and comparison before gating the data to the CPU [Jouppi 89]. Whether this gating is done via explicit multiplexors or via output enables onto a tri-state bus, there is likely to be an incremental delay in

---

[18] The page offset and block offset bits are those unaffected by the translation.

the cache access time as compared to a direct-mapped implementation of the same size. Depending on the physical constraints, the additional access width may mandate broader static RAMs. Within a single product family, wider yet shallower RAMs are invariably slower than the by-one and by-four versions. A wide physical organization may result in additional loading on critical address and data lines, causing further degradation in the cycle time. The accumulated time penalty is even more severe when the cache/CPU interface would otherwise allow the hit/miss information to arrive after the data [Horowitz 87]: there is no opportunity to use this additional time since the choice of which piece of data to present to the CPU depends on which tag within a set, if any, matches.

The cycle time penalty of an increased set size can be reduced by using faster RAM technology for the tags. This allows for overlap of the tag comparison with a portion of the data access. Many integrated cache controllers do this by integrating the tag RAM onto the same IC as the comparators and control logic [Cole 88]. Depending on the block size and the physical organization of the cache, the data portion is sometimes deeper than the tag portion. This too can help hide the tag comparison time.

These degradations are most severe for large caches made of discrete RAMs. For integrated caches, they are all substantially reduced. Since the performance of a RAM array degrades as it becomes less square [Duncombe 86], any moderately large array fetches several words simultaneously. The multiplexors needed in a set-associative design are then necessary regardless of the cache organization: the challenge is to complete the tag fetches and comparisons early enough that the control signals do not delay the data. In a full custom VLSI design, circuit design techniques and the optimization of the physical and logical organizations can minimize the cycle time degradation due to set associativity.

Rather than quantifying these various temporal and physical costs, the benefits associated with the improved miss ratio are translated into equivalent cycle time changes. If the implementation of set associativity impacts the cache/CPU cycle time by an amount greater than this break-even value, then adding set associativity is detrimental to overall performance.

Figure 4-5 confirms previously reported results for the effects of set associativity on miss rate [Agarwal 88, Hill 87]. As in Figure 4-1, the X axis plots the combined size of the equal I and D caches, and the Y axis plots the miss rates for the single-level model system (Figure 3-5) for various sizes and associativities. For each cache size, a doubling in associativity is accompanied by a halving of the number of sets. Random replacement is used regardless of the set size. The change from direct-mapped to two-way set-associativity drops

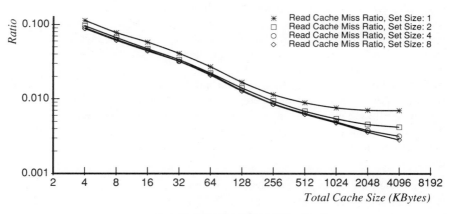

Set-Associative Read Miss Ratio

Figure 4-5

the miss ratio[19] by about 20% for caches up to about 256KB total. Smaller improvements are seen for set sizes above two. For caches greater than 256KB, the relative improvement in the miss ratio increases because the caches are virtual and many processes use the same portion of their respective virtual address spaces. For these large caches, interprocess, or extrinsic,[20] misses constitute a large fraction of the total. Due to the overlap between the address usage between processes, few of these interprocess conflicts are eliminated by adding more sets. In contrast, increasing the set associativity allows two or more processes to coexist in the cache without fighting one another.

As in the previous section, the tradeoff between cycle time and set associativity is investigated by varying both parameters simultaneously. Figure 4-6 shows the effect on execution time of cache size, set associativity and cycle time. The memory model is the same as was used previously, with the cycles per memory reference varying as in Table 4-1. In contrast to Figure 4-3, a change in associativity has a significant performance effect on the smaller caches. For a 4KB combined cache size, a change in set size from one to two results in a 10% improvement in the execution time. For large caches, the improvement is much less significant. Since the miss rate is smaller for larger

---

[19] Called the miss ratio spread by Hill [Hill 87].

[20] See Section 3.4.

caches, the main memory accounts for a smaller proportion of total execution time. A constant percentage decrease in the number of memory accesses corresponds to a smaller percentage decrease in total execution time.

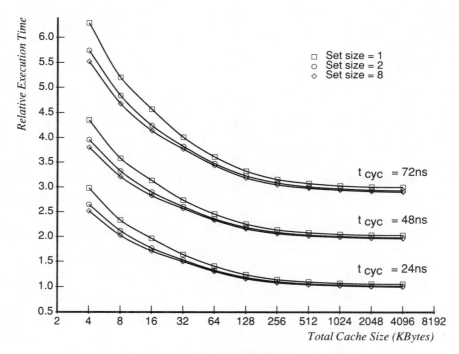

Speed - Set Size Tradeoff: Execution Time

Figure 4-6

Vertical interpolation between the lines for the direct-mapped caches allows estimation of the cycle time that a direct-mapped machine would need to match the performance of a set-associative design of the same size. The difference between the cycle times of the two machines is the amount of time available for the implementation of set associativity. If increasing the set size degrades the cycle time by more than this difference, then there is a net decrease in performance.[21]

Figures 4-7 through 4-9 map the cumulative break-even degradations over the cycle time of a direct-mapped cache for set associativities of two, four and eight across the explored design space. The boundaries between the shaded regions are the contours at 2ns through 10ns at 2ns intervals. They show the portions of the design space in which more or less time is available for the break-even implementation of associativity.

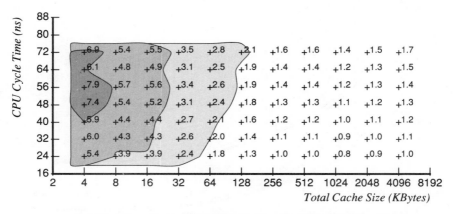

Set Size Two Cumulative Break-Even Implementation Times

Figure 4-7

There are several important observations to make from these graphs. Most significantly, the numbers are uniformly small. Only for a total cache size of less than 16KB is the break-even point more than 6ns. Six nanoseconds is the worst-case *data-in* to *data-out* time for an Advanced-Schottky (AS) multiplexor [TI 86]. More important is the delay from *select* to *data-out*. No point matches the 11ns along this path for this high-speed part. The conclusion is clear: it is unlikely that set associativity ever makes sense from a performance

---

[21] As noted in Section 4.1, the 56ns design is abnormally inefficient, to the extent of introducing non-monotonicities in the performance as a function of cycle time. While this did not significantly affect those results, it severely distorted the analysis of set associativity. As a result, the data for the 56ns case has been smoothed to be more representative. Quantization effects can be significant and deceiving.

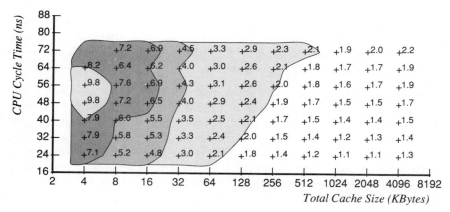

Set Size Four Cumulative Break-Even Implementation Times

Figure 4-8

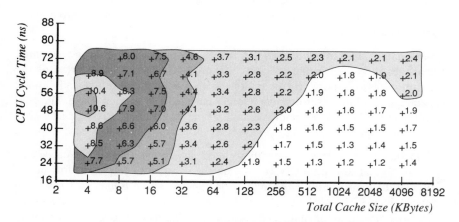

Set Size Eight Cumulative Break-Even Implementation Times

Figure 4-9

perspective for caches made of discrete TTL parts. On the other hand, in an integrated environment, where the caches are likely to be smaller and the cost of implementing set associativity is reduced, an increase in set size may be beneficial. In addition, the difference in incremental break-even times between set size two and four is small: at most 2.4ns. The difference between four and eight is even smaller. This indicates that set associativity greater than two should be implemented only if it is forced by the virtual memory constraints or if there is essentially no additional cycle time penalty.

For the smaller cache sizes, the break-even difference is not monotonic with cycle time. For larger caches, there is a slight positive correlation. The non-monotonicity is a result of the quantization effects and the uneven changes in the cache miss penalties from one scenario to the next. For large caches, the performance is a much smoother function of cycle time, which translates to a better behaved tradeoff function. The larger relative improvement in the miss ratio seen for large caches does not result in a significant cycle time advantage. In general, the proportion of a cycle that is equivalent to a set-associativity change increases with decreasing cycle time.

As with the speed – size tradeoff, if a less aggressive memory system were used, the increased cache miss penalty would more significantly affect the smaller cache sizes. In that regime, the miss rate improvement brought on by an increase in the associativity would be more significant than with the simulated memory model. The result would be larger differences between equivalent cycle times and a greater opportunity for performance improvement through the implementation of set associativity.

An analytical examination of the associativity tradeoffs has the potential advantages discussed in the previous section: insight into the sources of the benefits of associativity, corroboration of the simulation results and limited generalization of those results over a larger portion of the design space. The goal is to relate the break-even implementation time to the associativity, cache size, and memory speed.

Equation 3.5 describes the conditions necessary for a change in the cache size to be performance-neutral. By combining the comparable equation for the set size with the expression for the total cycle count given in Equation 3.7, we can relate a change in associativity to a change in cycle time. The change in the cycle time needed to maintain a constant level of performance across a doubling in the associativity is the incremental break-even time, Δt_{IBE}. Figures 4-7 through 4-9 plot the cumulative times, Δt_{CBE}, which are the differences in cycle times between a direct-mapped cache and an associative one. These times are linearly proportional to the mean memory access time, $\bar{t}_{MMread}$, the fraction of reads in the reference stream and the accompanying change in the miss rate:

$$\Delta t_{IBE}(C,A,B,t_{L1}) = -\frac{N_{Read}}{N_{Read}+N_{Store}\overline{n}_{L1write}} \times \overline{t}_{MMread} \times \Delta m(\mathbf{C}) \quad [4.3]$$

$$\Delta t_{CBE}(C,A=a,B,t_{L1}) = \sum_{i=1}^{\log_2 a} \Delta t_{IBE}(C,A=2^i,B,t_{L1})$$

As was mentioned earlier, Hill shows that the relative change in the miss rate that accompanies a change in associativity is independent of the size of the cache [Hill 87]. The ratio of the miss rates across a change in associativity, $r(A)$, is a function of the set size and, to a much lesser extent, the block size:[22]

$$r(A=a) = \frac{m(\mathbf{C}(C,A=2a,B))}{m(\mathbf{C}(C,A=a,B))}$$

Both a simple analytical analysis by Smith based on a bilinear miss ratio model [Smith 78a] and Hill's empirical data indicate that the miss ratio ratio approaches one from below as the set associativity increases. Smith's analysis also confirms the independence of the cache size found by Hill. As observed in the simulation results, the incremental improvements in the miss rate become vanishingly small as the associativity increases.

The break-even implementation time for a doubling in the set associativity then becomes dependent on one minus the ratio of miss ratios, $1-r(A)$, the weighted proportion of reads in the reference stream, the cache miss ratio before the doubling and the mean main memory read access time:

$$\Delta t_{IBE}(A=2a) = t_{A=a} - t_{A=2a} = (1-r(A=a))\frac{N_{Read}\, m(A=a)\,\overline{t}_{MMread}}{N_{Read}+N_{Store}\overline{n}_{L1write}}$$

$$= \frac{T_{MM}(A=2a)}{T_{L1}}(1-r(A=a))$$

---

[22] This ratio of miss ratios is equivalent to Hill's miss ratio spread, which defines it as the relative change in the miss ratio when the associativity is halved.

$$mrs(A=a,B) = \frac{m(\mathbf{C}(C,A=a,B))}{m(\mathbf{C}(C,A=2a,B))} - 1 = \frac{1}{r(A=a)} - 1$$

$$\Delta t_{CBE}(A=a) = \sum_{i=1}^{\log_2 a} \frac{T_{MM}(A=2^i)}{T_{L1}}\left(1 - r(A=2^{i-1})\right)$$

$$= \frac{T_{MM}(A=a)}{T_{L1}}\left(\frac{m(A=1)}{m(A=a)} - 1\right) \qquad\qquad [4.4]$$

In these equations we can observe all the empirically observed phenomena. Since the miss ratio ratio, $r(A)$, approaches one for increasing associativity, the incremental break-even time goes to zero, as the associativity increases, causing the cumulative break-even time to plateau. The ratio of the fully associative cache miss ratio and a direct-mapped cache miss ratio sets the upper bound on the cumulative break-even times. Also, as the cache size increases, the miss ratio, $m(A)$, and the total main memory access time, T_{MM}, decline, causing the incremental break-even times to drop dramatically. The break-even times are independent of the cycle time, except through the transfer period of the mean main memory time. As the cycle time increases, the transfer period, measured in nanoseconds, also increases, causing the mean main memory fetch time and the break-even time to follow suit.

The previous section showed that the miss ratio drops uniformly with increasing cache size until the number of mandatory misses becomes significant. For large caches, where the direct-mapped miss ratio flattens out, the ratio of miss ratios is no longer independent of the total size. That it significantly increases with C causes the incremental break-even times to stop declining, and even to increase slightly at the largest cache sizes. In the simulated system, the minimum occurred at about 1MB of combined cache size (See Figure 4-7).

Smith's analysis of workloads showed a variation of between three and five to one in the fully associative miss ratios as a function of cache size [Smith 85a]. In the absence of any information about the dependence of the miss ratio ratio, $r(A)$, on the workload, it is reasonable to expect a comparably large overall dependence of the break-even times on the workload. This underscores the importance of having traces that accurately reflect the operating system and the multiprogramming characteristics of the target system when deciding on this organizational parameter.

To summarize, this section confirms Hill's finding that it is difficult to build a set-associative cache that has higher overall performance than a comparable direct-mapped cache. Though clearly true for larger caches composed of several integrated circuits, this is also true for the medium sized caches that the previous section shows are performance-optimal. Associativities greater than two are unwarranted except when mandated by other factors, such as the virtual memory constraints. The amount of time available for the implementation of set-associativity is linearly dependent on the cache miss penalty and on the magnitude of the miss rates, which translates to a fairly wide variation depending on the system configuration and workload. More significantly, the break-even time is independent of the cycle time.

4.3. Block Size – Memory Speed Tradeoffs

Of all the organizational parameters, the block size is unique in that it affects performance through the miss ratio and the cache miss penalty. Furthermore, in determining the cache miss penalty, it interacts with parameters external to the cache: the memory latency and transfer rate.

The block size is very commonly confused with the fetch size. To summarize the definitions presented in Section 2.1, the block size is the amount of data memory in the cache associated with a tag. The fetch size is the amount of data retrieved from main memory at one time. The confusion between the two stems from two sources: first, the nomenclature for blocks and fetches is not standardized across the industry. It is often not clear where an author is referring to one or the other or both when using one of several near or partial synonyms. Second, the two are frequently identical in size. This facilitates the use of block or line size for both. Throughout most of this section, the two are assumed to be equal. Section 4.3.2 specifically deals with the case of different block and fetch sizes. In the remainder of this section, unless clearly indicated, "block size" is used in the traditional way as a short form for "equal block and fetch size." As a reminder of this convention, "block/fetch size" is occasionally used instead.

Increasing the fetch size generally decreases the miss ratio because of the spatial locality of references: the high probability that data in the vicinity of a referenced word is likely to be referenced in the near future. The miss ratio decreases because the expected utility of a word adjacent to and brought in with a referenced word is greater than the expected utility of the word that it is replacing in the cache. Data that is further away from the current reference has a lower probability of being used soon. Therefore the mean utility of the words being brought in decreases with increasing fetch size. When the mean utility of the fetched words drops below the mean utility of the words in the cache, the miss ratio begins to rise again. The mean utility of data in a cache is primarily a function of the cache size: small caches only contain things that were relatively recently used and so have a higher likelihood of being used again because of the temporal locality of the program. For each cache size there is an optimal fetch size that minimizes the miss ratio.

There is secondary effect on the average utility of data in the cache that is dependent on the block size: for a constant cache size, as the block size increases, the number of blocks in the cache decreases. As the number of tags is reduced, there is less opportunity to hold a lot of widely distant data in the cache. Except in pathological cases, however, this effect only comes into play for very small caches. In addition, there are important interactions between the block size and the write strategy. For instance, as the block size increases, the effective penalty of a write miss increases since more potentially good data is invalidated.

When these two factors that tend to increase the miss rate start to dominate over the declining benefit of spatial locality, then the miss rate begins to increase with further increases in block size. There is an optimum combined block and fetch size with respect to the miss rate; it is a function of the degree of locality in the program. Smith has shown how the cache miss rate varies with the cache size and block size [Smith 87a].

The block/fetch size that optimizes system performance is significantly smaller than that which minimizes the miss rate. The performance-optimal block size depends on the characteristics of main memory. The memory read access time, or alternatively, the cache miss penalty, can be expressed in the form $la + \frac{B}{tr}$, where la is the latency in cycles to the first word, tr is the transfer rate in words per CPU cycle and B is the block/fetch size in words. This equation illustrates the difficulty with large block sizes: each doubling of the block size doubles the second term, to the point where it completely overwhelms the latency. The impact of these large cache miss penalties can be lessened somewhat through the use of more complicated fetch strategies: for example, early continuation (allowing the processor to continue once the desired word is received from memory), load forwarding (starting the fetch from the desired word or sub-block) or streaming (channeling incoming memory data to both the CPU and the cache). Smith points out that if the miss penalty is of the form $la + \frac{B}{tr}$, then the block size that minimizes the mean read time depends only on the product $la \times tr$, and not on either factor independently.

Though the read access time is the main component of memory's contribution to the total execution time, it is not the only component. In particular, the mean time that reads are delayed by writes or other memory operations, $\bar{n}_{ReadDelay}$, can be folded into the latency. For real systems, then, we can reasonably expect the optimal block size to depend to some degree on the other memory and cache parameters that influence the mean read delay time.

Cache blocks can be implemented horizontally, vertically or in some combination of the two. The distinction between the two organizations blurs somewhat for an integrated, or on-chip, cache. In a horizontal implementation, each word of the block is in a separate RAM: all the words in the block are accessed in parallel. This allows for wide paths between memory and the CPU, though multiplexors are needed somewhere between the cache RAMs and wherever the data is used in the CPU. In a vertical implementation, some or all of the words in a block reside in a single collection of RAMs that are indexed by the block offset; this allows the block size to be larger than the path to the CPU without the impediment of a multiplexor in the critical cache read path. On the other hand, in vertical implementations, increasing the block size decreases the depth of the tag store with respect to the data store. This may have some advantage in set-associative implementations that rely on shorter tag access times to minimize the cycle time penalty that normally is associated with set-associative designs. Horizontal implementations have the disadvantage that increasing the block size inevitably also increases the amount of multiplexing necessary to retrieve the desired word from the block. The resulting impact on the cycle time is frequently ignored. In addition, there is a link between the block size and the main memory transfer rate; increasing the transfer rate by adding width to the memory bus forces blocks to be horizontally implemented at least to the width of the bus. The alternative, cycling the cache at twice or four times the backplane's frequency, is indicative of an imbalance in the system design. Large block sizes also have the advantage for integrated caches that they increase the ratio of tag bits to data bits in the cache. In environments with a finite amount of area available for a cache, increasing the block size effectively increases the area available for data [Alpert 83, Agarwal 87a] and consequently the cache size.

Figure 4-10 confirms Smith's miss ratio results for the Harvard organization used in the simulations. It shows the miss ratios and relative execution time of the default organization (separate 64KB I and D caches) with a 260ns latency memory.[23] The block size that minimizes the miss ratio is 32W on the data side, and somewhat greater than 64W on the instruction side – a reflection of the greater locality within the instruction stream. Despite this disparity, throughout this experiment both caches are consistently given the same block and fetch sizes.

The other parameters in the graphs that follow are the main memory's latency and transfer rate. The latency is represented by the read and write operation times and the recovery time, all three of which are made equal (See Section 3.3.2). The latency typically includes address decoding and buffering, dynamic RAM access and any error detection and correction. Here, it is varied from

---

[23] A 260ns latency makes for a 12 cycle read request for a block size of four and a cycle time of 40ns.

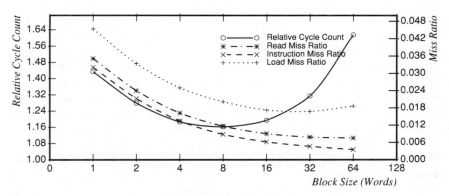

Block/Fetch Size Dependencies:

1.0W per cycle, 260ns latency

Figure 4-10

100ns (three 40ns cycles) to 420ns (eleven 40ns cycles). The lower bound is representative of an aggressive design using fast DRAMs and no ECC. The other extreme, 420ns, is in excess of a very conservative memory board plugged into a generic, low performance backplane. The transfer rate ranges from four words in one cycle to one word in four cycles. These rates translate to peak bandwidths of 400MB/s and 25MB/s, respectively, for a 40ns cycle time. For very small block sizes, a large transfer rate is of no benefit, as the minimum transfer period is one cycle, even if only a quarter of the backplane's width is being used.

Figure 4-11 shows how the total execution time varies with the three parameters that affect the cache miss penalty. In comparison to the cache speed and size parameters, the memory system design has a relatively small impact on performance. Assuming a reasonable choice of block size, the execution time only doubles across the entire range of memory systems. This reflects the moderate size of the caches and their low miss rates.

On each of the curves, representing a particular memory and backplane implementation, an optimal block/fetch size can be estimated by fitting a parabola to the lowest three points and finding its minimum. Figure 4-12 plots these minima as a function of the memory characteristics. Over most of the range, an increase of 80ns (two cycles) in the latency causes an increase in the execution time of between 3% and 6%. Similarly, a halving of the peak transfer rate increases the execution time by between 3% and 13%. These ranges shrink slightly if the block size is restricted to binary values. The sensitivity of execution time to changes in transfer rate is largely independent of the latency, and vice versa.

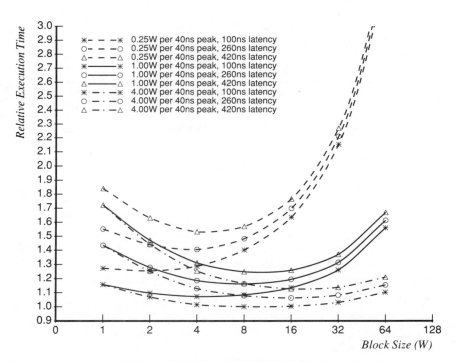

Execution Time versus Memory Parameters:

64KB/64KB Split I/D Cache

Figure 4-11

Figure 4-13 tests the first-order derivation that the optimal block size is dependent only on the product of the two memory parameters. The non-integral optimal block size is plotted against the product of the latency and the transfer rate. Each line corresponds to a single transfer rate, with the points representing the latencies of three, five, seven, nine and eleven cycles. The line segments

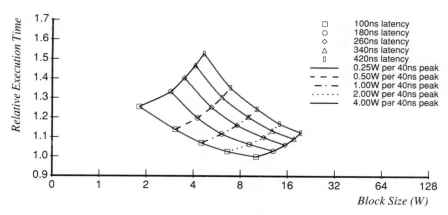

Optimal Block/Fetch Size: 64KB/64KB Split I/D Cache

Figure 4-12

overlap, verifying that the optimal block size is indeed a function of the memory speed product, $la \times tr$. Since the block size of choice is solely a function of this product, as DRAM and backplane technologies improve, their influences tend to cancel each other, leaving the best block size relatively unchanged.

Note also that since the selection of the block size is dependent on the main memory characteristics and not the CPU cycle time, it is inappropriate to use "cycles" as the unit of time in discussing this tradeoff. Main memories' latencies and transfer rates are specified in terms of nanoseconds. In synchronous systems, these are generally rounded up to the nearest integral number of CPU cycles, once the value of the cycle time is determined.

An experienced engineer might expect that a good design would equalize the transfer time and the latency. The dotted line in Figure 4-13 shows the block size choice that balances the two components of the miss penalty. Clearly, the optimum block/fetch size does not follow from this strategy. When the memory product is small and the memory technology is superior to the backplane's, the optimum block size is larger than expected. In the region above the dotted line, more than half the time is spent transferring data. Similarly, when the product is high – indicating that the memory technology is poor with respect to the backplane – the optimal block size is smaller than one might expect. Below the dotted line, the latency period is greater than the transfer period, so more than half the time is spent waiting for memory to present the first word.

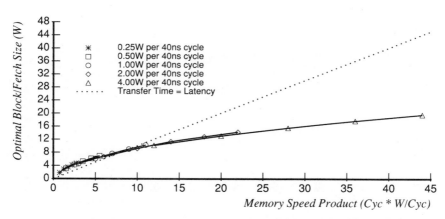

Optimal Block/Fetch Size versus Memory Speed Product:

64KB/64KB Split I/D Cache

Figure 4-13

For caches smaller than 132KB, the general shape and position of the web of optimal block and fetch sizes is relatively unchanged. However, for larger caches, one starts to see significantly larger optimal block size. Recall that two factors cause caches with much larger block sizes to have poorer miss rates: a decreasing mean expected utility of the incoming data and a reduction in the number of tags. For very large caches, this latter term, which is dominant for small and medium sized caches, is much less significant. The result is an increase in the optimal block sizes; Figure 4-14 shows that for a 2MB total cache size, the best block size approaches 16 and 32 words for many plausible memory systems.

The primary conclusion is that without special mechanisms to reduce the cache miss penalty, optimal block/fetch sizes are reasonably small and relatively invariant. For the central portion of the design space, the best binary block size was either four or eight words. Since the transfer rate, tr, and latency, la, are inversely linked through the cycle time to their cache independent counterparts, LA and TR, and since the optimal block size is only a function of $la \times tr$ (or equivalently, $LA \times TR$), the block size of choice is completely independent of the CPU cycle time.

Again, some algebraic manipulation of the equations of Section 3.4 provides some insight into the mechanisms at work and allows generalization of these

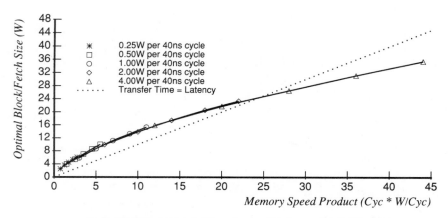

Optimal Block/Fetch Size versus Memory Speed Product:

1MB/1MB Split I/D Cache

Figure 4-14

observations. If one is strictly interested in minimizing the mean reference time, that is, $N_{Total}/(N_{Read}+N_{Write})$, then the optimal block/fetch size, found by equating to zero the derivative of the total cycle count with respect to the block size, is strictly a function of the memory speed product. Intuitively, it doesn't depend on the total time spent fetching data, but only on the ratio of the time spent transferring data to the time spent waiting. Neither doubling both nor changing the units of time alters the tradeoff.

The inverse function specifies the appropriate memory speed product given a block size. Since the two functions are one-to-one, they are equivalent. The optimal memory product is related to the block size, the miss ratio, and the rate of change of the miss ratio with respect to the block size:

$$ la \times tr \;=\; - \left(B + \frac{m(\mathbf{C})}{\frac{\partial m(\mathbf{C})}{\partial B}} \right) \;\approx\; - \left(B + \frac{m(\mathbf{C})\,\Delta B}{\Delta m(\mathbf{C})} \right) $$

This relationship between the optimal block size and the memory characteristics can be simplified by defining the ratio, $R(B)$, of the miss rate for block size of $2B$ to that for a block/fetch size of B. The best memory product for each block size is equal to the block size, modified by a term dependent only on this ratio of ratios:

$$R(B=b) = \frac{m(\ \mathbf{C}(C,B=2b)\ )}{m(\ \mathbf{C}(C,B=b)\ )}$$

$$la \times tr = B\left(\frac{2R(B)-1}{1-R(B)}\right) \qquad [4.5]$$

This multiplicative factor determines the optimal block size. To probe its characteristics, we need a model of the ratio of miss ratios, $R(B)$, on which the optimal block size solely depends. Smith developed such a model for fully associative caches [Smith 87a]. Having measured miss rates for a variety of small and medium cache and block sizes, Smith fit the observed ratio of ratios to a continuous function of the block and cache sizes. For fully associative unified caches up to 32KB, and block sizes up to 32 words, the ratio of miss ratios is given by:[24]

$$R_{S=1}(C,\frac{B}{2}) \approx e\left(1+\frac{a}{4B+f\log_2 4C-\log_2 4B}\right)\left(1+c(\log_2 4B-2)^d\right)$$

where

$$a = 2.656 \quad b = 4.197 \quad c = 2.357 \quad d = 0.247 \quad e = 0.113 \quad f = 0.667$$

The ratio of ratios for direct-mapped caches, $R(B)$, can be obtained from this fully associative ratio by defining $g(B)$, the ratio of the miss rate for a fully associative cache to a direct-mapped cache. Hill shows, as discussed in Section 4.2, that $g(B)$ is relatively independent of the cache size C [Hill 87]. The desired ratio, $R(B)$, is related to Smith's model through the ratio $\frac{g(B)}{g(2B)}$:[25]

$$g(B=b) = \frac{m(\ \mathbf{C}(C,S=1,B=b)\ )}{m(\ \mathbf{C}(C,A=1,B=b)\ )}$$

---

[24] The factors of four result from Smith's definition of the cache and block size in bytes rather than words. Though accurate for cache sizes between 32B and 32KB, Smith's equation becomes increasingly inaccurate for larger cache sizes. It is usable in the calculation of the optimum block size for cache sizes up to about 256KB.

[25] This ratio declines from a high of 1.009 for a block/fetch size of one word to 0.887 for 64 words. It indicates that improvement in the miss rate due to the addition in set-associativity declines as the block size increases.

$$R(B=b) \ = \ \frac{g(B=b)}{g(B=2b)} R_{S=1}(B=b)$$ [4.6]

Using measured values of the set-associative miss ratio ratio, $g(B)$, and Smith's model, we can calculate values of $R(B)$, shown in Figure 4-15, for a variety of cache sizes. These values can be corroborated by comparing the predicted optimal block size with that calculated by Equation 4.5 with these values and the experimentally observed values. Figure 4-16 shows the results of these two techniques for three cache sizes: 8KB total, 128KB total and 2MB total. The lines show the values predicted by Smith's empirical model, and the hollow symbols are the measured values, obtained identically to those in Figure 4-13. The close correspondence between the two methods of predicting the optimal block size within the region of validity of Smith's model (32B to 32KB) indicates that there is little difference between the optimal block size of equal sized split and unified caches. Outside that domain, the model significantly underestimates the optimum block size. Much of the error in the estimate for large caches is due to an increase in the relative change in miss ratios across the range of associativities, $g(B)$ (See Section 4.2).

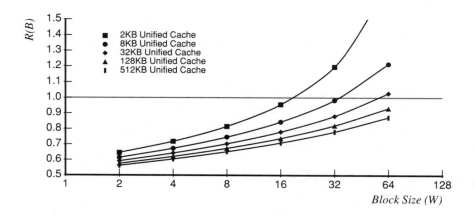

Block/Fetch Size Miss Ratio Ratio, R(B)

Figure 4-15

For each cache size, the ratio of miss ratios, $R(B)$, grows with increasing block size, indicating the declining incremental benefits from further additions

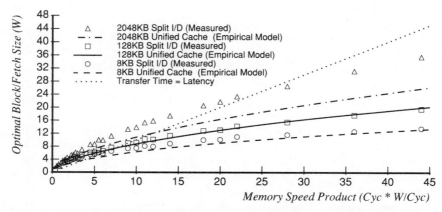

Optimal Block Size versus Memory Speed Product: Model Evalution

Figure 4-16

to the block size. The ratio is 1.0 at the block and fetch size that minimizes the miss ratio. At that value, the multiplicative factor, $\frac{2R(B)-1}{1-R(B)}$, goes to infinity. Clearly, the performance-optimal block size is always less than this miss ratio optimal block size, regardless of the memory system.

As the block size increases, the multiplicative factor, $\frac{2R(B)-1}{1-R(B)}$, decreases, causing the optimum block size curve in Figure 4-13 to bend over in a vaguely logarithmic fashion. For larger caches, the dependency of $R(B)$ on B decreases, so that the characteristic curve becomes more linear, which has the effect of increasing the optimum block size for a given $la \times tr$ product. This increase makes intuitive sense since the miss rates for larger caches are smaller and they reach their minimum at larger block sizes. Since $R(B)$ varies less, the curves bend less, meaning that for larger caches, the naive choice of equal latency and transfer periods, given by $B = la \times tr$, is more reasonable.

A potential simplification to this analytical model is to make the ratio of miss ratios across a block size change, $R(B)$, a constant averaged over a range of block sizes of interest [Killian 88]. The consequence of such a change is to linearize the relationship between the memory speed product and the optimal block size. Depending on the method used to arrive at a single value of $R(B)$, the linearized form could either consistently overestimate the optimal block size or, alternatively, underestimate the block size for low memory products while overestimating for large values of $la \times tr$.

Since larger fetch sizes are beneficial specifically because of the spatial and temporal localities exhibited by programs, one expects the optimal block and fetch size to be highly dependent on the degree of locality in the workload or application. Smith noted the variability of the cache miss rates but did not pursue the issue of sensitivity of the optimum block size [Smith 87a]. Killian measured the values of $R(B)$ for nine non-trivial unix programs[26] for split instruction and data caches up to 512KB each and most block sizes up to 16 words [Killian 88]. Harmonically averaged over the block sizes measured, the values of $R(B)$ varied quite dramatically for smaller caches, although less so for larger ones. For instance, for a 16KB data cache, the average value was 0.70, but the range was 0.86 to 0.58. One extreme indicates a modest benefit from increasing the block size, while the other is very close to the theoretical minimum of 0.5. The result is a wide range in optimal block size as a function of speed product from one program to another. Even for larger caches, where there was consistently less variation in $R(B)$ (for example, 0.66 to 0.52 for the combined effect of a 64KB instruction cache and a 64KB data cache), there was substantial variation in the presumed constant of proportionality between the block size and memory speed product: when inserted into Equation 4.5, these values yield $la \times tr = 0.23B$ and $la \times tr = 0.92B$, respectively. This range indicates close to a factor of four difference in the optimal block size across programs. The ratio of the maximum to minimum optimum block size varied erratically from three to 24 depending on the program being run and the cache type and size. Of all the organizational parameters, the choice of the block size is by far the most workload dependent.

Interestingly, three programs[27] had non-monotonic miss ratio ratios for their data streams. Particularly for small cache sizes, the relative improvement due to an increase in the data cache block size started out small, then increased before falling again to no improvement at very large sizes. Presumably this is due to some characteristic stride to the data references related to the utilization of their data structures.

4.3.1. Optimal Block Size with Cycle Time Degradation

The discussion thus far has focused on the minimization of the mean access time. The linear relationship between the mean access time and the cycle count implies that in the absence of any changes to the cycle time, minimizing one is

---

[26] as1, ccom, espresso, hspice, nroff, spice2g6, spice3a7, tex and timberwolf compiled for the R2000 processor using optimizing C and FORTRAN compilers.

[27] espresso, nroff, and timberwolf.

equivalent to minimizing the other. The question thus arises: how does the relationship between the optimal block size and the memory parameters change if there is a cycle time penalty associated with longer blocks? Figures 4-17 and 4-18 show the behaviour of the optimal block/fetch size in the face of a 1% cycle time degradation per doubling in block size for the default cache organization. For the 40ns base CPU cycle time, this corresponds to 0.4ns additional delay for each additional 2:1 multiplexor needed in a horizontal implementation. In the first of these figures, the unfilled symbols show the optimum block size and performance level with no cycle time degradation (referred to in the key as the reference model), while the filled symbols indicate the optimal choice with the cycle time degradation. Each of the five small numbers is the performance degradation from the corresponding reference scenario, assuming the optimal non-binary block size in both scenarios. In Figure 4-18, the solid and dashed lines indicate the optimal block size with and without the cycle time degradation, respectively.

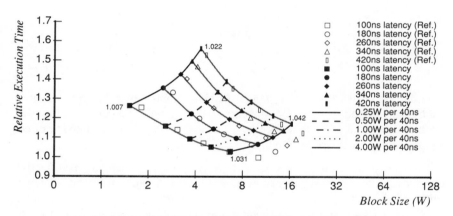

Optimal Block/Fetch Size: 1% Cycle Time Degradation

Figure 4-17

Figures 4-19 and 4-20 duplicate the experiment with a 5% change per increment in block size. The effect of the increased cycle time degradation is sufficiently strong that the optimum block and fetch size never exceeds eight words, even for the highest transfer rate and shortest latency. Also, the function of optimum binary block size is no longer a single valued function of the memory speed product, $la \times tr$. In both these experiments, the changes in cycle

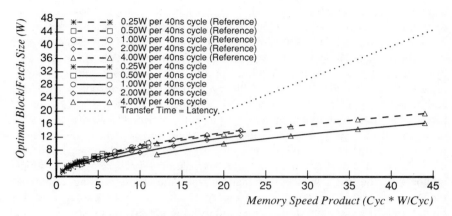

Optimal Block/Fetch Size versus Memory Speed Product:

1% Cycle Time Degradation

Figure 4-18

time are assumed to be small enough that the number of cycles per memory fetch is unchanged. If this is not the case, and the total cycle count decreases as the block size and cycle time increase, then the degradation's depressing effect on the optimal block size would be reduced.

Interestingly, degrading the cycle time is equivalent to changing the effective transfer rate. This correspondence manifests itself in Figures 4-17 and 4-19 by a shift in the mesh of points along the lines of constant latency, and in Figures 4-18 and 4-20 by shifting downwards the individual line segments, each of which corresponds to a particular transfer rate.

As before, the algebraic investigation of this behaviour begins by balancing the relative cycle time and cycle count effects. At the optimum block/fetch size, a change in block size causes an equal percentage change in the cycle time and in the total cycle count:

$$\frac{1}{t_{L1}} \times \frac{\Delta t_{L1}}{\Delta B} = -\frac{1}{N_{Total}} \times \frac{\Delta N_{Total}}{\Delta B}$$

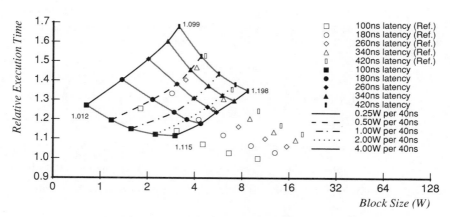

Optimal Block/Fetch Size: 5% Cycle Time Degradation

Figure 4-19

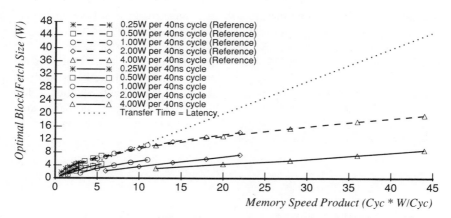

Optimal Block/Fetch Size versus Memory Speed Product:

5% Cycle Time Degradation

Figure 4-20

When this equation is rearranged, the relative cycle time degradation size becomes related to total transfer time, the total main memory latency time, and the optimal block size through the ratio of miss ratios, $r(B)$:

$$-\frac{\Delta t_{L1}}{t_{L1}} = (R(B) - 1)\left(\frac{N_{La}}{N_{Total}}\right) + (2R(B) - 1)\left(\frac{N_{Tr}}{N_{Total}}\right) \qquad [4.7]$$

The total number of cycles spent in transferring data, N_{Tr}, is the number of read misses times the transfer time, $\frac{B}{tr}$. The total number of cycles spent waiting for a transfer to begin, N_{La}, is simply the number of read misses times the number of latency cycles per miss, la.

This balance between the changes in the cycle time and the cycle count can be used to show equivalency between a cycle time degradation and a decrease in the transfer rate. One way to express the shift in the web in Figure 4-17 is to find the change in transfer rate and latency with and without the cycle time penalty for a given performance level and block size. Given an execution time, T_{Total}, and a block size, B, let (la_a, tr_a) be the memory characteristics with a constant cycle time and (la_b, tr_b) be the memory characteristics with a fractional cycle time penalty. The four equations below specify the problem of determining la_a and tr_a in terms of la_b, tr_b, and B. The first equates the performance levels of the two systems: the products of their cycle times and cycle counts must be the same. The second relates the two cycle times according to the block size: an additional multiplicative factor of k is added for each bit in the block index. The third and forth reiterate that the two points in question are each optimal in their environments, according to Equation 4.7 above: they respectively balance the changes in cycle times and cycle counts.

$$T = t_a N_{Total_a} = t_b N_{Total_b}$$

$$t_b = t_a k^{\log_2 B}$$

$$-\frac{\Delta t_a}{t_a} = 0 = (R(B) - 1)\left(\frac{N_{La_a}}{N_{Total_a}}\right) + (2R(B) - 1)\left(\frac{N_{Tr_a}}{N_{Total_a}}\right)$$

$$-\frac{\Delta t_b}{t_b} = (R(B) - 1)\left(\frac{N_{La_b}}{N_{Total_b}}\right) + (2R(B) - 1)\left(\frac{N_{Tr_b}}{N_{Total_b}}\right)$$

These equations reduce to a pleasantly symmetrical pair that incrementally relate the two pairs of memory characteristics, the block/fetch size and a convenient measure of the accumulated cycle time degradation, $K(B)$:

$$K(B) = \frac{k-1}{k^{\log_2 B} - 1}$$

$$la_a = la_b + \frac{2R(B)-1-K(B)}{R(B)K(B)N_{Total}}\left(\left(1-R(B)\right)N_{La_b} + \left(1-2R(B)\right)N_{Tr_b}\right)$$

$$= la_b + \Delta la$$

$$\frac{B}{tr_a} = \frac{B}{tr_b} + \frac{1-R(B)+K(B)}{R(B)K(B)N_{Total}}\left(\left(1-R(B)\right)N_{La_b} + \left(1-2R(B)\right)N_{Tr_b}\right)$$

$$= \frac{B}{tr_b} + \Delta\frac{B}{tr}$$

The ratio between the incremental change in the latency and the transfer period, $\frac{B}{tr}$, is related to the miss ratio ratio, $R(B)$, and the aggregate cycle time degradation, $K(B)$:

$$\frac{\Delta la}{\Delta\frac{B}{tr}} = \frac{2R(B)-1-K(B)}{1-R(B)+K(B)}$$

Using Smith's empirical model to determine this ratio as a function of B shows the disparity in the relative shifts in the latency and transfer rate. Figure 4-21 shows that for a 1% incremental degradation, that is $k = 1.01$, the magnitude of the ratio is substantially less than one for the block sizes of interest. For small block sizes, adding the cycle time degradation increases the effective latency and decreases the transfer period. For larger memory speed products, both characteristic times decline.[28] The sign of the change of the transfer period also flips, but only when the miss rate is beginning to climb with increasing block size ($R(B) > 1$). Note also that the lines of constant latency

---

[28] The inverse relationship between the transfer period and the transfer rate means that a decrease in the transfer period corresponds to an increase in the transfer rate.

in Figures 4-12 and 4-17 are uniformly two cycles apart, while the lines of constant transfer rate are separated by between one and four cycles, depending on the transfer rate and the block size. Thus, a fixed change in the transfer period translates into a varying amount of lateral shift, depending on the region of the graph. This accounts for most of the apparent warping of the grid in these figures.

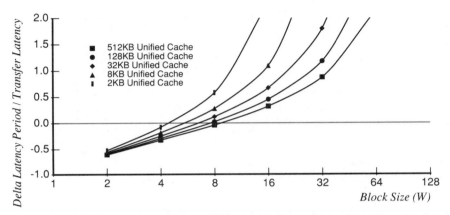

Ratio of Absolute Incremental Changes in Transfer and Latency Periods

Figure 4-21

Intuitively, the similarity between an erosion in the cycle time and a change in the effective transfer rate is explained in terms of equivalent influences. The incremental cycle time degradation model increasingly penalizes large fetch sizes. A drop in the transfer rate has a similar negative effect on performance that also becomes more pronounced for larger fetch sizes.

In conclusion, even a small cycle time penalty can significantly reduce the optimum equal block and fetch size below that which minimizes the mean access time. If the penalty is small and the cache reasonably large, the degradation is equivalent to a reduction in the transfer rate. The effective reduction in transfer rate is small for low block sizes and transfer rates and for large caches, but can easily surpass a factor of two for the opposite conditions.

4.3.2. Independent Block and Fetch Sizes

It is becoming increasingly common to have a fetch size that is larger than the block size [Freitas 88]. This is typically done in conjunction with a more complicated fetch strategy that allows for early continuation of execution as soon as the requested block or sub-block is received. In this section, the block size and fetch size vary independently, but fetches still occur only on misses and execution is still suspended until the entire fetch is complete. The following section will deal with the additional ramifications of a complicated fetch strategy.

Recall from Section 2.1 that the fetch size need only be larger than a sub-block, while the block size needs to be a binary number of sub-blocks. Therefore, the fetch size can in fact be smaller or larger than the block size. Though it is uncommon to have a read fetch size that is smaller than the block size, both cases will be examined here.

Formally, the desire to free both the block and fetch size variables comes from the realization that the mean read time, the product of the miss penalty and the miss rate ($(la + F/tr) \times m(B, F)$), is actually dependent on two independent variables separately: the block size, B, and the fetch size, F. In particular, the miss penalty is only dependent on the fetch size and the memory characteristics. A designer might therefore reasonably select the fetch size that is most closely suited to the memory system and then select the block size that minimizes the miss ratio given that block size.

It is straightforward to illustrate that the decreasing miss ratio with increasing equal block and fetch sizes is essentially due to the increasing fetch size. Figure 4-22 shows the instruction and data miss ratios for the standard scenario with the fetch size varied from one word through 64 words. The block size is a constant four words, and the sub-block size is one word. Comparison with Figure 4-10 shows that for fetch sizes greater than four words, the miss ratios are essentially identical.

Recalling the discussion of the influences on the miss ratio from the beginning of Section 4.3, note that as the block size increases, there is a slight negative impact on the miss rate because of the reduction in the number of tags. For the default cache size and associativity, and a fetch size of 16 words, the overall miss ratio increases from 0.0087 to 0.0090 as the block size increases from one word to 16 words. All of that change occurs in the data cache since there is no interference between reads and writes in the instruction cache: once a block is loaded by a fetch, it must remain in the cache until a cache miss to a conflicting block forces it and all other blocks loaded at the same time to be replaced. In this case, the data cache load miss ratio increases from 0.0161 to 0.0173, while the instruction fetch miss ratio is constant at 0.0062.

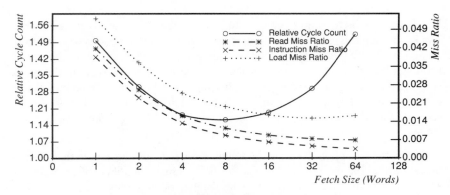

Fetch Size Dependencies:

1.0W per cycle, 260ns latency

Figure 4-22

For block sizes greater than the fetch size, this degradation in the miss ratio with increasing block size becomes more dramatic and affects both the instruction and data caches. By the time the block size reaches 64 words, the instruction and load miss ratios have reached 0.0084 and 0.0277, respectively, for a combined read miss ratio of 0.013.

Thus, given this fetch strategy, there is no intrinsic advantage to having a block size greater than the fetch size. For the instruction cache, there is no advantage to having a block size smaller than the fetch size. For the data cache, there is a miss ratio preference for a block size that is as small as practical.

Figure 4-23 shows the results of an experiment in which both the block and fetch sizes were varied over the range one word to 64 words. For each set of memory characteristics, a two dimensional array of execution times was the result. By fitting parabolas first in one direction and then the other, the optimal non-binary fetch and block size could be estimated along with the best-case performance. The figure shows the web of the optimal fetch sizes and performance levels. Again, the hollow symbols indicate the base level scenario of equal block and fetch sizes. The web of points for the optimal block size looks very similar. It is slightly shifted to the left, indicating optimal block sizes that are slightly smaller than the optimal fetch sizes.

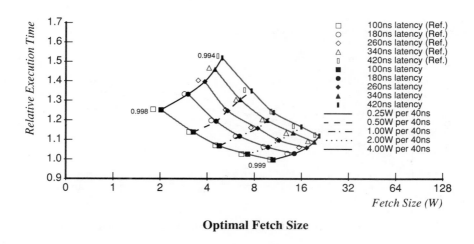

Optimal Fetch Size

Figure 4-23

The most significant observation is that there is only a small increase in the optimal fetch size and a negligible improvement in the performance level (less than 0.6%). Clearly, selecting equal block and fetch sizes is a very good choice. Figure 4-24 shows the optimal block and fetch sizes for each memory speed product. The dashed lines again represent the baseline case of enforced equal block and fetch sizes. Freeing up the block and fetch sizes allows the fetch size to increase fractionally and the block size to decrease slightly. When restricted to binary sized blocks and fetches, the best case is occasionally equal blocks and fetches and occasionally fetches of two blocks.

The question that then arises is why was the optimal block size not significantly smaller than in the default scenario. The answer is write effects. Even though the write policy was selected to minimize the performance impact of writes (See Appendix B), the block size's impact on the read miss ratio was so small that it was overwhelmed by the block size's impact on the write performance. Specifically, as the block size decreased, the number of discrete writes to main memory increased since each fetch could replace a number of dirty blocks, each with potentially different tags. Each of these dirty blocks would translate to a separate write to main memory, each with its own latency and overhead. For a constant fetch size, as the block size decreases, the backplane and memory utilization also increase. This in turn increases the probability that a cache miss fetch will be delayed by a write to main memory in progress. The resulting increase in the average cache miss penalty overwhelmed

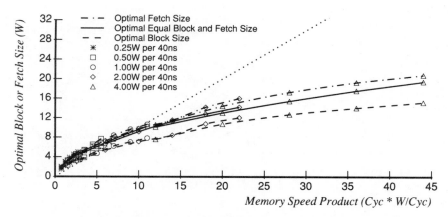

Optimal Block and Fetch Sizes versus Memory Speed Product

Figure 4-24

the decrease in the cache miss ratio that directly results from the smaller block size. Combining writes from different blocks into block writes requires a significant increase in the complexity of the write buffer and is only somewhat successful at mimicking the effect of a large block size. Basically, just as larger fetches make the most of the memory bandwidth for reads, large blocks make the most of it for writes.

There is another important aspect to the interaction between the write policy and block size. For the experiments performed here, the write hit time was a constant two cycles, regardless of the block size. However, with write-through caches, the write hit and miss time are both dramatically minimized for writes equal in size to the block size. In this case, there is no need to check the tags before performing the write into the data portion. For machines with write-through primary caches, this strongly biases the block size towards the most common size of write operation: typically, one word.

The differences in the behaviour and locality of reference between the instruction and data reference streams significantly change the cache design tradeoffs in the two halves of a split instruction/data cache. Given that the block size on the instruction side has no performance impact provided it is less than or equal to the instruction cache fetch size, there are really three free variables in the design of a split cache: the instruction block/fetch size, the data fetch size and the data block size. The optimal size for each of these can be estimated by finding the instruction block and fetch sizes that minimized the instruction and data reference components to the total execution time observed in the experiment illustrated by Figures 4-23 and 4-24. Inaccuracies in this technique are caused by the failure to accurately account for changes in the contention for main memory that exists between the instruction and data streams as a result of different instruction and data block sizes. These errors are likely to be small and not consequential at the level of optimal binary block and fetch sizes. Figure 4-25 shows the estimated optimal instruction block and fetch size, data fetch size, and data block size. As expected, the best instruction cache fetch size can be substantially larger than the best combined cache or data cache fetch size: for most values of the memory speed product, it is either 8, 16 or 32 words. The best data cache fetch size should be about half as big as the instruction cache fetch size, and the data cache block size should be equal to or half as big as the data cache fetch size.

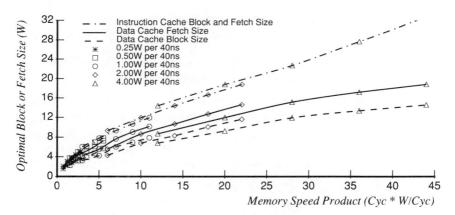

Optimal Block and Fetch Sizes versus Memory Speed Product

Figure 4-25

The conclusion to be drawn here is that the fetch size is properly selected with regard to the memory characteristics, while the block size needs to be selected in conjunction with the write policy. For the write-back data cache and write buffers simulated here, that implies a fairly long block size – usually equal to or slightly less than the fetch size.

4.3.3. Optimal Block Size with Alternate Fetch Strategies

This section explores the second half of the traditional rationale for larger fetch sizes: the use of more complicated fetch policies facilitates parallelism between CPU execution and memory activity. It is commonly believed that aggressive fetch strategies, including prefetching, can significantly improve miss ratios and, consequently, system-level performance. However, the improvements in the miss ratio that accrue from a complicated fetch strategy can be particularly misleading because the potential benefits of these techniques are only achieved if certain specific inherently temporal criteria are met. For instance, if prefetched data does not arrive before it is needed, or if the memory or cache is busy when needed by the CPU, then the amount of time saved by the fetch strategy is less than predicted.

There are a large number of details involved in fully specifying an involved fetch strategy. The consequence of this complexity is that the complete design space of fetch strategies is large and horribly convoluted. Rather than trying to systematically explore all the options, simulation results for a few of the more effective alternative fetch strategies will be presented along with an analysis of the underlying phenomena behind their successes and failures.

There have been a number of studies of fetch strategies [Rau 77b, Rau 77a, Smith 86] and of prefetching in particular [Bennett 82, Gindele 77, Lee 87, Rau 77c, Smith 78b, Smith 85a]. For the most part, though, these have concentrated on the reduction in the miss rate that stems primarily from the increase in the fetch size or initiation of a fetch prior to a miss occurring.

Three of the main design parameters of a fetch strategy are:
1. When does a fetch occur.
2. Which word is returned from main memory first.
3. When is the CPU allowed to continue execution.

The alternatives for the first design decision are 1) consider initiating a fetch on every memory reference, and 2) fetch only on a cache miss. The two most common alternatives for the second decision are 1) begin with the lowest address, and 2) start with the desired word. From there, the fetch usually proceeds with increasing addresses, wrapping around to the start of the fetch unit if necessary. This is sometimes referred to as a wrapping fetch [Hennessy 90], or a "desired word first" fetch. The simple approach to the third question is to wait until the entire fetch is complete before resuming execution. A common alternative, though, is to release the CPU from its stall as soon as the data it requires is available. This is often called early-continuation or early restart.

Traditionally, a machine is said to be prefetching data if either 1) a fetch on a cache miss retrieves more than one block of data (fetch size > block size) and CPU execution is resumed after the desired word or block is returned, or 2) a fetch can be initiated as a result of a reference to the cache, regardless of whether or not a cache miss was encountered. Smith categorizes these two cases as Class 1 and Class 2 respectively [Smith 78c], or alternatively as "Fetch on Fault" and "Fetch Always" respectively [Smith 78b].

If fetches are initiated regardless of whether a miss occurred, or if the CPU is allowed to proceed before the fetch is complete, then the next major point of differentiation of fetch strategies is what happens if a miss is encountered while a fetch is in progress. Again, the common simple case is to wait out the current fetch until the bus and memory are again available. A more aggressive alternative is to abort the fetch in progress and start a new one to satisfy the new miss.

The choice of fetch strategy is integrally linked to the amount of hardware in the cache and memory subsystems. The data paths around the RAM array and the peak bandwidth into the RAM array determine the maximum number of tag and data accesses per cycle. The synchronous/asynchronous nature of the backplane bus can allow for interleaving of incoming data accesses with further CPU reads and writes. The predictability of CPU references, the basic cache organization (split or unified), and the penalty for stalling the CPU favour some designs over others. A fully specified fetch strategy consists of a myriad of details, each of which can subtly affect the effectiveness of the cache. It is important to realize that the fetch strategy affects both halves of the performance equation: most often the primary concern is to tune the fetch strategy to minimize the cycle count, but frequently the cache's cycle time is impacted. For instance, seemingly innocuous decisions can increase the amount of logic in the hit/miss detection circuitry, with significant repercussions. Another common pitfall is the need to add or widen a multiplexor in the critical read access path of the cache.

So far, only the simplest possible fetch strategy has been used in the trace-driven simulations: complete the entire fetch, beginning with the lowest address, before allowing the CPU to continue. Two other fetch strategies implemented in the simulator (See Section 3.3.1) are called *nbdwf* and *adwf*. The first, *nbdwf*, fetches one block's worth of data on a cache miss, beginning with the desired word and wrapping around when the end of the block is reached. The CPU is restarted as soon as the referenced sub-block is received. The caches are assumed to be dual ported so that the CPU can continue to use the caches normally, unhindered by the fetch in progress. If a new miss is encountered, the existing fetch is allowed to complete before a new fetch is initiated. The second strategy, *adwf*, is a more aggressive strategy that greedily tries to satisfy the

CPU's immediate needs as quickly as possible. In this case, a miss aborts any fetch in progress and causes a new fetch to be initiated. The CPU is again restarted as soon as possible. Neither of these fetch strategies are technically prefetching strategies – the block and fetch sizes are identical, and fetches are initiated only on misses.

Figures 4-26 through 4-29 compare these fetch strategies with the simple default fetch strategy. The figures again use the same format as do Figures 4-17 and 4-18: hollow symbols and dashed lines indicate the reference scenario. These graphs assume no cycle time penalty associated with the implementation of these fetch strategies. Any such penalty would reduce the improvements obtained.

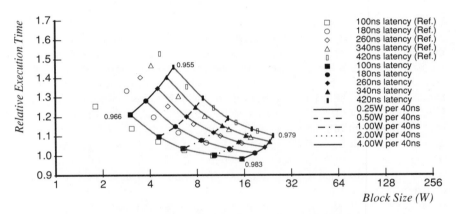

Optimal Block/Fetch Size: nbdwf Fetch Strategy

Figure 4-26

The major observations from these empirical results are:

1. The performance improvements are relatively small: 4% maximum for the aborting case (*adwf*) and 4.5% for the non-blocking strategy (*nbdwf*). The smallest improvements are a meager 0.8% and 1.7%, respectively.

2. The fetch strategies, particularly the less aggressive *nbdwf*, behave like an incremental improvement in the transfer rate. The characteristic matrix shifts along the lines of constant latency.

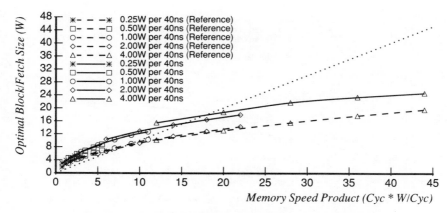

Optimal Block/Fetch Size versus Memory Speed Product:

nbdwf Fetch Strategy

Figure 4-27

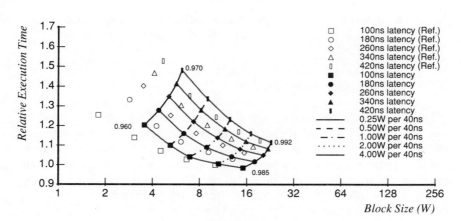

Optimal Block/Fetch Size: adwf Fetch Strategy

Figure 4-28

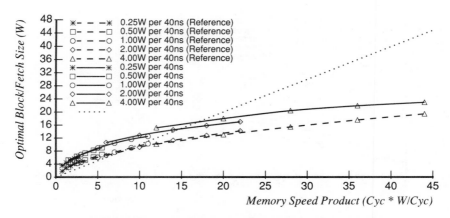

Optimal Block/Fetch Size versus Memory Speed Product:

adwf Fetch Strategy

Figure 4-29

3. The optimal block sizes are quite unaffected. A larger binary block size is indicated only over a fairly limited range of memory speed products.

4. The more aggressive strategy did not perform consistently better than the less aggressive one.

There are two fundamental reasons for this poor showing. The first is that the baseline choice of an optimally selected block and fetch size does a very good job of exploiting as much of the locality in the program as possible, given the specific memory system at hand. Second, cache misses are very tightly clustered and correlated. When a strategy has a good chance of fetching something to reduce the miss rate, it frequently lacks the time to do so. Furthermore, when there is a lot of time between misses, it is difficult to know what to fetch.

Complex fetch strategies are at a disadvantage because there is a relatively small region of the design space where they have a significant opportunity for improving on the default case. Consider the maximum possible benefit as a function of backplane utilization, as measured by the fraction of all cycles spent waiting on main memory.

A large cache or a fast memory system yields a low bus utilization – an indication that the processor is not spending very much time waiting on cache misses. In this case, even a large reduction in miss rate will not dramatically improve the system-level performance, merely because the memory component of the total cycle count is small to begin with.

At the other extreme, when the backplane utilization is high, there is very little time between misses, and the execution time is dominated by the memory component of N_{Total}. This regime is characterized by small caches and long cache miss penalties. When the mean time between satisfying one miss and incurring the next is less than the memory fetch time, then any benefit derived by the use of that bandwidth is likely to be offset by a penalty to the next cache miss. An alternative way of viewing this situation is that as memory utilization approaches 100%, the misses are so frequent that there is no better alternative than to wait for the next miss and deal with it as quickly as possible. The speedup obtained by various fetch strategies, particularly non-prefetching policies, drops off as memory utilization rises.

Only in the middle regime, representing a balanced system with modest bus utilizations, do improved fetch strategies have enough resources available to them to make a significant impact on the memory component of the total execution time. Figure 4-30 reveals this middle region by plotting the bus utilizations and speedups for the two fetch strategies and two cache sizes: the 8KB total and the default 128KB total.[29] The line tracks the best observed speedup as a function of the bus utilization. It illustrates that even aggressive strategies are of little benefit when the memory hierarchy plays a dominant role in the execution time of a program.

Above and beyond this limitation of resources, the task of improving on the simple case is made significantly harder by the temporal clustering of cache misses. Figure 4-31 shows this clustering by plotting the cumulative distribution of the interval between cache misses, measured in instructions, as a function of the block/fetch size for the default 128KB (total) split I/D organization. The value for each interval is the probability of two successive misses being separated by less than that number of instructions. As the block size is increased, the probability of short intervals between misses is decreased. However, since spatial and temporal locality are just that – local in nature – the probability of large gaps between misses does not increase as dramatically as we might hope.

---

[29] Some of the points in Figure 4-30 show a degradation in the execution time when the greedy fetch strategy (*adwf*) is added. When the miss rates are high, the instruction and data streams unproductively fight each other for the available bandwidth. This conflict reduces the mean transfer size to the detriment of the total cycle count: a designer cannot blindly add complexity with the expectation that performance will improve.

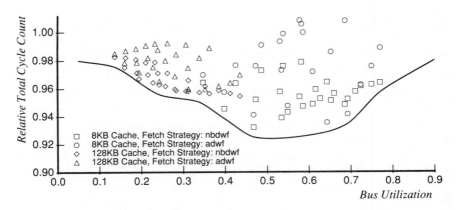

Relative Performance Improvement versus Bus Utilization

Figure 4-30

For example, for a block size of 64W, fully 50% of all misses are encountered within 16 instructions of their predecessors. Regardless of the block size, if a cache and memory system have just finished satisfying a miss, they had better be prepared to handle another soon.

This idea is further corroborated by Figure 4-32. For all the simulated cycles in which an instruction and data reference were issued simultaneously[30], it plots the probability of encountering an instruction miss, a data miss, and the two cross-conditional probabilities. It shows that instruction and data misses are very strongly correlated. For this cache size, given that an instruction miss has occurred, the probability of also encountering a data miss (P(Dmiss|Imiss)) is between 1.3 and 4.2 times greater than the overall data cache miss rate, depending on the block size. The same applies to the probability of an instruction miss given a data miss (P(Imiss|Dmiss)). The frequent need to fetch something into both caches before progress can be made inhibits the usefulness of long fetch sizes used in conjunction with fetch strategies that allow the CPU to potentially continue when the desired word is received.

---

[30] For the RISC traces, the number of cycles in which both an instruction and data reference are initiated is equal to the number of data references. This is because the R2000 architecture is a load-store architecture and the CPU model facilitates single-cycle execution with a Harvard organization (See Section 3.3.2).

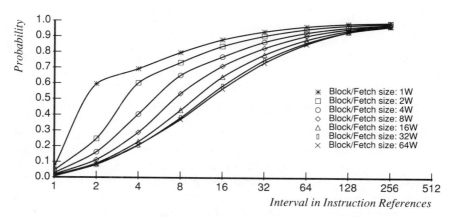

Cumulative Distribution of the Interval Between Cache Misses:

64KB/64KB Split I/D Cache

Figure 4-31

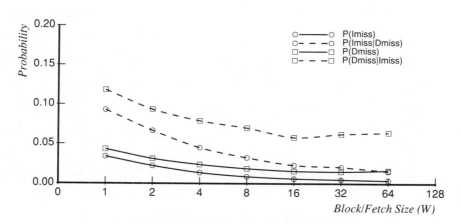

Joint Instruction and Data Miss Probabilities

Figure 4-32

These phenomena that detract from the performance improvement obtained by complicated non-prefetching strategies also hinder prefetching strategies. Figure 4-33 shows the web of optimal equal block and fetch sizes and best performance levels for a "Fetch Always" prefetch strategy [Smith 78b]. On all memory references, two addresses are generated: the address of the desired word, a, and the address in the next block in main memory, $a+B$. If the first address misses in the cache, a main memory fetch is initiated to that address into the cache. The block comes in with the desired word first and wraps around at the end of the block. The CPU is released from its stall as soon as the required data is received from memory. If the first address hits in the cache, then the required data is passed on to the CPU without any delay. The second address is checked against the tags simultaneously with the first. If the first hits in the cache and the second misses, then a fetch is initiated for that block. It comes in according to the same algorithm. The CPU is unhindered by the prefetch in progress. Only if it encounters a cache miss while a prefetch is active will it be stalled unnecessarily. In this case, it waits until the prefetch completes before initiating the new fetch of the word currently required. This strategy is similar to *nbdfw* above with an added "Fetch Always" feature; that is, fetches can be initiated on every reference, regardless of whether a cache miss is encountered.

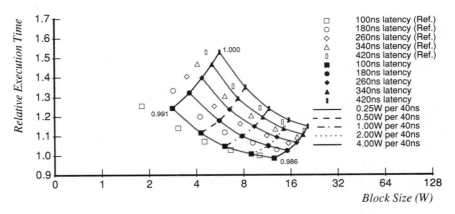

Optimal Block/Fetch Size: Fetch Always Strategy

Figure 4-33

Recall that there are two major classes of prefetching strategies. This strategy from the first group is characterized by fetches potentially being initiated on every reference. The second group have fetch sizes greater than the block size. Figure 4-34 shows the comparable web of points for a prefetch strategy of the second class. It is a linear prefetch strategy in that the block size is one word and on a cache miss a fetch is initiated for the desired and subsequent $F - 1$ words. As before, the CPU resumes execution as soon as the desired word is received from memory, and thereafter instruction execution is unhindered by the incoming data from memory. Indeed, as simulated, data is available to the CPU on the same cycle in which it arrives from memory. This allows instructions to be streamed into the CPU from the bus and executed directly without any pipeline stalls. This is commonly referred to as instruction streaming [Freitas 88]. If a miss is encountered while instructions or data are coming in, then the CPU stalls until the current fetch is finished before starting up a new one. Write-backs are complicated in this fetch strategy in that a miss can replace up to F dirty lines, each with potentially different write-back addresses. The strategy simulated here assumes write buffers capable of grouping as many dirty words as possible together into write operations before sending them on to the bus. Without such a write policy, the number of write operations grows with the fetch size, negating any improvement due to the early release of the CPU.

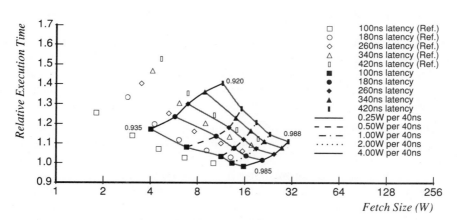

Optimal Fetch Size: Prefetch on Fault Strategy

Figure 4-34

Both these figures show a disappointingly small amount of performance improvement over the simple default case, especially given the amount of extra hardware required to implement such a strategy. Depending on the particulars of the design and the utilization of the caches, the minimum additional hardware to implement one of these strategies is a significant amount of control logic, while the worst case is an additional set of tags and several new data paths into and out of the data array. Though the fetch always strategy did not increase the optimal fetch size very much, the prefetch on fault consistently increased it by at least a factor of two. Its web of points is also the most distorted of all the fetch strategies presented. This is an indication that it is the most complicated strategy, with the most special cases, especially in its write policy. It is also an indication of the unpredictability and non-uniformity of its performance improvement.   This data does not imply that all prefetch strategies are ineffective. Rather, the lesson to be learned here is that they are not necessarily effective.   A complicated strategy, be it prefetching or not, must be carefully thought out and extensively simulated to ensure that all the potential benefit is being realized and that the designer's efforts are not being wasted.

These results are just for 64KB/64KB split instruction/data caches. For other cache sizes and associativities, these fetch strategies may do better. As the cache size increases, the mean time between cache misses increases, signalling greater resources available to the fetch strategy. However, memory's contribution to the total execution time decreases with increasing cache size, so it is harder to make a large impact on the overall performance. The converse applies to smaller caches. The net result is that though a fetch strategy may do somewhat better as the cache size is varied, it is unlikely to perform dramatically better in comparison to the simple default case. It has also been noted in the literature that prefetching works best when applied only to instructions [Smith 78b]. That the above policies were applied to both instructions and data indicates that there is some room for improvement over the absolute results presented here.

Regardless, the dilemma of designing an effective fetch strategy is straightforward: when it is clear what to do, there is not enough time to do it, and when there is an abundance of time, it is unclear what should be fetched. The default strategy with an appropriately chosen block size does a good job of balancing the memory characteristics with the temporal and spatial localities of the workload to make the most of available bandwidth. It is very difficult to do significantly better, even with arbitrarily large amounts of hardware.   Also, aggressive fetch strategies do not necessarily significantly increase the optimal block size over the simple case.

In conclusion, over a wide range of memory characteristics, cache sizes and fetch policies, the best choice for a binary equal block and fetch size is either four, eight, or sixteen words.   Except for the smallest caches, only a small performance penalty results from a choice that is incorrect by a factor of two. Only for very large caches, which are of dubious value, is the optimal block/fetch size more than 16 words.   Fetch sizes greater than 16 words are practical for instruction caches in conjunction with memory systems with very high memory speed products. Otherwise, only a significantly different workload could justify long blocks for smaller caches. Any sort of cycle time penalty associated with the longer block size will further reduce the size of choice. For instruction caches, it does not make any sense to have a block size different than the fetch size. However, for data caches, the fetch size is most appropriately selected according to the memory system, and the block size, which has a small impact on the miss ratio, is best selected to work well with the write strategy. For the write-back caches simulated here, the best instruction block/fetch size was about twice as large as the best data fetch size, which in turn was about twice as large as the best data block size. Complicated fetch strategies can improve performance a small amount, but the clustering of misses and the reality of spatial locality imply that they are fighting an uphill battle. In practice, aggressive fetch strategies do not significantly increase the optimal block size over the simple case.

4.4. Globally Optimum Cache Design

Each section of this chapter has focused on the temporal tradeoffs involving a single organizational parameter. The significant influences of the other variables on each of these tradeoffs have been discussed, but only within the context of their effects on the tradeoff under examination. This section summarizes and integrates these results into a unified framework for determining the globally optimum cache.

Section 4.1 stressed the importance of appropriately balancing the cycle time and the cache size. For the organization and memory system simulated, the optimal cache size is likely to end up between 32KB and 128KB, depending on the specifics of the relationship between the cache size and cycle time. We have yet to identify how this tradeoff is dependent on the underlying assumptions of set associativity and block size.

At the optimal cache size, for an incremental change in the size, the relative change in cycle time is proportional to the absolute change in the miss rate (Equation 4.1). For the simulated system, over much of the region of interest, a doubling in the cache size resulted in a 31% decrease in the miss rate. Section 4.2 shows that an increase in set associativity from one to two produces a 20% drop in miss rate over that same range. Therefore, for a set-associative cache, all of the speed – size tradeoff curves in Figure 4-4 shift to the left by slightly less than one binary order of magnitude. That shift increases the optimal cache size for a set-associative cache by an amount that depends on the specifics of the function relating cache size and speed.

In Section 4.3, the ratio of miss ratios for a doubled block size, $R(B)$, was in the range of 0.6 to 0.7 for most cache and block sizes (Figure 4-15). Thus, increasing the block size by a factor of two decreases all the miss ratios between 30% and 40%. This corresponds to a shift in the curves of constant performance of between one and two cache sizes. However, the block size also affects the mean memory access time, which in turn linearly influences the equilibrium cycle time change. The fractional change in the main memory fetch time is linearly dependent on block size and inversely proportional to the sum of the memory speed product and the block size:

$$\frac{n_{MMread}(2B)}{n_{MMread}(B)} = 1 + \frac{B}{la \times tr + B}$$

Depending on the memory speed product and the initial block size, the change in the cache miss penalty can either reduce or totally overwhelm the left shifting effect of the miss rate. The reference scenario has a block size of four, so for memory speed products below two, the optimum cache size would be increased by doubling the block size, and for speed products less than about five, the shift in tradeoff is less than one-half of a binary order of magnitude. Only for memory speed products above 20 does increasing the block size over four words consistently shift the lines of constant performance to the left by more than one-half of a cache size. When the relationship between the optimal block size and miss penalty is factored in, moving the block size from four words towards the optimum uniformly shifts the size tradeoff of Figure 4-4 to the left. The amount of shift increases with the magnitude of the difference between the optimal block size and the starting point. In Figure 4-4, that initial block size is four words.

Increasing the block size has a similar effect on the set-associativity tradeoff. The break-even implementation time is linearly related to the change in the miss ratio and the memory fetch time (Equation 4.3). For memory speed products less than two, the break-even times increase with increasing block size; for products greater than five, the break-even times always decrease. For a product of 20, the range of the percent decrease in the break-even times, shown in Figures 4-7 through 4-9, ranges from 30% for large caches (small $R(B)$) to 18% for small caches (large $R(B)$).

The effect of the memory characteristics on the block size tradeoff was considered in depth in Section 4.3. The latency and transfer rate's effect on the set associativity and total size tradeoffs is identical to the block size's influence through the miss penalty: the linear relationship between the mean memory fetch time and the balancing change in cycle time equates a percentage change in the fetch time to a change in the cache size. Specifically, since a doubling of the cache size is equated to a 31% drop in the miss and absolute miss ratios change ($\Delta m(C)$), a change in the fetch time of the same proportion – regardless of whether it derives from a change in the latency, the transfer period, or both – shifts the curves of constant performance by one factor of two to the left.

The problem at this point is to reconcile these intertwined tradeoffs to find the globally optimum cache organization for a given set of technology options. The specific implementation details specify the cache cycle time as a function of all the organizational parameters, including fetch and write policies.

Section 3.1 formally states the cache design problem as a minimization of a function of four variables: cache size, set associativity, block size and cycle time. Machines with the same execution time define surfaces of constant performance in this four-dimensional space. The lines of constant performance, shown in Figure 4-4, really constitute a single cross-section of those surfaces of constant performance. Right and left shifts are one way of relating the different cross-sections to one another. The set of realizable implementations is a set of points in this four dimensional space, each of which lies on some particular surface of constant performance. The optimal cache organization and implementation is the one that lies on the surface of lowest total execution time. The fact that the shape and position of the four-dimensional surfaces depend on the memory characteristics further complicates the optimization problem. Changes in the latency and transfer rate affect the various cross-sections differently, reflecting varying influences of the main memory access time. The goal is to solve this problem regardless of these input parameters.

Fortunately, the straightforward relationships among the various cross-sections make the optimization problem conceptually tractable. Specifically, the various cross-sections appear as lateral shifts of one another. Since a lateral shift of the lines of constant performance in one direction is identical to a shift of the axis in the other direction, all of the cross-sections can be represented on one graph by using different axes: Figure 4-35 displays all four design dimensions simultaneously, allowing the direct performance comparison of machines anywhere within the four dimensional space covered. The lines of constant performance of Figure 4-4 are reproduced with several sets of X and Y axes, one for each pair of block size and associativity. The warping of each pair of axes is computed so as to map each cross-section onto the reference set of curves representing a set size of one and a block size of four words. Translation of the cycle times along the Y axis was necessary to match the performance levels for infinite sized caches.

The accuracy of the simulation results is only slightly reduced by the warping process. Figure 4-36 shows symbols for all six cross-sections after the mapping process. Near the center of the graph, the maximum error in the performance estimate associated with the merging of the cross-sections is less than 3% – much less than the performance variation observed across workloads. Despite its accuracy, Figure 4-35 is not meant to determine an absolute answer, but rather to help select a few organizations for more detailed design and simulation.

The combined graphical representation of the design space in Figure 4-35 does not account for changes in the memory characteristics, the fetch strategy, or the write policy. Properly speaking, a different cache comparison chart is needed for each combination of these variables. However, by introducing the concept of effective cache size, the one chart can be used directly for a wide variety of memory systems, fetch strategies and write policies with little or no degradation in its accuracy.

The memory system used in the generation of Figure 4-35 has a transfer rate of one word per cycle and a fixed latency of six CPU cycles, regardless of the cycle time. However, it was noted earlier that a proportional change in the memory access time can also be equated to a change in the cache size. Naturally, the memory access time is dependent on the block size as well as the latency and transfer rate. If the memory characteristics are different from those chosen for the chart, the ratio of the actual fetch time to the presumed fetch time (both based on the same actual block size) determines the amount of the change that needs to be applied to the cache size to get the effective cache size. An increase in access time moves the point left, to lower performance levels, by about one binary order of magnitude per factor of 1.39 in the access time; conversely, a decrease in the access time from the assumed value increases the effective cache size by a factor of two for every multiple of 0.72 difference between the actual and presumed memory fetch times.

For example, to determine the relative performance level of a machine with a 24ns cycle time direct-mapped, 64KB/64KB split instruction data cache with a block size of four words and memory system with a two words per cycle transfer rate and a latency of 100 ns, the first step is to determine in CPU cycles the cache miss penalty. In this case it would presumably be five cycles of latency and four cycles of transfer period for a total of nine cycles. For this block size, the chart assumed six cycles of latency and eight cycles of transfer period for a total of fourteen. The ratio of the two is 0.643, which is 1.41 factors of 0.72. That is, $0.72^{1.41} = 0.643$. Since this is an improvement in the cache miss penalty, the effective cache size will be bigger than the actual cache size. Therefore the effective cache size to be used on the chart is the real cache size (128KB) increased by 1.41 powers of two ($128K \times 2^{1.41}$), or approximately 340KB. For a cache size of 340KB, set size of one, block size of eight words and cycle time of 24ns, the chart indicates a relative execution time of 1.38 times the best case for the chart. This technique provides acceptable accuracy for effective cache

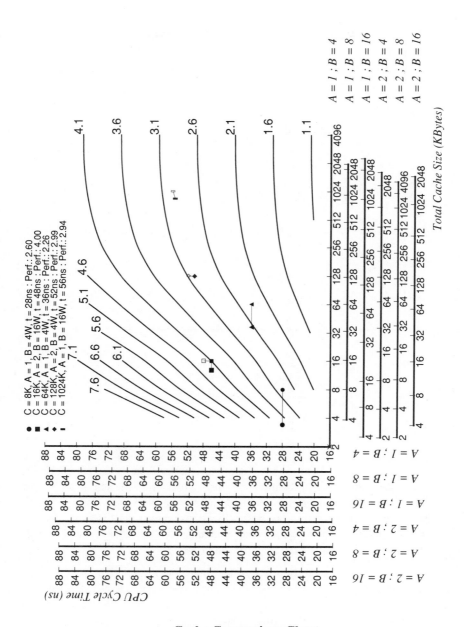

Cache Comparison Chart

Figure 4-35

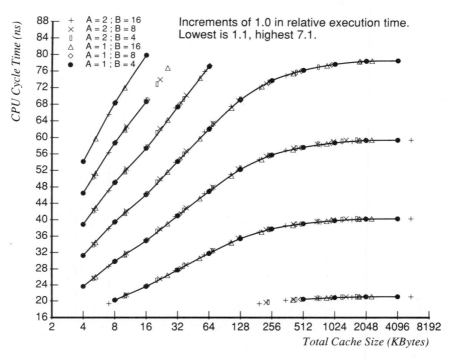

Lines of Constant Performance

Figure 4-36

sizes that are up to a factor of four larger or smaller than the actual cache size. Beyond that, the bus utilization of the actual system starts to become significantly different from the "equivalent" system with the standard memory system. The difference in the bus utilizations causes a difference in their respective performance levels through a change in the frequency and duration that memory reads are delayed by writes in progress.

Of course, time is entirely relative. To determine the relative execution time for machines with cycle times less than 20ns, one need only scale all units of time appropriately to get an effective cycle time between 20ns and 80ns. For instance, consider a machine with a cycle time of 16ns, a block size of 16 words and a 44 cycle cache miss penalty. Since the cache miss penalty is specified in terms of cycles, not nanoseconds, the total cycle count is independent of the cycle time. This machine's cycle count is the same as that of a second machine with a 48ns cycle time and a 44 cycle cache miss penalty. The difference is that execution time of the first machine is one third of that of the second machine. The relative execution time of the second machine can be found from Figure 4-35 chart via the procedure above[31] to be 3.5. Therefore the relative execution time of the first machine is on the order of 1.17.

Section 4.3.3 has shown that complicated fetch strategies can be modelled as a change in the effective latency and transfer rate; the change in the effective transfer rate is generally the more significant of the two. For instance, in Figure 4-29, one can see that for a block size of eight words, a memory latency of 180ns and a transfer rate of one word per 40ns, the *adwf* fetch strategy behaves very similarly to the simple default fetch strategy with a memory system with 180ns of latency and transfer rate of two words per cycle. Thus to make use of the chart, the cache miss penalty needed to determine the effective cache size would be calculated with the equivalent transfer rate instead of the actual one. If this equivalency is appropriately understood, either exactly through simulation or approximately through analytical estimation, the effect of the fetch strategy can be folded into the calculation of the mean memory access time and into its resulting shift. Care must be taken, though, since the mapping between the actual memory characteristics and the equivalent ones for the simple fetch strategy are dependent on the cache size, associativity and block size. Specifically, the figures in Section 4.3.3 are generally applicable across wide ranges of the design space. With this said, though, with judicious use of engineering approximations, Figure 4-35 can be used to compare machines with different fetch policies, albeit with reduced accuracy.

Up to this point, the choice of write strategy has been consistently ignored. All simulation results, including the cache comparison chart, are for a write-back cache with an ample supply of write buffering. The assumption throughout is that the write buffer is successfully able to hide the write-back traffic to the extent that the memory fetch time, ($n_{Mmread} = la + \frac{B}{tr}$), and the average memory access time, ($\bar{n}_{MMread} = n_{MMread} + \bar{n}_{ReadDelay}$), are negligible. The validity of this assumption is explored in Appendix B. Clearly, this will be less true as the bus utilization increases, but the simplification is generally adequate. The effect of a different or noticeable write strategy can also be incorporated into the comparison by noting its contribution to the mean memory access time and adjusting the effective memory latency appropriately prior to determining the effective cache size.

---

[31] The ratio of the cache miss penalties is $\frac{44}{6+16} = 1.83 = 1.39^{1.835}$. The effective cache size is $128KB / 2^{1.835} = 49KB$.

Figure 4-35 facilitates the quick comparison of radically different implementations. The solid symbols scattered about it indicate the performance levels of the following five machines. As a matter of convenience only, they all have the same memory system (300ns of latency and one word per cycle transfer rate):

circle:	($C=8K$, $A=1$, $B=4W$, $t_{L1}=28$),	Performance = 2.60
square:	($C=16K$, $A=2$, $B=16W$, $t_{L1}=48$),	Performance = 4.00
triangle:	($C=64K$, $A=1$, $B=4W$, $t_{L1}=36$),	Performance = 2.26
diamond:	($C=128K$, $A=2$, $B=4W$, $t_{L1}=52$),	Performance = 2.99
rectangle:	($C=1024K$, $A=1$, $B=16W$, $t_{L1}=56$),	Performance = 2.94

Of these machines, the second has significantly worse performance, the third is clearly the fastest, and the other three are comparable. If these were five organizations under consideration for a design, then the second could be discarded outright, and further investigations should concentrate on refining the cost and performance of the 64KB total, 36ns machine in relation to the other three. As in Section 4.1, we have here a situation in which the best performing computer does not have the fastest cycle time. In particular, the third machine has a cycle time that is 22% slower than the first machine, despite the fact that it performs 15% better. Furthermore, since the third machine's basic cycle time is longer, it could be less expensive and easier to manufacture than the first.

For each configuration, three symbols are plotted. The small hollow symbol plots the size and time using the axes of the reference scenario. This is the best estimate of the execution time ignoring the block size, set associativity and actual memory characteristics. The small filled symbol uses the appropriate set of axes based on the cache's set and block sizes, but still does not take into account the fact the cache's miss penalty is different from the default for its block size. Finally, the placement of the large filled symbol accounts for the actual cache miss penalty. The horizontal line between the smaller filled symbol and the larger one represents the difference between the actual cache size and the effective cache size along the axis that is appropriate based on the set associativity and block size. In all but a single case, at least one of the smaller symbols is obscured.

This chart is physically possible because changes in organizational variables can be transformed into changes in other variables that have the same impact on performance. More formally, it is possible because the function that maps the organizational and temporal parameters to the system-level performance is well behaved in that the effects of the various inputs are remarkably independent of each other. Specifically, the transformation is possible because the change in memory system is equivalent to a change in cache size, and a change in associativity and block size is equivalent to a change in cache size and cycle time:[32]

$$T_{total}(\mathbf{C}(C,A,B), la, tr, t_{cyc}) = T_{total}(\mathbf{C}(\alpha C, A, B), la_{ref}, tr_{ref}, t_{cyc})$$

$$= T_{total}(\mathbf{C}(\alpha\beta C, A{=}1, B{=}4), la_{ref}, tr_{ref}, \gamma t_{cyc})$$

Since the warping is not uniform across the design space, the parameters that define the warping (α, β and γ) are not constants. The crucial decomposition necessary for the creation of this chart is that cache size is modified by parameters ($\alpha(B, la, tr)$ and $\beta(C, A, B)$) that are independent of the cycle time, and the cycle time is modified by a parameter ($\gamma(A, B, t_{cyc})$) that is independent of the cache size. This decomposition stems primarily from the specification of the memory characteristics in terms of CPU cycles so that the total cycle count is also independent of the cycle time:

$$T_{total}(\mathbf{C}(C,A,B), la, tr, t_{cyc}) = N_{total}(\mathbf{C}(C,A,B), la, tr) \times t_{cyc}$$

In summary, Figure 4-35 makes a rapid exploration of the design space practical, to the extent that enumeration of all the feasible implementations is conceivable. However, it should be noted that although the enumeration of a large number of cache configurations on a single graph is possible, the specific results of Sections 4.2 and 4.3 can simplify the task. Those sections describe the viability of set-associative designs and the range of block sizes best suited to the specific memory subsystem. The general guidelines developed there can help the designer develop an understanding of the underlying principles and the circumstances under which set associativity and large block sizes make sense.

The first step towards a reasonable algorithm for global optimal cache design derives from an understanding of the tradeoffs involving each of the primary organizational variables. Rationalization of the interaction between those tradeoffs allows for their formulation within a common framework: this chapter developed a single graphical representation of performance function across a large portion of the entire design space. For the first time, the direct comparison of the performance levels of widely dissimilar organizations and implementations is possible. This comparison chart accommodates the variations in memory system characteristics and, to a lesser extent, in the fetch

---

[32] Most of the change is in the cache size. The warping of the cycle time is only required to account for the small performance differences between very large caches of different block, fetch and set sizes.

and write strategy.   It is intended to be used to quickly select a few cache organizations for detailed analysis and simulation.

Chapter 5

Multi-Level
Cache Hierarchies

O, I were damn'd beyond all depth in hell,
But that I did proceed upon just grounds
To this extremity.

– Othello V(2):136

5.1. Introduction

Two significant implications for computer design are embedded in the results of Chapter 4. First, once the cache size is increased to the 64KB level, there is little room for further improvement. An implementor has no apparent way to increase significantly the performance of the memory hierarchy and the system through the application of more hardware: increasing the cache size or adding set associativity at the expense of cycle time is likely to be detrimental; and exchanging the cache RAMs for more copies of a smaller and faster variety may not reduce the cycle time if additional multiplexors or additional buffering is needed as a result of the switch.

The second implication involves the evolution of computer organization in the face of continued improvements in implementation technologies. A fundamental question confronting computer implementors is what sort of memory hierarchy is needed to keep high performance machines running at close to their peak rates. The mean cycles per reference must be kept reasonably low in the face of decreasing cycle times. Figure 4-35 indicates that for high-speed CPUs, it is advantageous to increase the cycle time to obtain a bigger cache. A small high-speed cache does not appear to be a good design. This conclusion directly confronts the designer's desire to increase performance by squeezing the cycle time.

Multi-level memory hierarchies present a way out of the dilemma. By having several levels of caching between the CPU and main memory, the goals of minimum execution time and cycle time are more easily achieved simultaneously. Section 5.2 illustrates the difficulty in making the most of short cycle time machines and the reason for the worsening of the problem as implementation technologies improve. It proceeds to introduce multi-level hierarchies as the next logical step in memory system design. Section 5.3 examines the design problem of multi-level hierarchies and some tradeoffs that differ between the design of individual levels in a hierarchy and the design of a single-level cache: the speed – size tradeoff, the viability of set associativity, and the choice of block size. Section 5.4 describes an algorithm for finding the best memory hierarchy to a given set of possible cache implementations. Finally, Section 5.7 summarizes the chapter.

5.2. Motivation

Many designers' intuition runs counter to the implication that one cannot necessarily improve system-level performance by adding more hardware to the memory hierarchy. The natural assumption is that time spent waiting on main memory is time wasted. We find it difficult to accept that this waste cannot be reduced or eliminated through the application of more hardware, especially in the form of larger caches. As things stand today, the largest source of degradation to the mean cycles per instruction is the memory hierarchy. Therefore, it is important to understand how this situation will change as implementation technologies improve.

If all delays within a system scale evenly, the basic tradeoffs do not change. If all the temporal parameters are divided by a common factor, the shape and position of the curves of constant performance remain the same, while the slopes, expressed in nanoseconds per doubling, scale down. The slopes remain constant when they are expressed as a fraction of the cycle time per doubling. If the main memory access time scales with the CPU cycle time, then unless there is a dramatic shift in the proportion of the cycle time needed to move from one RAM size to the next, the optimal cache size is not likely to change significantly as technologies improve.

Unfortunately, it is difficult to scale main memory access time with the CPU cycle time. Chip-to-chip and board-to-board communication time and control logic already make up a significant fraction of the latency period. Buffering and decoding will take up a larger fraction of the latency as dynamic RAM access times decrease. Transfer rates are limited by physical dimensions and fundamental electrical properties of materials. Adding width to data paths quickly becomes impractical due to the number of wires involved. Since both the main memory latency and transfer time will scale less than linearly with improvements in integrated circuit technologies, the cache miss penalties, expressed in cycles, will increase as cycle times continue to decrease. This in turn favours larger caches and set associativities. The overall effect is to drive the designer further away from the goal of a tight CPU cycle time and a small cache to match.

However, there is another way to interpret the data – one which exposes a solution. The hidden variable in the plots of the speed – size design space is the cache miss penalty. As the cycle time is varied from 20ns though 80ns, the cache miss penalty goes from 14 to 8 cycles. Table 5-1 rephrases the size – cycle time tradeoff in terms of the cache miss penalty. For each cache size, the first column is the total cycle count divided by the number of references. Since there are two caches, the value drops below one for large caches. The second column contains the cycle time degradation equivalent to a doubling of a cache size, expressed as a fraction of the CPU cycle time. For instance, in Figure 4-4 the slope for the constant performance curve for a 24ns, 4KB cache was 11.5ns. So when the cache miss penalty was 13 cycles, a doubling of the cache size was worth 48% of the cycle time.

The table makes two points. For small caches, with their high miss ratios, the mean cycles per reference is a strong function of the miss penalty. Since we would prefer not to increase the cache size at the expense of the cycle time, the cycles per reference can be kept low only if the trend of increasing cache miss penalties is reversed. The second point is that the fraction of a cycle that is equivalent to a doubling of cache size increases with the cycles per memory read. This means that as the miss penalty decreases, a doubling of the cache size is less likely to be beneficial; this tendency foreshadows a desirable decrease in the optimal cache size with decreasing cache miss penalty.

Two distinct conclusions appear when the cache design problem is observed from this perspective of a fixed cycle time and a varying miss penalty. First, if the cache miss penalty is short enough, the optimal cache size and cycle time are reduced to the point at which the CPU again limits the system cycle time. Second, since the number of cycles per reference is approximately a linear function of the miss penalty, any desired memory hierarchy performance goal can be attained, regardless of the cache size, by a sufficient reduction in the miss

Cycles Per Read	Cache Size							
	4 KB		**16 KB**		**64 KB**		**256 KB**	
	Cycles Per		Cycles Per		Cycles Per		Cycles Per	
	Ref.	size×2	Ref.	size×2	Ref.	size×2	Ref.	size×2
13	2.49	0.48	1.64	0.28	1.17	0.16	0.95	0.05
12	2.37	0.44	1.58	0.27	1.14	0.15	0.94	0.04
11	2.19	0.37	1.49	0.23	1.10	0.14	0.92	0.04
10	2.08	0.32	1.43	0.19	1.08	0.12	0.91	0.04
9	1.92	0.34	1.35	0.20	1.04	0.11	0.89	0.03
8	1.75	0.30	1.27	0.15	1.00	0.10	0.88	0.03

Memory Performance versus Cache Miss Penalty

Table 5-1

penalty. Since the cycles per reference goal is achieved through the reduction of the miss penalty, the CPU cycle time remains unaffected. Furthermore, these conclusions are independent of the actual CPU cycle time and apply equally to 80ns systems and 5ns systems.

The original question was "How can a short cycle time machine reach some desired performance level?" The data in Table 5-1 indicates that the question should be posed as: "What cache miss penalty is required?" Not surprisingly, the solution to the problem of building a memory system that responds in three or five 10ns cycles is identical to the answer to the historical need for high performance memory subsystems and reduced main memory latencies: a cache. The design of a second cache between the CPU/cache and main memory poses the same set of questions as the first level of caching, but with a different set of parameters, constraints and goals. The overall conclusion is that as the disparity between main memory times and CPU cycle times continues to grow, the only way to deliver a consistent proportion of the peak CPU performance is through the use of a multi-level cache hierarchy.

5.3. Intermediate Cache Design

The problem of designing a multi-level memory system has two parts: the design of the individual caches that make up the layers, and the selection of the caches that work best together to maximize the problem. As in Chapter 4, a combination of trace-driven simulation results and simple analytical modelling will be used to examine the design of individual caches. The selection process is then the subject of Section 5.4.

5.3.1. Decomposition of the Hierarchy

The simulation model used to generate the empirical results of this chapter is described in Section 3.2. A small split first-level cache (4KB total) is followed by a larger, unified, second-level cache (512KB). The CPU cycle time is fixed at 10ns, while the main memory parameters are the same as those used in the default single-level cache organization. Both caches are write-back, with a substantial amount of write buffering (four blocks worth) between the cache and the next level. Figure 5-1 shows the miss ratios for this hierarchy as the L2 cache size is varied. Local metrics refer to parameters measured relative to the input stream to a given level, while global metrics are measured with respect to the CPU reference stream. Thus, the L2 local read miss ratio is the number of L2 misses divided by the number of read requests reaching the second-level cache, while the global miss ratio is the same number of misses divided by the number of reads in the input stream. The solo L2 miss rates result when the L1 cache is removed entirely, and the larger cache is the only one in the system. Also, recall that the caches between a cache and the CPU are called the upstream, or predecessor, caches, and those between it and main memory are called the downstream, or successor, caches.

From Figure 5-1 we can see that if the first-level cache is small and the second cache is significantly larger than the first, then the global L2 miss and transfer ratios are independent of the existence of the L1 cache. This independence has the important consequence that activity downstream of L2 is completely independent of L1's organizational and temporal parameters. The overall hierarchy design problem can therefore be decomposed to some extent into the design of the individual layers. Clearly, interdependencies between layers still exist: Section 4.3 demonstrated the interaction between the optimum block size of one layer and the access time of the next. Unfortunately, the effectiveness of the upstream levels[33] determines the strength of the tradeoff

---

[33] A cache's miss ratio is an inverse measure of its effectiveness at filtering references and reducing traffic downstream.

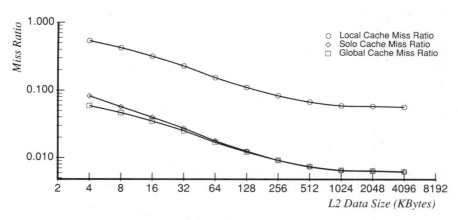

L2 Miss Ratios: 2KB/2KB Split I/D L1 Cache

Figure 5-1

between the L2 cache's organizational and temporal parameters. However, provided this minimum size increment is maintained between the layers of the hierarchy, the scope of these inter-cache dependencies is limited to adjacent pairs.

As the first-level cache increases in size, Figure 5-2 shows the unified L2 miss ratios for a substantially larger L1 size (16KB/16KB). Not only does it clearly illustrate the absurdity of having a second-level cache that is smaller than the L1 cache, but it also indicates that as the first-level cache becomes bigger, the characteristics of the reference stream reaching the subsequent level change. The presence of the predecessor cache noticeably perturbs the L2 global miss ratio from the solo miss ratio, even for very large caches. The independence of the layers of the hierarchy weakens as the size of the upstream cache increases.

The chief difference between the design of the first (or only) layer of the hierarchy and the design of any subsequent levels is the effect of the cache's cycle time. In the previous chapter, we assumed that the cache cycle time is identical to, and determines, the CPU cycle time; this cycle time is a continuous variable. In contrast, the access time of subsequent levels is a discrete variable. The limited range of the cycle time variable does not alter the tradeoffs; it merely renders some of the tradeoffs distinct by limiting the number of choices. More significantly, a cache's cycle time now only affects the time that the CPU spends waiting on this particular layer. In contrast, the first level's cycle time affects all cycles. Since the temporal parameters are now expressed in cycles

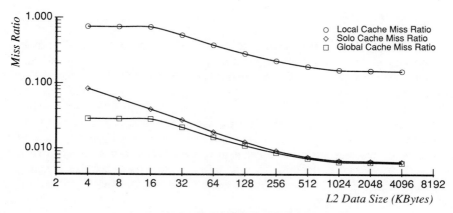

L2 Miss Ratios: 16KB/16KB Split I/D L1 Cache

Figure 5-2

instead of nanoseconds, cycle counts are a direct measure of execution time: the magnitude of the CPU cycle time is not relevant to the tradeoffs.

The amount of time that a cache waits idly for something to do differs substantially between the first and subsequent levels. For the aggressive CPU model used in the simulations (see Section 3.3.2), the first-level caches are used very heavily: only 20% to 30% of the time involves waiting for either a subsequent layer to present requested data or for the CPU to issue a new reference. In contrast, the second-level cache is consistently idle most of the time. This difference suggests that strategies for overlapping operations that are ineffective in a single-level cache design may be more effective in the downstream levels of a multi-level hierarchy. Unfortunately, the clustering or burstiness of cache misses demonstrated in Section 4.3.3 propagates down the hierarchy and continues to hamper the effectiveness of complicated fetch strategies. Throughout the hierarchy, the simple strategy of fetching an entire block before proceeding performs nearly as well as more aggressive policies.

The following sections contain a discussion of how the presence of upstream caches and the quantization of the cycle time affect the tradeoffs examined in Chapter 4. We begin by looking at the tradeoff between the speed and size of a second-level cache, before commenting briefly on the viability of set associativity and the choice optimal block sizes.

5.3.2. Speed – Size Tradeoffs

As in the previous experiments, the tradeoff between a temporal and an organizational parameter is investigated by varying the two simultaneously and comparing their relative effects on performance. Figure 5-3 shows the relative execution times for such an experiment where the two variables are the L2 speed and size. The L2 size is varied across the same range as in the previous experiments: from 4KB to 4MB. The L2 cycle time is varied from one CPU cycle through ten cycles. The L2 cycle time represents the basic SRAM access time: reads that tag hit are completed in this time, and writes take two such cycles. Since the L1 cache is write-back, all read and write references reaching the L2 cache are the L1 block size in length. If either cache has a vertical implementation of blocks, the transfer of a block from the L2 to the L1 cache must proceed serially, thus increasing the L2 access time.

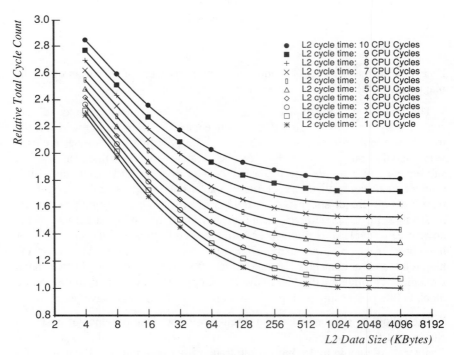

L2 Speed - Size Tradeoff: 2KB/2KB Split I/D L1 Cache

Figure 5-3

The interdependencies between L1 and L2 organizational parameters, such as the link between their block sizes, have an effect on the L2 cycle time, which is defined as the time needed to satisfy a read request from the upstream cache. Because of this, the L2 cache miss penalty is not legitimately linked solely to the L2 cycle time, as it was in the single-level experiments of Chapter 4. In those experiments, since the main memory latency was specified to be a fixed number of nanoseconds, the latency portion of the miss penalty, expressed in CPU cycles, changed with the CPU cycle time. This link between the memory characteristics and the speed half of the speed – size tradeoff is eliminated in this experiment: the total cache miss penalty and memory write operation times are kept entirely constant.

Perhaps the most noteworthy characteristic of the curves in Figure 5-3 is that they are more linear for small cache sizes than those of the corresponding figure in Chapter 4 (Figure 4-3). This linearity stems from two sources: the independence of the latency and the cycle time, and the interaction between the cache levels that occurs if there is not a significant increment between their sizes. The main evidence for the second effect is the increasing separation between the solo and the global miss ratio curves in Figure 5-1 for small L2 sizes. Simply put, an 8KB L2 backing a 4KB L1 performs better than an 8KB cache alone. This improvement in miss rate reduces the cycle count and straightens the curves for small L2 sizes in comparison to the cycle count and curves for the solo caches discussed in Chapter 4.

The linearization of the small L2 region is evident in the design space representation of the tradeoff as well (see Figure 5-4). Though the lines of constant performance are straighter than in the single cache case, the change is relatively minor in that the fundamental shape of the curves or the tradeoff regions remains quite unaffected. In this case, the boundaries between the shaded regions correspond to 0.75, 1.5, 2.25 and 3.0 CPU cycles per L2 doubling. Since the CPU cycle time is 10ns, in the leftmost region a quadrupling of the L2 size is beneficial if the total access time degradation is less than 60ns – a very substantial change. Again, there is a strong pull towards caches greater than 64KB. Since the curves do not become quite as flat for very large caches as they do in the single-level case, it is likely that caches greater than 128KB will be optimal, given reasonable implementation constraints; the slope of the curves do not fall below 2.5ns per doubling until the L2 cache size rises above 512KB.

The proportion of the total execution time spent waiting on the L2 cache varies considerably. Figures 5-5, 5-6 and 5-7 break down the total cycle count according to the level of the hierarchy delaying the CPU. The contribution of the L2 cache is further broken down into the cycles spent satisfying read hits, read misses, and delays to reads caused by writes to the L2 cache that are in

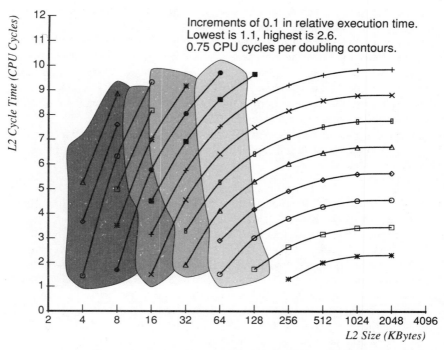

Increments of 0.1 in relative execution time.
Lowest is 1.1, highest is 2.6.
0.75 CPU cycles per doubling contours.

Lines of Constant Performance: 2KB/2KB Split I/D L1 Cache

Figure 5-4

progress. For a small L2 size, the main memory time dominates, as it would in a single-level hierarchy. The balance between read hit and read miss times reflects the very poor local cache miss ratio when the two caches are comparably sized.

Interestingly, as the L2 cycle time increases, the main memory time decreases slightly, despite the fact that none of its parameters have changed. As the L2 cycle time increases, the utilization of the L2 – main memory bus decreases, and so main memory writes are more effectively hidden between MM read accesses . Thus the total time that L2 cache misses are delayed by main memory writes in progress decreases. However, the increase in the total cycle count due to the increase in the L2 cycle time is much greater than this minor drop in the number of delay cycles. effect.

With the given set of experimental parameters, for L2 caches in the 64KB to 256KB size range and for access times around five or seven CPU cycles, the

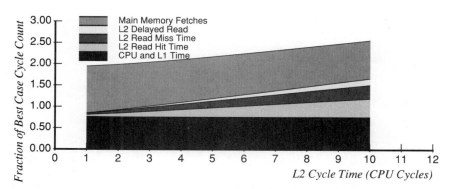

Cycle Count Breakdown: 8KB Unified L2 Cache

Figure 5-5

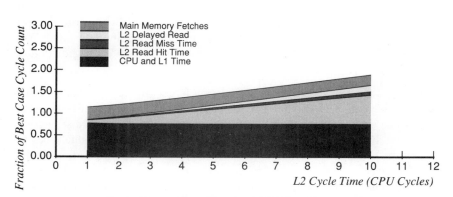

Cycle Count Breakdown: 128KB Unified L2 Cache

Figure 5-6

majority of the total execution time is spent accessing the first-level cache, and the contribution to the execution time decreases with the depth within the hierarchy.

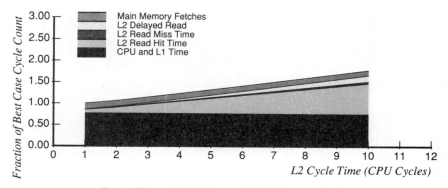

Cycle Count Breakdown: 2048KB Unified L2 Cache

Figure 5-7

One consequence of the increase in the depth of the memory hierarchy is an increase in the number of external parameters on which the tradeoffs can depend. In addition to the main memory parameters, the new external factors are the effectiveness of the upstream caches – primarily determined by their size – and the CPU cycle time; the latter determines the vertical scaling of Figure 5-3.

Figure 5-2 showed the L2 miss ratios for a larger first-level cache (32KB). The low cache miss ratio of the 32KB L1 cache dramatically decreases the performance impact of the second-level cache. Despite the increased separation between the lines of constant performance in Figure 5-8, the individual lines of constant performance have roughly the same shape and slope. The effect of the larger L1 cache is to limit the maximum slope of the lines and to dramatically cut the magnitude of the performance improvement possible, but this only slightly increases the optimal L2 size.

A slower main memory increases the penalty of a miss. As in Section 4.1, this increases the slope of the lines of constant performance. Figure 5-9 shows the L2 design space for the default L1 cache, given a main memory that is twice as slow as that in the default scenario. Since memory times are measured in CPU cycles, this graph looks much like a graph for the original memory with a CPU cycle time of 5ns. The only substantial difference is the scale of the Y axis and, correspondingly, the magnitude of the slopes. The effect of the slower memory, then, is to shift the shaded regions to the right by approximately a factor of two in cache size.

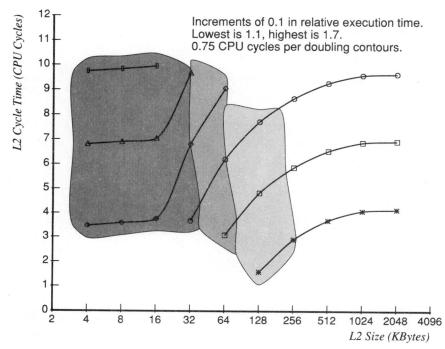

Lines of Constant Performance: 32KB Split I/D L1 Cache

Figure 5-8

Table 5-2 lists external parameters and their effects on the speed – size tradeoff as measured by the regions of slope of the lines of constant performance.

An analytical exploration of the L2 tradeoffs begins with the general equation relating the total cycle count to the global miss rates and cycle times in a multi-level cache hierarchy that was given in Equation 3.10. For a two-level hierarchy with negligible write effects, the equation becomes the sum of the time spent doing reads at each of the three layers of the hierarchy plus the cycles spent doing writes into the first-level cache:

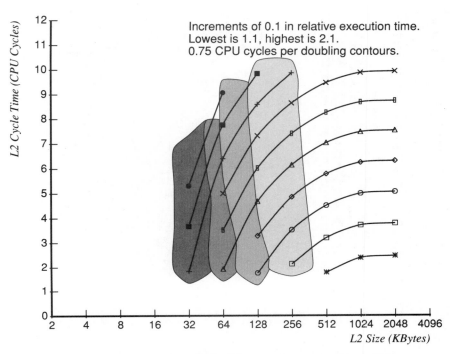

Lines of Constant Performance: Slow Main Memory

Figure 5-9

$$N_{Total} = N_{Read} n_{L1} + N_{Read} M_{L1} n_{L2}$$

$$+ N_{Read} M_{L2} n_{MMread} + N_{Store} \overline{n}_{L1write} \qquad [5.1]$$

When the derivative of the cycle count with respect to the L2 cache size is set equal to zero, the tradeoff between the second-level cache's size and cycle time, $t_{L2} = t_{CPU} \times n_{L2}$, is exposed. As in Chapter 4, an optimal configuration is obtained by balancing the relative change in the cycle time and the relative change in the cycle count:

Increase in:	Effect on Figure 5-3:
L1 Size, Associativity or Block Size	Reduces the overall performance variation. Reduces the slope of the lines of constant performance. Shifts the knee in the curves of constant performance to the right.
L1 Cycle Time	Reduces the slope of the lines of constant performance for small L2. Increases the separation, expressed in nanoseconds, between the lines. Shifts the curves of constant performance to the left.
Main Memory Latency	Increases the slope of the lines of constant performance for small L2. Shifts the curves of constant performance to the right.
Transfer Rate	Reduces the slope of the lines of constant performance for small L2. Shifts the curves of constant performance to the left.

Influences on the L2 Speed – Size Tradeoff

Table 5-2

$$\frac{1}{\bar{t}_{MMRead}} \frac{\partial t_{L2}}{\partial C_{L2}} = -\frac{1}{M_{L1}} \frac{\partial M_{L2}}{\partial C_{L2}} \qquad [5.2]$$

Equation 5.2 is very reminiscent of the balancing equation, derived in Section 4.1, that related the change in the CPU cycle time to the change in the miss rate (Equation 4.1):

$$\frac{1}{\bar{t}_{MMread}} \frac{\partial t_{CPU}}{\partial C} = -\frac{N_{Read}}{N_{Read} + N_{Store} \bar{n}_{L1write}} \times \frac{\partial m(C)}{\partial C}$$

In moving from the single to the multi-level environment, the fractional content of reads in the reference stream in the single-level case disappeared because the cycles spent doing writes to the first-level cache are unaffected by the L2 cycle time; in its place is the inverse of the L1 (global) miss ratio – a potentially large number. For the 4KB cache in the simulation experiment, the L1 miss ratio was 10.9%. This new factor represents a dramatic shift in the speed – size tradeoff in favour of larger caches.

In Section 4.1, Agarwal's cache miss model was used to show an inverse square relationship between the rate of change in the miss ratio and the cache size. Given a reasonable increment between the sizes of the caches, the relationship will also hold for the L2 global miss ratio for most large and medium sized caches. Admittedly, the relationship breaks down somewhat for larger L1 caches, but this effect will be considered in detail later. Disregarding temporarily the change in the left-hand side of Equation 5.1, the presence of the L1 cache increases the optimal cache size by a factor equal to the inverse square root of the L1 miss ratio.

The model and Figure 4-1 both verify that for the range of caches under investigation, a doubling of the cache size decreases the miss rate by a constant factor, which was observed to be about 0.69. Thus, the lines of constant performance for a second-level cache shift to the left by about a third of a binary order of magnitude in cache size for each doubling of the L1 size. Assuming that the marginal cycle time cost of increasing the cache is independent of cache size, the L1 cache would have to increase eightfold for the optimal L2 size to double. Across Figures 5-4 and 5-8, the L1 size increased by a factor of eight, and the lines of constant performance shifted by a factor of 1.74 – close to the 2.04 predicted by this model. Any changes in the L2 cycle time due to this increase in the L2 size would naturally affect the speed half of the speed – size tradeoff. This could either reduce or enlarge the actual increase in the optimal L2 cache size, depending on the local characteristics of the cycle time as a function of the cache size.

As was noted earlier, the inverse square relationship between the derivative of the miss rate and the cache size does not hold for very large caches. The miss ratio hits a plateau once the number of conflict misses drops below the number of misses due to non-stationary behaviour. At this point, the change in miss rate for a change in cache size drops to zero. For caches in this region, the presence of the other levels in the cache hierarchy does not change the tradeoff: further increases in the cache size are never worthwhile, regardless of how small the cycle time penalty is.

The impact of the main memory access time, $\bar{t}_{MMread}$, is the same in this situation as in the single-level case. Specifically, a proportional change in the cache miss penalty inversely modifies the cycle time half of the balancing equation, Equation 5.2. As in Section 4.1, increasing the L2 cache miss penalty skews the speed – size tradeoff towards larger caches.

5.3.3. Set Size Tradeoffs

The L1 cache miss ratio also appears in the equations for the incremental break-even times for the implementation of set associativity. The increase in cycle time, in nanoseconds – which exactly balances an improvement in the miss ratio due to doubling the associativity – is equal to the product of the change in the global miss ratio, the mean main memory access time, and the inverse of the L1 miss ratio:

$$\Delta t_{IBE} \;=\; -\,\frac{1}{M_{L1}}\,\overline{t}_{MMread}\,\Delta M_{L2}$$

With only a single level of caching (Section 4.2), break-even times for large caches were consistently much too low to warrant a set-associative implementation. Within a multi-level hierarchy, though, the break-even times can be substantially larger, depending on the effectiveness of the upstream cache. Figures 5-10 through 5-12 show the cumulative break-even implementation times for the default 4KB L1 cache and a memory system comparable to that used to generate Figures 4-7 through 4-9. The shaded regions are bounded by the 10ns through 40ns contours.

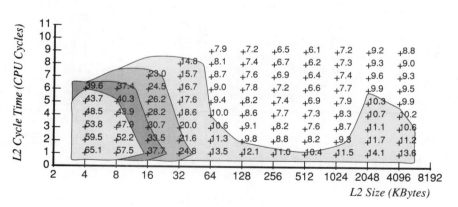

Set Size Two Cycle Time Tradeoff

Figure 5-10

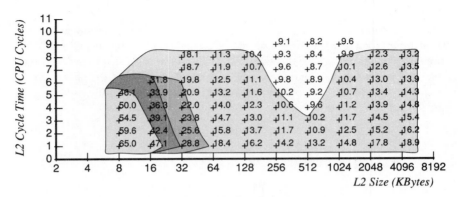

Set Size Four Cycle Time Tradeoff

Figure 5-11

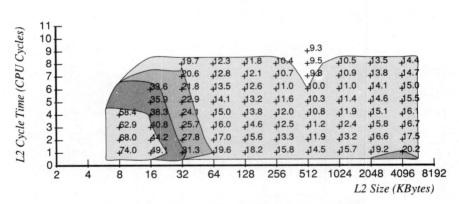

Set Size Eight Cycle Time Tradeoff

Figure 5-12

For this base scenario and most of the L2 sizes and cycle times of interest, the designer has between 10ns and 20ns at his or her disposal in the implementation of eight-way set associativity. These times, which correspond to between one and two CPU cycles, increase as the L2 size decreases. When there is a small increment in size between the two caches, and the direct-mapped L2 local cache miss ratio is close to one, the addition of set associativity causes a large relative change in the effective L1 cache miss penalty. Given a 4KB total L1 cache, an eight-way set-associative 8KB L2 unified cache is substantially better at reducing the memory traffic than a direct-mapped cache of the same size.

Figures 5-10 through 5-12 show a noticeable decrease in the cumulative break-even times with increasing L2 cycle time. In contrast, Figures 4-7 through 4-9 show the opposite trend. This difference is easily explained in terms of changes in the memory model used in the two systems. As noted at the beginning of Section 5.3.2, in the two-level model the main memory access time is entirely decoupled from the L2 cycle time, while in the single-level model, the transfer period is a fixed number of CPU cycles, regardless of its cycle time. The increase in the transfer period, measured in seconds, with increasing cycle time affects $\bar{t}_{MMread}$, and thus the break-even times. With this influence removed, the break-even time should be independent of the L2 cycle time. There are, however, other factors that come into play. Figure 5-6 shows a decrease in the amount of time that L2 misses are delayed by main memory writes in progress as the L2 cycle time increases. Thus, the mean memory access time, $\bar{t}_{MMread}$, decreases with increasing L2 cycle time. The improvement in the L2 miss rate with the additional set associativity accentuates this decrease in the time spent waiting on main memory to be free, since the main memory utilization is proportional to the L2 miss ratio. Overall, changes of up to 70% in cumulative break-even times across the range of L2 cycle times are observed. This is an example of a significant effect that can be accurately diagnosed only with the aid of a detailed cycle counting simulator.

In Section 4.2, the 11ns *select* to *data-out* time for a FAST multiplexor is introduced as a likely minimum implementation overhead for a discrete set-associative cache. In Figure 5-12 in particular, a large portion of the design space falls below that cutoff. However, recall that a 4KB L1 size was used. Since each doubling in the L1 size decreases its miss ratio by about 28%, the L2 break-even times will increase in the same proportion. As the size of the upstream cache increases, the benefit of set associativity also increases. If the size increments between layers of the hierarchy are small, on the order of four or eight, then the cumulative break-even times are uniformly greater than 17ns and reach as high as 45ns. If the L1 cache is small, then the L2 cache is also small enough that the break-even implementation times are substantially greater than their minimum, and if the second-level cache is larger, then so is the first level, and, consequently, so is the L1 miss ratio multiplier.

To put these large break-even times into perspective, remember the motivation for introducing more levels into the memory hierarchy: a reduction in the mean L1 cache miss penalty to improve performance and a decrease in the optimal L1 size. For a single-level cache, even when it increased the performance, associativity was added reluctantly because it increases the system cycle time. Increasing the set size also increased the unfortunate disparity between the optimal cycle time and the minimum CPU cycle time. On the surface, then, it is dissatisfying to have the L1 miss ratio multiplier effectively increase the L2 cycle time. Again, when viable, adding associativity presumably increases the L2 cycle time. The fundamental difference, though, is that adding set associativity to the L2 cache is in fact reducing the mean L1 miss penalty to its minimum, despite the potentially large increase in the L2 cycle time: in this case, associativity helps reach the goal of short CPU cycle times and small L1 caches.

5.3.4. Block Size and Fetch Size Tradeoffs

In Section 4.3, we observed the interaction between the block size, the fetch size and the main memory characteristics. From the perspective of an arbitrary layer in a multi-level cache hierarchy, the optimal choice of block size involves at least the layer in question and its successor. If the tradeoff also involved its predecessor, as the size and associativity tradeoffs do, the problem of finding a globally optimal memory hierarchy would be severely complicated.

Fortunately, the block and fetch size choices do not involve any of the upstream caches. Figure 5-13 shows the behaviour of the optimal equal block and fetch sizes as a function of the memory characteristics for the 512KB second-level cache of the default two-level model. It assumes no cycle time penalty for longer block sizes and uses the same simple fetch strategy. This figure describes the best choice for a 512KB unified cache. The optimal block sizes are similar to those shown in Figure 4-14 for a single-level, 2MB split I/D cache.

The independence of the optimal block/fetch size from the previous layers of caching is illustrated by equating to zero the derivative of the total cycle count with respect to the block size. This derivative has two components: one dependent on the upstream cache's miss ratio and the partial derivative of the cycle time with respect to the block size, and one dependent on the memory characteristics and the global miss ratio:

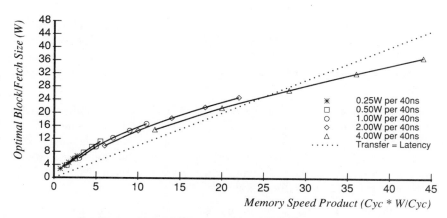

Optimal L2 Block/Fetch Size versus Memory Speed Product

Figure 5-13

$$0 = \frac{\partial N_{Total}}{\partial B}$$

$$= N_{Read} M_{L1} \frac{\partial n_{L2}}{\partial B} + N_{Read} \left(\left(la + \frac{B}{tr} \right) \frac{\partial M_{L2}}{\partial B} + \frac{M_{L2}}{tr} \right)$$

If the L2 cycle time is completely independent of the block size, then the term that is dependent on $\frac{\partial n_{L2}}{\partial B}$ vanishes. In the absence of a cycle time degradation, the relationship between the memory speed product, $la \times tr$, the optimal block/fetch size and the miss ratio ratio across a doubling of the block size, $R(B)$, is the same as in the single-level case, given in Equation 4.5:

$$la \times tr = B \left(\frac{2R(B) - 1}{1 - R(B)} \right)$$

However, if there is a degradation in the L2 cycle time due to the implementation of longer block sizes, the multiplication of the partial derivative, $\frac{\partial n_{L2}}{\partial B}$, by the L1 miss ratio implies that a large degradation in the cycle time is necessary to produce a significant change in the optimal block size. In Section 4.3, a 1% degradation per factor of two in the block size noticeably affects the optimal block size. With an L1 miss rate of 0.10, a dramatic 10% degradation is needed to have a comparable effect: as the effectiveness of the upstream cache increases, the choice of block/fetch size becomes more insensitive to any cycle time effects.

As in the single-level case, if the block and fetch sizes are allowed to be different, the optimal fetch size is determined by the downstream memory speed product, and the optimal block size is primarily determined by interactions with the write strategy. Again, if the block size's influence on the global miss ratio is small, for write-back caches, choosing equal block and fetch sizes is a good choice, with near optimal performance.

In a multi-level cache hierarchy, the downstream level may be a cache instead of the main memory. In this case, we need to define the memory speed product appropriately so that we can draw upon the experience gained in analyzing single-level hierarchies. Thus far, a cache's access time has been represented by the number of CPU cycles needed to satisfy a fetch, n_{Li}. To accurately define the speed product, this quantity must be broken down into its constituent parts that correspond to the main memory's latency and transfer time. The first step is to define the cache's internal cycle time, t'_{Li}, which is some integral multiple of the CPU cycle time. The total read access time is defined as n'_{Li} internal cycles. Each internal cycle is classified as either a transfer cycle or a latency cycle, depending on whether data is being passed up the hierarchy. The number of latency cycles, n'_{la}, plus the number of transfer cycles, n'_{tr}, equals the total number of internal cycles per read. The mean latency used in the calculation of the speed product, $\overline{n}'_{la}$, is the cache-hit latency, plus the mean delay in internal cycles to satisfy a cache miss. This is dependent on the cache's miss ratio and penalty. Assuming that the upstream cache is requesting an entire block, the memory speed product is the predecessor's block size, B_{Li-1}, multiplied by the ratio of the mean latency period and the transfer period: $la \times tr = \dfrac{B_{Li-1} \times \overline{n}'_{la}}{n'_{tr}}$. If the ratio of the transfer period and the request size is not a constant, then the speed product of the cache is a function of the upstream block size that it will be used to select. In this case, the best block size must be selected by comparing the total cycle counts for each of the possibilities.

Caches normally exhibit a much narrower range of memory speed product than main memories. Whereas some mainframes have speed products above 30 [Smith 87a], most caches have latencies and transfer periods of just a couple of sub-cycles. Smaller memory speed products translate to smaller optimal block sizes within cache hierarchies.

In practice, having the fetch size of one cache larger than the block size of the next is inefficient. If this is true, more than one tag access and comparison is needed to ensure that a read request can be satisfied. Since groups of sets in the second cache are always accessed together on reads, the performance can only improve if the second-level cache's block size is increased to the fetch size of the previous one. Thus, if the fetch size is generally restricted to be identical to the block size, then it is suboptimal to have a non-monotonic block size with increasing cache depth. Similarly, in the absence of cycle time variations, it does not make sense to have the upstream cache's block size be less than the bus width between the caches. Under such circumstances, increasing the block size to the bus width reduces the miss rate without incurring a cycle count penalty.

Given these practical upper and lower bounds on the block size, the optimal block size is a function of the downstream cache's latency and the transfer rate of the connecting bus. This function is the same as the one described in Section 4.3 for a single level of caching. It appropriately balances the latency and transfer periods, regardless of the source of the data. The latency used to calculate the memory speed product is the mean latency of the downstream cache, which is dependent on its miss rate and mean cache miss penalty.

5.3.5. Summary

In conclusion, the existence of upstream caches clearly affects the speed – size tradeoff of a second-level cache. The global miss ratio of the previous cache multiplicatively modifies the balance between the change in the cycle time and change in the miss ratio that exists at the optimal design point. The upstream hierarchy reduces the number of references reaching a cache without affecting its global miss ratio. This dramatically increases the importance of a low miss rate in comparison to a short cycle time.

Equating the effect of the upstream cache to a change in cache size is straightforward. Assuming that the inverse square relationship between cache size and miss rate holds, the addition of a 4KB L1 cache, with a 10% miss rate, should shift the lines of constant performance about to the right by seven binary orders of magnitude. The actual observed shift between Figures 4-4 and 5-4 is about 3.5 powers of two. The difference is accounted for by the change in block size (1.5 factors of two), the removal of write cycles from the balance (0.7 factor of two), and changes to memory model (one factor of two). Locally, a doubling in the L1 cache size is shown to shift the curves of constant performance about 0.24 powers of two to the right.

A shift in the curves of constant performance of seven binary orders of magnitude translates to a factor of 128 increase in the optimal size of the cache only if the change in the cycle time per doubling is constant. At any point in time, the available technologies determine the specific characteristics of the cycle time as a function of the cache size. If in the vicinity of the optimum, the change in the cycle time per doubling of the cache decreases, then the change in the optimal cache size due to the presence of the L1 cache will be greater than the shift in the curves. Alternatively, if that all-important function is locally increasing, a shift in the curves will result in a smaller increase in the optimal L2 size. However, given the strength of the influence of the upstream cache, the optimal cache size is likely to increase by at least a few binary orders of magnitude. For any one design, the exact amount of the increase in the optimum cache size is highly dependent on the specific implementation constraints.

Improving the miss rate of the upstream cache increases the viability of set-associative second-level caches. Break-even implementation times are multiplied by the inverse of the previous cache's global cache miss ratio. Increasing the set associativity, even at the expense of a significant increment in the L2 cycle time, minimizes the mean L1 cache miss penalty and, therefore, helps reduce the optimal L1 size, as desired.

The choice of block size is essentially independent of the presence of any upstream caching. The only effect of such caches is to reduce the impact of changes in cycle time resulting from increases in the block size. Within cache hierarchies, the block size is likely to be small in comparison to the expected single-level and final-level cache block sizes.

Somewhat unfortunately, but not unexpectedly, the empirical and analytical results indicate that the strong motivation to increase the L2 cache size at the expense of its cycle time remains relatively unchanged from the analysis of a single-level hierarchy in Chapter 4. In the absence of a strong incentive to build significantly faster L2 caches with access times below five CPU cycles, the basic L1 tradeoff does not change sufficiently to justify the small fast L1 caches.

5.4. Optimal Memory Hierarchy Design

The ultimate goal of a computer implementor is to design a memory hierarchy that maximizes the overall performance of his or her machine. This task involves deciding on the number of layers of caching, as well as the organizational and temporal parameters. So far, this book has addressed the single-level cache design problem and changes in that problem that occur when considering a cache in a multi-level memory hierarchy. This section considers the problem of selecting caches from the available realizable implementations to produce a memory hierarchy that minimizes the overall execution time.

Dynamic programming – a well-known technique for finding the minimum cost path through an annotated graph [Larson 78] – can be used to make this selection optimally without enumerating all possible hierarchies.

More formally, the set of possible caches can be represented by a set of tuples, $C_j(C, A, B, M, t'_{min}, n'(B_{Li-1}))$. For each cache we need to know the organization, the solo miss ratio, the minimum internal cycle time and the number of internal cycles needed to satisfy a read request. The read access time is a function of the request size, which can be assumed to be between the upstream bus width and the block size, as discussed in the previous section. The optimization problem is to select from this set of caches a memory hierarchy comprised of a sequence of caches, $C_{L1} \cdots C_{Ln}$, such that total execution time is minimized. The CPU cycle time is assumed to be equal to the minimum internal cycle time of the first-level cache. The operating cycle time of all the other chosen caches is the smallest value that is greater than or equal to the cache's minimum cycle time and that is also an integral multiple of both the CPU cycle time and the previous cache's cycle time. The block and cache sizes can be restricted to monotonically increasing values as a function of the cache depth without affecting the optimality of the solution.

An exhaustive search of the complete design space is not practical, since each cache is potentially followed by any larger cache or main memory. Of course, for each cache size, there can be more than one implementable cache. Given $c(j)$ candidate caches of size 2^j bytes,[34], the number of potential memory hierarchies starting with a cache of size 2^j is given by the product of one more than the number of caches of each size greater than 2^j:

$$c(j) \prod_{k=j+1}^{j_{max}} c(k) + 1$$

Figure 5-14 illustrates the size of the design space to be searched. The circle for each cache size represents all $c(j)$ possible caches of size 2^j bytes. Thus, the arc between level j_1 and level j_2 is really $c(j_1) \times c(j_2)$ individual arcs between the $c(j_1) + c(j_2)$ caches at the two levels. For example, if an average of three associativities and four block sizes are considered for every size between 128B and 4MB, there are over 6×10^{16} potential memory hierarchies to be evaluated. Though one could develop effective pruning heuristics based on the restriction

---

[34] In this section, n indicates the depth of cache hierarchy not including main memory, i is reserved for an index into a particular cache hierarchy, $1 \le i \le n$, and j and k are used to index into the set of candidate caches ordered by their sizes. Thus 2^j and 2^k are the sizes of the jth and k^{th} candidate caches.

on the block sizes and the analysis of the individual tradeoffs described up to this point, a much simpler method for finding the best hierarchy exists.

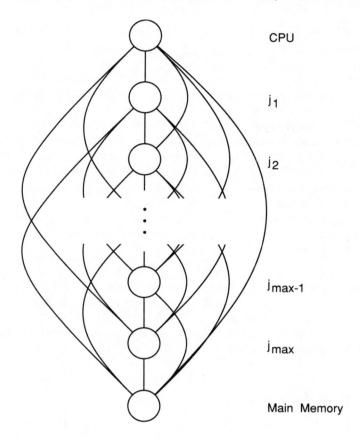

Memory Hierarchy Design Space

Figure 5-14

On the surface it seems that a simple, one-pass algorithm is impossible due to the structure of the dependencies. Specifically, the cache size and set associativity tradeoffs depend on the miss rate of the upstream cache, while the optimal block size depends on the downstream cache's characteristics. There also appears to be an upstream dependency between the cycle times, in that a cache's cycle time must be a multiple of the previous cache's internal cycle time. This dependency is actually bidirectional. It can equivalently constrain a downstream cache to a cycle time that is an integral multiple of a preselected upstream cache, or an upstream cache to a cycle time that is an inverse integral of a downstream cache.

Mathematically, the execution time being minimized is given by the sum of the total read times at each of the levels in the hierarchy, plus the total write time in the first-level cache. Each cache's read time is equal to the product of the predecessor's global cache miss rate and this cache's cycle time, here expressed as the product of its internal cycle time and its read access internal cycle count:

$$T_{Total} = N_{Store} \overline{n}_{L1write} t'_{L1} + N_{Read} n'_{L1} t'_{L1}$$

$$+ N_{Read} M_{L1} n'_{L2}(B_{L1}) t'_{L2} + N_{Read} M_{L2} n'_{L3}(B_{L2}) t'_{L3}$$

$$+ \cdots + N_{Read} M_{Ln-1} n'_{Ln}(B_{Ln-1}) t'_{Ln} + N_{Read} M_{Ln} t_{MM} \qquad [5.3]$$

Each internal cycle must be an integral multiple of its predecessor's internal cycle time:

$$t'_{L1} = t_{CPU}$$
$$t'_{L2} = K_1 \times t'_{L1}$$
$$t'_{L3} = K_2 \times t'_{L2}$$
$$\cdots$$
$$t_{MM} = K_n \times t'_{Ln} \qquad\qquad K_i \in \mathbf{I}, \ t'_{Li} \geq t'_{min}(C_{Li}) \ \ 1 \leq i \leq n$$

Equation 5.3 dispells the illusion that the dependencies simultaneously involve upstream and downstream caches [Gygax 78]. Each term involves parameters of at most two caches. If each arc between every two potential caches in Figure 5-14 is annotated with the total read time of the downstream cache, then the problem of finding the minimum path from the CPU to the main memory is solved in a straightforward manner by the use of dynamic programming [Larson 78]. This would be possible except that the downstream cache's operating cycle time is dependent on the upstream cache's internal cycle time, and that is unknown before its predecessor has been selected, and so on. Thus, unlike regular dynamic programming, in which the arcs are first labelled and then traversed, the labelling and traversing must be done together.

The simultaneous annotation and traversal of the graph begins with the smallest cache size. These caches can only be the first-level cache in a hierarchy because the size is a strictly monotonic function of the hierarchy depth. The only possible contribution of these caches to the best memory hierarchy is, therefore, their total read time, $N_{Read} n'_{L1} t'_{L1}$, and their total write time, $N_{Store} \overline{n}_{L1write} t'_{L1}$. The sum of these two values is the value attached to the lone arcs between these caches and the CPU. These values are immediately propagated to the nodes representing these caches. For the caches of this minimum size, finding their cycle times is not a problem since they can only be their respective minimum cycle times.

For the next larger cache size, each cache can be either a first- or a second-level cache. If one of these caches is the first-level cache in the optimal hierarchy, its cost is the same sum of the total read and write times that was just calculated for the smallest caches, so that sum can be attached to the arc joining the CPU to the cache. If the cache is to be the second level of the hierarchy, then its cycle time will be an integral multiple of the cycle time of its predecessor, the L1 cache. In this case, the cache's contribution to the overall execution time will be its total read time, including the effect of its upstream partner, $N_{Read} M_{L1} n'_{L2} (B_{L1}) t'_{L2}$. Since the cycle time of each of the smaller caches is known, we are able to label each arc. Once all the arcs are annotated, the minimum cost between the cache in question and the CPU can be found by adding each arc's cost to the accumulated cost of the node at its upstream end. The arc which yields the lowest value is marked as the path back to the CPU, the sum of that arc's cost and the accumulated cost of the cache it leads to becomes this cache's accumulated cost, and, finally, the cache's cycle time is set equal to the value used to calculate the selected arc's cost.

This process continues, progressing to ever larger cache sizes. By the time a cache is processed, all the smaller caches already have had their optimal cycle time determined, so that the arcs leading from the larger cache to each of the smaller ones can be labelled unambiguously. Finally, the main memory is considered and the minimum total cost is found, along with its read access time. Thus, the optimum hierarchy is the unique path up the graph, along the selected arcs, to the CPU.

This dynamic programming algorithm for finding the globally optimal cache hierarchy given a set of possible cache implementations is illustrated graphically in Figures 5-15 and 5-16. For the sake of conceptual simplicity, the figure only shows a single implementation for the smallest cache size, and two possible implementations of a larger size, in addition to the nodes for the CPU and main memory. Figure 5-15 shows the graph with all its annotations, and a bold arc to each caches optimal predecessor. Figure 5-16 follows the algorithm as it progresses down the graph, annotating arcs and accumulating minimum total costs.

Each of the nodes (caches) is marked with the minimum cycle time, t'_{min}, the read access cycle counts for the various block sizes, $n'(B_{Li-1})$, the block size and miss ratio, and an empty slot for its accumulated cost, O. Each arc is eventually annotated with a cost, $r(Li,Li-1)$, the downstream cache's cycle time on which the arc's cost is based, and a boolean marker used to indicate the optimal hierarchy. The block size for the CPU is taken to be one word, and its accumulated sum is set to zero. Main memory's latency, transfer rate and minimum internal cycle time are used to calculate its read access internal cycle count as a function of the request size, $n'_{MM}(B_{Li-1})$.

The outer loop of iteration involves visiting each node in turn, starting at the top (smallest caches) and concluding with main memory at the bottom. For each cache, the inner loop queries in turn all the incoming arcs, each of which leads to a potential predecessor. For each arc, the cycle time of the larger cache must be determined by finding the smallest integral multiplier between the two internal cycle times that satisfies the downstream cache's minimum requirement. The arc is then labelled with its cost: the upstream cache's miss rate multiplied by the downstream cache's cycle time and read access cycle count:

$$r(Li,Li-1) \;=\; N_{Read} M_{Li-1} \, n'_{Li}(B_{Li-1}) \, t'_{Li}$$

If the arc points to the CPU, then it is labelled with the sum of the cache's minimum cycle time and the write time:

$$r(L1) \;=\; N_{Read} \, n'_{Li}(B=1) \, t'_{min} \;+\; N_{Store} \, \bar{n}_{L1write} \, t'_{min}.$$

After all of the arcs are labelled, the minimum accumulated cost for the cache is found by adding each arc's cost to the accumulated cost of the node that it points to. The arc that yields the lowest sum is marked as the preferred arc, and the cycle time that it mandates is assigned to the cache.

After all the nodes have been visited, the optimum upstream hierarchy for each cache is found by following the marked arcs all the way to the CPU, and the globally optimum memory hierarchy is found by following the single set of arcs that connect the CPU with the main memory. The memory's accumulated cost is the minimum total execution time possible given the possible caches.

Bellman's Principle of Optimality guarantees the legitimacy of this simultaneous annotation and traversal of the graph [Bellman 57]. The principle states that given an optimal path between the two extremes of the graph, any subportion of that path must be the optimal route between its end points. For all

C1:
$$t'(C1,CPU) = t'_{min}(C1)$$
$$r(C1,CPU) = N_{Write}\bar{n}_{L1write}\,t'(C1,CPU) + N_{Read}\,n'_{C1}(1)\,t'(C1,CPU)$$
$$O(C1) = O(CPU) + r(C1,CPU)$$
$$t'(C1) = t'(C1,CPU)$$

C2:
$$t'(C2,CPU) = t'_{min}(C2)$$
$$r(C2,CPU) = N_{Write}\bar{n}_{L1write}\,t'(C2,CPU) + N_{Read}\,n'_{C2}(1)\,t'(C2,CPU)$$
$$t'(C2,C1) = K_1 \times t'_{C1}$$
$$r(C2,C1) = N_{Read}\,M_{C1}\,n'_{C2}(B_{C1})\,t'_{C2,C1}$$
$$O(C2) = \min\left\{\; O(CPU) + r(C2,CPU)\,,\, O(C1) + r(C2,CPU)\;\right\}$$
$$t'_{C2} = \text{one of }\left\{\; t'(C2,CPU)\,,\, t'(C2,C1)\;\right\}$$

C3:
$$t'(C3,CPU) = t'_{min}(C3)$$
$$r(C3,CPU) = N_{Write}\bar{n}_{L1write}\,t'(C3,CPU) + N_{Read}\,n'_{C3}(1)\,t'(C3,CPU)$$
$$t'(C3,C1) = K_1 \times t'_{C1}$$
$$r(C3,C1) = N_{Read}\,M_{C1}\,n'_{C3}(B_{C1})\,t'(C3,C1)$$
$$O(C3) = \min\left\{\; O(CPU) + r(C3,CPU)\,,\, O(C1) + r(C3,CPU)\;\right\}$$
$$t'_{C3} = \text{one of }\left\{\; t'(C3,CPU)\,,\, t'(C3,C1)\;\right\}$$

MM:
$$t'(MM,CPU) = t'_{min}(MM)$$
$$r(MM,CPU) = N_{Write}\bar{n}_{L1write}\,t'(MM,CPU) + N_{Read}\,n'_{MM}(1)\,t'(MM,CPU)$$
$$t'(MM,C1) = K_1 \times t'_{C1}$$
$$r(MM,C1) = N_{Read}\,M_{C1}\,n'_{MM}(B_{C1})\,t'(MM,C1)$$
$$t'(MM,C2) = K_2 \times t'_{C2}$$
$$r(MM,C2) = N_{Read}\,M_{C2}\,n'_{MM}(B_{C2})\,t'(MM,C2)$$
$$t'(MM,C3) = K_3 \times t'_{C3}$$
$$r(MM,C3) = N_{Read}\,M_{C3}\,n'_{MM}(B_{C3})\,t'(MM,C3)$$
$$O(MM) = \min\left\{\; O(CPU) + r(MM,CPU)\,,\, O(C1) + r(MM,C1)\,,\right.$$
$$\left. O(C2) + r(MM,C2)\,,\, O(C3) + r(MM,C3)\;\right\}$$
$$t'_{MM} = \text{one of }\left\{\; t'(MM,CPU)\,,\, t'(MM,C1)\,,\, t'(MM,C2)\,,\, t'(MM,C3)\;\right\}$$

Optimal Design Procedure

Figure 5-15

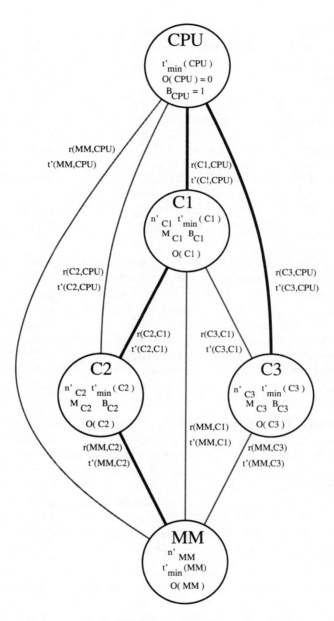

Optimal Design Procedure (cont.)

Figure 5-16

the caches in the optimal hierarchy, the upstream hierarchy between a cache and the CPU is the one that minimizes the total access time to that depth. This means that once the optimal path between a cache and the CPU is found, the cache's cycle time is fixed and is independent of the downstream caches.

Notice that a cache's miss ratio is only needed after its optimal predecessor has been determined. This facilitates ensuring that the size increment is large enough to warrant the use of the cache's solo miss ratio instead of the upstream-specific global miss ratio, $M_{Li-1}(\mathbf{C}_{Li-1}, M_{Li-2})$. Although the true global miss ratio can easily be substituted throughout this procedure, the guaranteed optimality of the algorithm is sacrificed if it makes a difference. When the global miss ratio is used in Equation 5.3, the terms depend on three levels of the hierarchy, meaning that the costs along individual arcs are no longer independent of the path above the upstream cache: Bellman's Principle may no longer hold.

The complexity of this algorithm is dramatically less than that of an exhaustive search. In essence, each arc is considered only once. The number of arcs in the graph is given by the number of legitimate successor-predecessor pairs. For a candidate of a particular size, the number of possible predecessors is equal to the number of smaller caches. The number of arcs is quadratic in the total number of candidates. In contrast, the size of the exhaustive search is polynomial of order the maximum possible depth of the hierarchy. For the rather extensive search space used as an example above, instead of 6×10^{16} possible hierarchies, only 1440 arcs would have to be evaluated using the dynamic programming technique.

A potential flaw in the optimality of this algorithm stems from the quantization of the cycle times. The cycle time (or, alternatively, its integral multiplier K) at one level of the hierarchy can sometimes be increased slightly from its minimum value to the benefit of the cycle count. For instance, for a minimum L1 cycle time of 24ns and a minimum L2 cycle time of 49ns, the straightforward application of the algorithm calls for an implementation that has a three cycle L1 miss penalty ($t_{L1} = 24ns$, $t_{L2} = 72ns$). Depending on the miss ratio, the hierarchy probably performs better if the L1 cycle time is increased fractionally to 25ns, so that the cache miss penalty drops to two cycles.

Recall that in Figure 4-3, the performance was not uniformly a monotonic function of the cycle time. For one combination of cache size and cycle time, the performance increased when the cycle time decreased. That anomaly was caused by exactly this phenomenon: an unfortunate choice of cycle time and a high cache miss rate and a relatively long cache miss penalty combine to noticeably perturb the performance function. Though this phenomenon is more likely to occur with smaller caches, as indicated by the miss ratio's role in the above inequality, that it occurred only once in Figure 4-3 constitutes strong indication that unfortunate quantization effects seldom cause a problem. Moreover, it is easy to check for the problem and adjust the cycle times accordingly while traversing the graph of candidate caches.

The algorithm as stated produces a suboptimal design if a fractional degradation, k, in one cache's cycle time facilitates a reduction by one in the integral multiplier, K, between the cycle times of the cache and its successor. The fractional degradation necessary to produce a change in the multiplier depends on the ratio of the upstream cycle time and downstream minimum cycle time and the ceiling of that ratio. If the ratio and its ceiling are markedly different, then there is a great deal of time wasted in the default downstream access time, and only a small change in the upstream cycle time is needed to trigger the change in the multiplier, K. In the above example, the ratio of the downstream minimum to the upstream cycle time is $\frac{49}{24} = 2.04$. Also, as the size of the multiplier increases, the fractional degradation needed to reduce it by one decreases:

$$ k = \frac{K+1}{K} \frac{\dfrac{t_{min}(Li+1)}{t_{Li}}}{\left\lceil \dfrac{t_{min}(Li+1)}{t_{Li}} \right\rceil} $$

The dynamic programming algorithm produces the wrong result if much time is spent in the downstream cache compared to the time spent in the upstream cache. The upstream cycle time should be adjusted if the ratio of the time spent waiting for reads at the two levels is less than the inverse of the percentage decrease in the upstream cycle time, $k-1$, minus the integral multiplier:

$$ \frac{1}{k-1} - (K-1) > \frac{M_{Li-1} \, n'_{Li}}{M_{Li} \, n'_{Li+1}} $$

If this relation holds, the execution time decreases if the upstream cache's cycle time is increased to the next inverse integral of its successor's minimum cycle time.

The designer will want to quantify the performance improvement due to the multi-level hierarchy. The best single-level or two-level hierarchy is determined by applying the dynamic programming algorithm to a subset of the entire graph. By restricting which arcs are taken, the maximum depth of the hierarchy can be constrained. The ratio of the main memory's accumulated sum before and after the restriction is the performance improvement, if any, that results from the additional hardware investment.

A difficult problem arises when the performance attained by the best memory hierarchy does not meet the performance goal. The only recourse is to attempt to design some better candidate caches, either by investigating new technology alternatives or by trying different fetch and write strategies as a means of eking some additional performance out of existing technologies.

5.5. A Detailed Example

The following example is fabricated to illustrate the application of the above hierarchy selection procedure and to illustrate some of its consequences. Since the example's purpose is to make the tradeoffs clear, the correspondence between technologies and cycle times is only loosely based in reality. However, the miss rates used are accurate.

A company undertakes building a new computer system from the ground up; the designers have been given *carte blanche* to produce the fastest machine they can, provided it can be used in an office environment and sold for under $100K. Naturally, they choose to build a RISC machine.[35] Using the latest ECL gate arrays, they decide that they can cycle the CPU at 10ns.

Table 5-3 lists 14 candidate caches, clustered into four groups based on size and implementation technology. The caches in the first group would be integrated onto the same chip as the CPU and use about 16K bits of storage for data and tags. Since the total area is kept constant, the data size can increase only if the block size also increases. The three candidates in this class are organized as separate instruction and data caches. However, we assume that the pin count of the die is too limited to permit the buses necessary for a split external organization. Therefore, all the remaining candidates are unified caches.

The second group of caches uses a moderate number of fast ECL RAMs (10ns to 15ns access times) to form caches that cycle around 20ns to 30ns. For this size (8KB to 32KB) and memory system, the optimal block size for a solo organization, as predicted by Figure 4-16, is four to eight words. The caches in the third set are made of fast CMOS static RAMs. Level conversions between the ECL CPU or L1 cache degrade the cycle time to the range of 50ns. Finally, caches in the largest group, also made of CMOS SRAMs, have internal cycle times that are half their access times. This reflects the difference between the

---

[35] This is, after all, 1990 [Mashey 86].

Cache	Type	C (KB)	S	B (W)	M	t_{min} (ns)	$n(1,2,4,8)$
CPU	I/D			1		10	1 – – –
A_1	I/D	1	1	1	0.57	10	1 – – –
A_2	I/D	2	1	2	0.27	12	1 – – –
A_3	I/D	2	2	2	0.23	14	1 – – –
B_1	U	8	1	1	0.205	20	1 – – –
B_2	U	16	1	2	0.090	26	1 1 – –
B_3	U	32	1	4	0.0395	32	1 1 1 –
B_4	U	8	1	4	0.0752	20	1 2 4 –
C_1	U	64	1	4	0.026	50	1 1 2 –
C_2	U	128	1	8	0.0078	52	1 1 1 2
C_3	U	128	4	8	0.0055	62	1 1 1 2
C_4	U	128	4	16	0.0035	62	1 1 1 2
D_1	U	1024	1	8	0.0044	40	2 2 2 3
D_2	U	1024	2	8	0.0035	45	2 2 2 3
D_3	U	1024	2	16	0.0021	45	2 2 2 3
MM	Maximum Transfer Rate: Latency: Memory Speed Product:					2 Words/50ns 300ns 12 Words	

Candidate Caches

Table 5-3

SRAM's read access time and the rate at which data can be gated to the upstream cache. Since this level must be the final layer of the hierarchy, only larger block sizes are given consideration.

Changes in the cache size and block size within each group indicate the presumed nature of the implementation of blocks within the cache. If the cache size increases with the block size, it is because additional width is added to each set. If the total size stays constant, then the width of the RAM array remains the same, and the implementation becomes increasingly vertical. Generally, blocks are implemented horizontally up to a width of two or four words, beyond which they are overlaid vertically.

Figure 5-17 shows the performance optimal hierarchy given these candidate caches. Only the arcs that form the path from optimal upstream hierarchies are shown. The costs are based on the distribution of references found in the eight traces used in simulations: 63% instruction fetches, 25% loads and 12% writes. Writes are not propagated past the L1 cache, where they take exactly two cycles. When the first-level cache is split I/D, load cache accesses and half of the write cycles are overlapped with instruction cache accesses. Within each circle, the middle number is the cache's minimum accumulated cost divided by the total number of references. The main memory's accumulated cost is the number of nanoseconds per reference for this hierarchy. The bottom number is the actual internal cycle time for the cache in its optimal hierarchy.

The globally optimal memory hierarchy, shown by the thickest arcs, is the on-chip A_2, followed by B_3, and C_4 off-chip. These caches are highlighted in Table 5-3. The best single-level hierarchy, indicated by the dashed lines in Figure 5-17, is B_4. The execution time per reference for the optimal single-level cache is 50.1ns, so the performance more than doubles when the additional two levels of caching are added.[36] The best two-level hierarchy is A_3, followed by C_2 cycling at 56ns. Their combined execution time per reference is 27.3ns, or 87% of the best-case performance.

This example underscores several key points made in previous sections and chapters. First, the small, three cycle, L1 cache miss penalty makes possible the small optimal L1 cache size: 2KB. Recall that the Cache Comparison Chart, Figure 4-35, depicts the design space for a memory latency of six cycles and a transfer rate of one word per cycle. A change in the cache miss penalty from seven to three cycles shifts the lines of constant performance by close to three binary orders of magnitude. The knee in the vicinity of 128KB moves to about 16KB, close enough to the 2KB that the slope of the curves at that point do not warrant abandoning the on-chip cache. The desirability of the on-chip configuration is increased by the split organization, and the substantial penalty is paid by the off-chip unified caches for serial instruction and data references. The

---

[36] The performance improvement resulting from increasing the depth from one to three is $\frac{50.1}{24.0} - 1 = 109\%$.

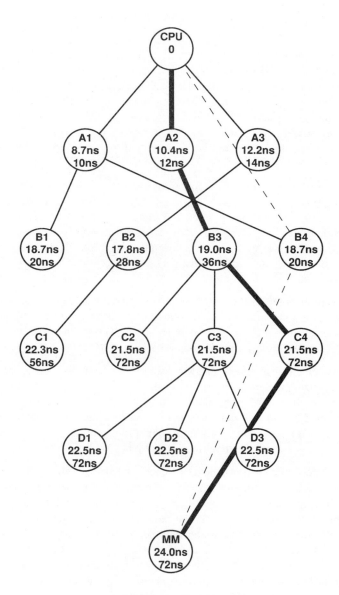

Optimal Cache Hierarchy

Figure 5-17

cache miss penalty of the second-level cache was also very small; only two L2 cycles are needed to fetch four words from the L3 cache.

The second important observation relates to the optimal single-level hierarchy. The best overall single-level machine, built around B_4 (8KB, 20ns), performs only 19% better than the best single-level CMOS machine, built with C_2 (128KB, 52ns). This indicates that the designers should seriously consider dropping their plans for an ECL processor if they are unwilling to build a multi-level hierarchy. They would also need to seriously question whether they can meet their target performance range with this memory and a single level of caching.

The third point is that if the hierarchy is restricted to at most one level of ECL caching (that is, only one split I/D cache from the first two groups), then the best choice is a different three-level hierarchy: B_4 (8KB, 20ns) followed by C_2 (128KB, 64ns) and D_3 (1MB, 64ns). In other words, when the L2 cache is limited to being large and slow, the optimal L1 size increases to compensate. This three-level hierarchy obtained a respectable 91% of the best-case performance.

The final layer in the best overall hierarchy was four-way associative. Its predecessor's miss ratio was 4%, which had a dramatic effect on the viability of set associativity. Its block size was 16 words, larger than expected for this main memory speed product (see Figure 4-16).

Most of the differences in the minimum cycle times were overshadowed by the quantization that occurs as a result of the requirement that cycle times be integral multiples of one another. When the upstream cycle time is already determined, organizational changes that improve the miss ratio at the expense of the minimum cycle time are clearly beneficial provided that the new minimum cycle time is not greater than the original integral cycle time.

The addition of a fourth level of caching gained nothing; the total execution time per reference for the best four-level hierarchy was 0.8% greater than the overall minimum. For each set of design constraints and technological alternatives, there is a particular hierarchy with a finite depth that maximizes the system-level performance. Increasing the depth of the hierarchy from one to two levels increased performance by 87%. Extending the hierarchy depth to three improved performance by only another 14%: as might be expected, the benefit of adding hardware to memory system is great initially, but the marginal benefits diminish rapidly.

5.6. Fundamental Limits to Performance

This chapter began with the observation that there was a finite limit to the performance that could be achieved with a single level of caching: beyond a certain point, performance is not improved through the addition of hardware or a reduction in the cycle time. It should not be surprising, then, that there is also an upper bound to the performance obtained with a multi-level memory hierarchy; given the set of realizable caches defined by the set of currently available technologies, there exists a unique multi-level hierarchy that minimizes the total execution time. Once the optimum is reached, the local miss ratio of any new cache is so close to one that the time spent accessing it is inevitably greater than the reduction of time spent reading from the hierarchy further downstream: there is an optimal depth to the hierarchy. In other words, the execution time cannot be arbitrarily reduced through the application of more hardware in the form of additional levels of hierarchy or of changes to specified caches. This section probes analytically the relationship between the limitations imposed by the implementation technologies and the performance-optimal hierarchy and the CPU cycle time that the hierarchy mandates. This hierarchy sets the upper bound on the performance level that can be obtained by a uniprocessor system with a given set of implementation technologies.

A first-order model of the cycle count with a multi-level hierarchy was presented in Equation 3.10. Once the CPU cycle time is distributed across the terms, the execution time becomes the sum of the time spent doing read accesses at each of the levels of the hierarchy, plus the time spent doing writes into the first-level cache.

$$T_{Total} = N_{Read}\left(t_{L1} + M_{L1}(C_{L1}) \times t_{L2} + M_{L2}(C_{L2}) \times t_{L3}\right.$$

$$+ \cdots + M_{Ln}(C_{Ln}) \times t_{MMread}\left.\right)$$

$$+ N_{Write} \times t_{L1} \times \overline{n}_{L1write}$$

The cycle time of each cache, t_{Li}, is equal to the number of CPU cycles that it takes to respond to a read request, n_{Li}, times the CPU cycle time, $t_{CPU} = t_{L1}$.

To push beyond this form, we need to relate a cache's miss ratio to its cycle time. Of all the thousands of cache implementations possible at any given time, only a few are truly practical: it never makes sense to use an organization when there exists another that has a smaller or equal minimum access time and a smaller miss ratio. Disregarding limitations on hardware resources, for each cache access time, the minimum miss ratio corresponds to some organization for which the minimum cycle time is no greater than that access time. For the set of technologies available at any given time, we can construct a graph that shows the best solo miss ratio attainable as a function of the cache access time. Figure 5-18 shows this function for three hypothetical years. The horizontal segments extending from the symbols that represent the few practical cache organizations is the true discontinuous function relating the minimum miss ratio and the cache access time for one of the three years. For that year, all other realizable cache implementations would lie above and to the right of at least one of those useful implementations. The smooth curves represent continuous approximations to the actual discrete functions.

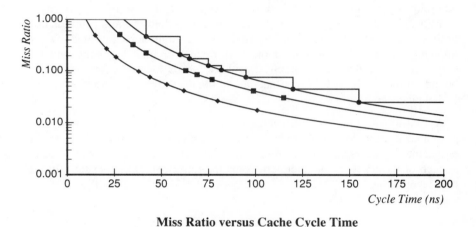

Miss Ratio versus Cache Cycle Time

Figure 5-18

Once a continuous minimum miss rate function is defined, the above performance model becomes a simple equation in n unknowns, ($t_{L1}, \ldots, t_{Ln}$), and one organizational parameter, (t_{MMread}):

$$T_{Total} = N_{Read} \left(t_{L1} + M(t_{L1}) \times t_{L2} + M(t_{L2}) \times t_{L3} \right.$$

$$\left. + \cdots + M(t_{Ln}) \times t_{MMread} \right) + N_{Write} \times t_{L1} \times \overline{n}_{L1write}$$

Since the continuous miss ratio function is well behaved and strictly decreasing, the optimum is attained when the partial derivative with respect to each of the cache cycle times is equal to zero:

$$\frac{\partial T_{Total}}{\partial t_{L1}} = 0 \quad \Rightarrow \quad 0 = 1 + M'(t_{L1}) \times t_{L2} + \frac{N_{Read}}{N_{Write}} \times \overline{n}_{L1write}$$

$$\frac{\partial T_{Total}}{\partial t_{L2}} = 0 \quad \Rightarrow \quad 0 = M(t_{L1}) + M'(t_{L2}) \times t_{L3}$$

$$\cdots$$

$$\frac{\partial T_{Total}}{\partial t_{Ln}} = 0 \quad \Rightarrow \quad 0 = M(t_{Ln-1}) + M'(t_{Ln}) \times t_{MMread}$$

provided

$$t_{Li} < t_{Li+1} < t_{MMread}$$

This formulation of the problem ignores the requirement that the cycle time of each cache be an integral multiple of its predecessor. In practice, though, this simplification has little effect. When integral multiples are enforced, the number of levels in the optimal hierarchy remains unchanged except over a few small ranges of values of t_{MMread}, where the depth is increased by one. The optimal performance level and CPU cycle time, however, are not significantly altered. The contribution due to writes in the final term of the first equation can be safely ignored because the low proportion of writes in the reference stream makes its significance less than the error associated with the continuous model of $M(t_{cyc})$. The final restriction on the ordering of the cycle times is necessary to ensure that the algebraic solution corresponds to a plausible memory hierarchy. Without it, the set of equations occasionally indicates an "optimal memory hierarchy" with cache cycle times greater than the main memory access time.

A useful approximation for the minimum miss ratio function is the ratio of the cycle time to a minimum CPU cycle time, raised to a negative exponent. Chow used this same power function in his analytical investigation of the memory hierarchy design problem [Chow 76].

$$M(t_{cyc}) = \left(\frac{t_{cyc}}{t_{min}} \right)^{e} \qquad e < 0 \qquad t_{min} < t_{cyc} < t_{MMread}$$

$$= 1 \qquad\qquad\qquad t_{cyc} < t_{min} \qquad\qquad [5.4]$$

The linearity of the miss ratio shown in Figure 4-1 suggests an exponent of about −0.54 for the relationship between a cache's size and its miss ratio. Section 4.1 argued that the link between a cache's cycle time was at most $O(\sqrt{C})$. Together, these two proportionalities indicate an exponent, e, less than −1; experience suggests an exponent in the general vicinity of −2.5. The dots on Figure 5-19 show the caches used in the example of Section 5.5, while the curves represent the miss ratio power function for a variety of exponents. Though the miss ratio function varies a great deal with the exponent, we will see that the basic characteristics of the optimal hierarchy are quite insensitive to its value of e.

The minimum cycle time, t_{min}, is not influenced by the choice of exponent since all of the curves are quite steep over the domain in the vicinity of t_{min}. This model parameter is fractionally smaller than the cycle time of the smallest implementable cache.

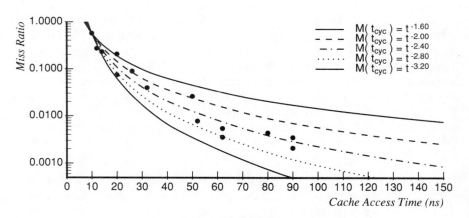

Miss Ratio versus Cache Access Time

Figure 5-19

The solution to this set of coupled equations is complicated by the fact that the optimum number of levels, n, is unknown. However, given a depth, the cycle times of all the caches that yield the minimum execution time can be directly computed from the exponent, e, and the ratio of the main memory access time and the minimum cycle time, $\dfrac{t_{MMread}}{t_{min}}$. The lack of a closed form for the preferred depth can be overcome by computing that execution time for all possible depths and recognizing that the smallest of them is the global minimum, T_{opt}. The optimal depth, n_{opt}, and the optimal CPU cycle time, t_{opt}, follow directly.

Figures 5-20 and 5-21 show the best attainable execution time and the optimal CPU cycle time as a function of the normalized main memory access time for a variety of exponent values. The plusses mark changes in the optimal depth, from zero at the extreme left to four or five for a t_{MMread} of 50 times t_{min}.

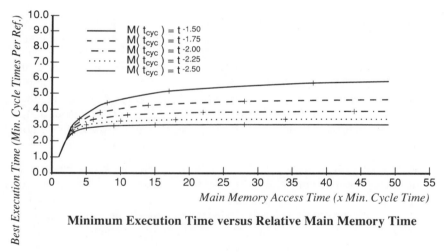

Minimum Execution Time versus Relative Main Memory Time

Figure 5-20

The good news is that even if main memory access times increase dramatically with respect to minimum CPU cycle times, neither the performance degradation due to the memory system nor the separation between the optimal and minimum CPU cycle times grow very rapidly. The depressing side of this news is that the amount of hardware needed to maintain this performance level appears to be formidable; five levels of caching sounds extravagant. As illustrated in the previous section, we are already operating in a region in which three or four levels of caching are optimal.

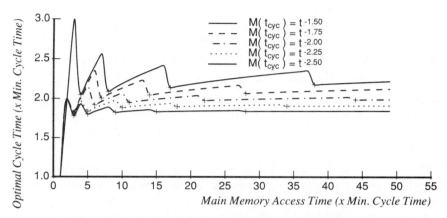

Optimal CPU Cycle Time versus Relative Main Memory Time

Figure 5-21

Interestingly, even when the integral cycle time multipliers are enforced, the optimal CPU cycle times hover between 1.85 and 2.25 times t_{min}, depending on the exponent. For this simple model of the miss ratio, these cycle times correspond to an optimal L1 miss ratio of between 0.22 and 0.29: about 0.5KB to 1KB direct-mapped or equivalent, regardless of the ratio of the main memory speed to the minimum CPU cycle time, or the optimal hierarchy depth.

The detailed example in Section 5.5 also illustrated that most of the benefit of a multi-level hierarchy comes from increasing the depth from one to two, with diminishing returns thereafter. This observation is corroborated by Figures 5-22 and 5-23, which show the same best attainable execution time and optimal CPU cycle time for hierarchies of limited depth. When only a single level of caching is employed, the performance degradation and optimal CPU cycle time continue to climb with increasing main memory access times. In contrast, when just two levels are used, the performance level is between 12% and 26% slower than the global optimum for main memory access times between 20 and 100 times t_{min}. Though squeezing out that additional performance is worthwhile in some applications, the cost in hardware and design effort for the addition levels of caching is probably not warranted under most circumstances.

The model's exponent was fixed at −2.5 for these two graphs. When the exponent is more negative, it is more important to have at least two levels in the hierarchy. Even though the performance of the best single-level cache improves with increases in the magnitude of the exponent, its performance improves less

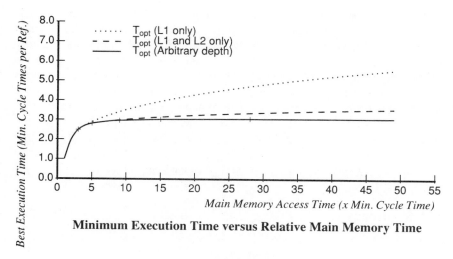

Minimum Execution Time versus Relative Main Memory Time

Figure 5-22

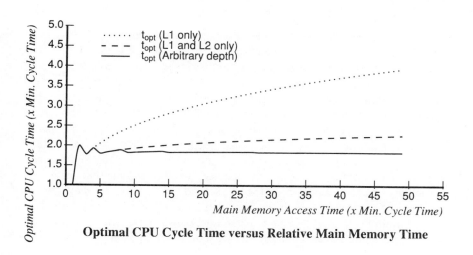

Optimal CPU Cycle Time versus Relative Main Memory Time

Figure 5-23

quickly than that of the global optimum. In other words, when the miss ratio is a more gradual function of the cycle time, a single level of caching does proportionately better, in comparison to the absolute best case.

Despite the approximate nature of the miss ratio and execution time models used, some significant conclusions are safely drawn. As the relative main memory access times increase, degradations in performance due to the memory hierarchy can be kept small through the introduction of additional levels to the memory hierarchy. As technologies improve, and minimum CPU cycle times decrease with respect to main memory times, the optimal CPU cycle times should continue to decrease with the minimum cycle times. Along the same lines, the optimal first-level cache remains quite small regardless of design conditions. Though the size and the speed of the best single-level cache increase noticeably with the main memory speed, the situation is dramatically improved when the depth is increased to just two levels of caching.

5.7. Summary

This chapter has focused on the multi-level cache hierarchies. The first portion has considered the differences between cache design for a single level of caching and for a part of a larger hierarchy. Experiments based on a two-level simulation model and a multi-level analytical model indicated how the choice of optimal caches varies between the two environments.

In particular, the speed – size tradeoff changes significantly when there is an upstream cache. All other parameters being equal, the presence of the 4KB first-level cache shifted the lines of constant performance to the right by about seven binary orders of magnitude. Changes in the L1 size have only a limited effect on the optimal cache size: four doublings in the L1 size are needed to shift the curves by one factor of two towards larger L2 sizes. In general, though, as the miss rate of the upstream cache decreases, the amount of performance improvement that is achieved through the addition of more layers of caching decreases dramatically. The presence of the upstream caches significantly improves the viability of set associativity, to the extent that large set associativity caches made of MSI TTL and static RAMs may be an improvement over their direct-mapped equivalents. Except for the peculiarities of the definition of latency and transfer rate between two cache layers, the choice of block size remains unaffected by the upstream hierarchy.

Also presented in this chapter is a dynamic programming algorithm that, given a set of possible cache implementations, finds the performance-optimal memory hierarchy. It differs from standard dynamic programming in that the graph of potential hierarchies is traversed as the costs of the arcs – which are the added execution time for each new cache to be added to the hierarchy – are evaluated. The requirement that caches have cycle times that are integral multiples of their predecessors implies that each arc's cost depends on the optimal path to its upstream end. This stipulation introduces the quantization effects that can cause a naive implementation of the algorithm to find a suboptimal hierarchy. To be certain that the best hierarchy is being found, the amount of wasted time introduced into a cache's access time by the integral multiplier must be compared to the cost at the previous level of eliminating that slack by increasing the upstream cache's cycle time. The algorithm makes a single pass over the graph and is $O(c^2)$ in the number of candidate caches.

A detailed example illustrates that even with today's technologies, a substantial amount of performance improvement is available through the use of cache hierarchies that are two or three deep. Most of the empirically and analytically predicted tradeoffs are visible in the hierarchies selected from just 14 candidate caches. The optimal depth was three, though the best two-level system did almost as well as the best three-level system (87% of the overall optimal performance).

This chapter concludes with an exploration of the fundamental limits to performance that can be obtained with a multi-level hierarchy. By assuming a power function for the miss ratio as a function of the cycle time, the optimal hierarchy for any given relative main memory access time can be calculated. This model corroborates the lesson of the detailed example: though the optimal number of levels may be large – upwards of five or six – very good performance can be obtained with just two or three levels. The requirement that cycle times be integral multiples of the upstream cycle times did not significantly affect the performance attainable, though it did occasionally increase the optimal depth of the hierarchy. Even as main memory access times become very long with respect to minimum CPU times, increasing the depth of the hierarchy limits the optimal CPU cycle time to about twice the theoretical minimum cycle time and the number of CPU cycles per reference to less than two.

Chapter 6

Summary, Implications and Conclusions

The real world is not easy to live in.

– Clarence Day

6.1. Summary

This final chapter summarizes the main results of this book and places them in the context of real-world cache design: when designing a machine for the marketplace, consideration must be given to many factors other than performance. This section highlights the systematic treatment of the various tradeoffs exposed in Chapters 4 and 5. Section 6.2 discusses memory hierarchy design for real machines and considers the impact of performance-directed design on that task; specific attention is given to aspects of system design that are seldom mentioned in the literature. It also includes a succinct set of guidelines intended to help designers better understand the consequences of performance-directed cache design.

This book tackles the optimal memory hierarchy design problem in two steps. First, the minimal hierarchy of a single cache is examined from the perspective of each of the three main organization parameters: the cache size, the set associativity, and the block size. These individual tradeoffs are then combined into a single cache comparison chart that allows the direct evaluation of the performance of a wide variety of organizations and implementations. The second phase demonstrates that multi-level hierarchies are the way to provide higher performance and to counter the growing tendency towards optimal caches that are large and slow. The design of a cache at an intermediate level is contrasted to the design of a single-level cache. Section 5.4 illustrates an algorithm for selecting the optimal multi-level hierarchy given a selection of implementable caches.

The data presented in the graphs throughout this book were generated with trace-driven simulation. The simulator used is able to accurately account for time at each level of a multi-level hierarchy (Section 3.3.1). It realistically models the temporal interactions between activity at the various levels and is therefore appropriate for an accurate study of the inherently time-dependent behaviour of complicated fetch and write strategies. This degree of accuracy and precision is a prerequisite for a credible study of memory hierarchies in which performance is the basis of comparison.

As a starting point for the simulation study, two base system models were developed (Section 3.3.2). The first, used throughout Chapter 4, has a single level of split instruction/data caching, while the second, used in Chapter 5, has two levels of caches; the L1 cache is small and also split into a Harvard organization, and the L2 cache is much larger and unified. The models were made as realistic as possible so that they would represent useful configurations. The single-level base system is modelled after a low-cost workstation built around a 25MHz RISC CPU, while the two-level system is representative of a higher performance ECL based server delivering about 75 MIPS sustained. The individual experiments discussed in each section start with one of these models. Up to four design variables are then varied across a wide range of values. Thus each experiment explores a multi-dimensional region of the whole design space. Each region has one of the two base scenarios at its center.

Eight large virtual address reference traces were used to generate the numerical data (Section 3.3.3 and Appendix A). Four were captured on a VAX 8250 running VMS or Ultrix and a variety of user and system programs. The other four traces were fabricated by interleaving between three and seven uniprocess traces obtained on a MIPS Computer System's R2000 architecture machine. Though the traces in this second set of four do not contain operating system references, the individual programs were interleaved according to the context switch distribution observed in VAX traces. In addition, the R2000 traces have preambles that precisely initialize the memory hierarchy cache prior to the warm-start boundary. Except for the lack of operating system references, the statistics gathered after the warm-start boundary are thus exactly the same as would be observed in a real system running those programs, regardless of the cache size. So while most traces of this length stop yielding credible results for cache sizes greater than about 256KB, these traces yield valuable data for much larger caches.

In tandem with the empirical study, analytical analysis, based on fairly straightforward models of execution time, reveals insights into the empirically observed behaviour and confirms the applicability of the results to a wide portion of design space. The performance-optimal cache configuration is investigated by equating to zero the partial derivative of the total execution time as a function of the various organizational and temporal parameters. This technique, while not useful for generating specific data points, is valuable for two reasons: first of all, it corroborates the empirical data and allows for extension of the general results beyond the limited region of the design space explored in the simulation study. Second, it gives great insight into the underlying phenomena and the reasons for the observed behaviour. The enhanced intuition about the nature of caches that the designer thus develops is much more valuable in the long run than all the concrete simulation results.

This book has concentrated almost exclusively on read effects. In both the empirical and analytical portions, write effects have been minimized through the selection of aggressive write policies or outright ignored through simplifying assumptions. This has been done because reads and writes occur at different rates, they have different miss ratios, and their cache hit and miss policies and penalties are radically different. In practice, and as shown in Appendix B, for write-back caches, reads generally dominate writes in their respective contributions to the overall execution time. Thus by concentrating on reads – that is, instruction fetches and loads – the problem of performance-directed cache design is simplified and clarified without a great loss in relevance. All of the empirical results presented in this book were generated with an aggressive write policy: write-back caches, no fetches on a write miss, and with large, wide write buffers between all levels of the hierarchy.

The first three substantive sections of Chapter 4 examine in detail the temporal tradeoffs in single-level cache design relating to each of the three main organizational parameters: cache size, degree of associativity and block size. In the first section, Figure 4-4 succinctly presents a spectrum of split I/D cache simulation results; lines of equal performance drawn through the speed – size design space allow the comparison of the performance levels of direct-mapped caches of different sizes and cycle times. The asymptotic shape of the curves, represented by the decreasing slope of the lines, delineates the tradeoff that exists between a cache's size and the system cycle time. The slopes of the lines, measured in nanoseconds per doubling of the cache size, determine whether it is worthwhile to exchange the cache RAMs for ones that are larger but slower, or conversely, smaller but faster. The magnitude of the slope of the lines is quite substantial for small caches: more than 10ns per doubling for 4KB and 8KB caches with the aggressive memory system used in the simulations. However, the lines of constant performance are essentially flat for cache sizes above 128KB. Consequently, for a wide variety of circumstances, the best cache size falls between 32KB and 128KB. Furthermore, the slopes of the curves and the resulting speed – size tradeoff are independent of the actual cache cycle time. Increasing main memory access times shifts the curves of constant performance to the right, towards larger caches. The exact amount of change in the performance-optimal cache size depends on the exact nature of the function between a cache's size and its access time. As CPU cycle times decrease, the tradeoff between cycle time and cache size remains a constant proportion of the cycle time only if the cache miss penalty decreases proportionately with the cycle time. Unfortunately, main memory access times are not decreasing as rapidly as CPU cycle times. This growing gap is at the heart of the motivation for multi-level cache hierarchies. Finally, the fundamental shape of the curves lessens the influence of the variation in the miss ratio as a function of the workload. Thus the choice of best cache size is less variable than would be indicated by an analysis of miss ratios alone.

In Section 4.2, the speed – associativity tradeoff for the same base system is quantified by deriving the break-even implementation times. If the difference between the cycle times for a direct-mapped cache and a set-associative cache is less than this value, the set-associative cache has a higher overall performance: otherwise, the direct-mapped cache is the better choice. For the same aggressive memory system, the break-even times ranged between 1ns and 8ns for two-way associativity, increasing to between 1.4ns and 11ns for eight-way associativity. For caches greater than 32KB, the values were uniformly less than 4ns: too small to justify a set-associative cache implemented with MSI TTL. For smaller, integrated caches, set-associative caches could be beneficial, though any cycle time penalty would degrade the performance advantage foreshadowed by the improvement in the miss ratio. The incremental break-even implementation times are sufficiently small beyond a set size of eight that very large associativities are never warranted strictly from the perspective of performance. Set sizes greater than four are usually implemented as a result of virtual memory and page size constraints. The break-even times are directly related to the change in miss ratio between the two scenarios, indicating the much greater applicability of set-associative caches to environments whose applications have chronically poor miss rates. The break-even implementation times are also directly proportional to the cache miss penalty. This means that if the number of CPUs per main memory access increases, then the break-even implementation times will increase as a percentage of the CPU cycle time. This signals a greater propensity towards set associativity as the gap between CPU cycle times and main memory cycle times continues to grow.

The tradeoffs involving the block size are investigated in four parts in Section 4.3. First, the link between the optimal block size and the main memory speed product (the product of the latency and transfer rate) is examined alone by excluding any complicating circumstances. The section begins by pointing out the important distinction between the block size and the fetch size. However, since in most systems they are identical, the standard usage of block size for the equal block and fetch size is used except when specifically talking about fetch strategies with different block and fetch sizes.

For each memory system, as characterized by a latency/transfer rate pair, the optimal, non-integral block size is found by locating the minimum of the curve of performance as a function of block size. The block/fetch size that maximizes performance is always less than the fetch size that minimizes the miss ratio. In essence, across a wide range of cache sizes and memory parameters, the best binary block size is one of 4, 8 or 16 words. Being off by one size does not cause a major performance loss. Near their minima, the lines of performance as a function of the memory parameters and the block size are quite flat. For straightforward fetch strategies, the block size that minimizes execution time is a function of the product of the main memory's latency and transfer rate, and not of either independently. When the product is low, indicating that the memory technology is superior to the backplane's, then it is better to spend more than one-half of the cache miss penalty transferring data. When the memory speed product is high, indicating a superior backplane, it is preferable to spend more than half of the total main memory access time waiting for the first word. Of the three primary organizational parameters – the cache size, set associativity and block size – the block size is most sensitive to the characteristics of the workload. The optimal block size was observed to vary by as much as a factor of four across programs. Programs that exhibit a higher degree of spatial locality benefit more from a larger fetch size. The cache size affects the optimal block size, with larger caches demanding larger block sizes. This is because large caches have lower ratios of miss rates across a change in block size.

When the possibility of some cycle time degradation with increasing block size is included in the performance model, the optimal block size is significantly reduced. Even for minute incremental changes in the cycle time, the decrease in the cycle count due to larger blocks is seriously offset by the degradation in the cycle time half of the performance equation. Interestingly, the effect is equivalent to a decrease in the transfer rate, particularly for small perturbations in the cycle time.

Section 4.3.2 specifically deals with the case of a simple fetch strategy but unequal block size and fetch size. The most important observation here is that the traditional reduction in the miss rate as a function of increasing "block size" is really due entirely to increasing fetch size. In fact, for a constant fetch size, the miss ratio actually slightly increases with increasing block size. Therefore the appropriate perspective to look at the previous results relating to the optimal equal block and fetch sizes is that the optimal fetch size is dependent on the memory speed product, and the optimal block size is dependent primarily on the write policy. Specifically, for the default split organization and standard write-back write policy with extensive buffering, the performance-optimal block size was somewhat smaller (up to a power of two) than the optimal fetch size. For instruction caches, there is no intrinsic advantage to having the block size be anything other than equal to the fetch size. Therefore, for a split cache system, there are three independent design variables: the instruction cache block and fetch size, the data cache block size, and the data cache fetch size. Again, for the default size and write policy and workload, the best instruction block size was typically 8, 16 or 32 words. The best data cache fetch size was about half the instruction cache fetch size and either equal to or twice as large as the best data cache block size.

Another example of the close dependence of optimal block size and the write strategy exists for write-through caches. For these caches both the write hit and write miss times are dramatically reduced when the write size is equal to the block size. In this case the tags need not be checked before the tag and data arrays are written. As a result, there is a strong preference for making the block size equal to the most common write size – typically one word.

Finally, Section 4.3.3 investigates the effectiveness of complicated fetch and prefetch strategies and their impact on the optimal block size. Two aggressive non-prefetching strategies and two prefetching strategies are presented. For this cache size the maximum performance improvement attained over the simple default fetch strategy is on the order of 8%, with most being under 4%. For only one of the prefetching strategies was the optimal block or fetch size increased significantly over the default case. Although these strategies are able to significantly reduce miss ratios in time-independent simulations, they are unable to achieve the full performance benefit suggested by the reduction in the miss ratio because the full benefit is obtained only under very specific temporal conditions. For instance, if prefetched data has not arrived by the time it is needed, then not all of the potential benefit is achieved. Complicated fetch strategies fail to live up to expectations for two fundamental reasons. First, only when the bus utilization is in the neighbourhood of 50% are there sufficient resources to make a significant dent in the memory's contribution to the overall execution time. Second, and more significantly, they are hampered by the strong temporal clustering of cache misses. For example, for the default caches, even with a block/fetch size of 64W, 50% of all misses occur within 16 instructions of the previous miss. Furthermore, instruction and data cache misses are strongly cross-correlated. Given that both an instruction and a data reference are being initiated on the same cycle, and if one flavour of miss has occurred in that cycle, then the probability that the other flavour also occurred is up to 4.2 times the overall miss ratio for the other variety. Fundamentally, the difficulty in designing a fetch strategy that significantly improves on the simple case is that when it is clear what should be fetched in order to reduce the miss ratio, chances are that there is not enough time to fetch it, and when there is plenty of time available between cache misses, it is unclear what should be fetched next.

The problem in dealing with each of the organizational parameters individually is that the three sets of tradeoffs are intertwined: the optimal cache size depends on the block size and set associativity; the set-associative break-even times depend on the block size and memory system, and so on. The last section of Chapter 4 conquers this problem by considering cache design as a whole. The plots of lines of constant performance, as in Figure 4-4, can be thought of as cross-sections of the surfaces of constant performance in the four-dimensional cache design space. Since changes in the organizational and memory system parameters can be translated into equivalent changes in the cache size, all the various cross-sections of interest can be mapped to one set of curves. This is done in Figure 4-35 – the most important figure in this book (See page 105). The mapping of all the various cross-sections is done two ways. The various relevant combinations of set associativity and block size are accounted for by their own separate sets of X and Y axes. All the different main memory systems are accounted for via the notion of effective cache size. A change in the cache miss penalty can be equated to a change in the cache size that has the identical effect on performance. Thus the difference between a system's actual cache miss penalty and the standard cache miss penalty on which the chart is based is equivalent to the difference between the cache's actual size and its effective size. The system's relative execution time is read off the chart by finding the system's cycle time and effective size on the appropriate set of axes and finding the value of the execution time surface at the intersection point that they define.

Figure 4-35 allows the direct comparison of caches across a large portion of the four-dimensional split cache design space for virtually any memory system. This figure enables us not only to ascertain which of several organizations performs best, but to directly measure the performance increment between the resulting systems. To some extent, the cache comparison chart can also account for other fetch strategies and write policies, but these procedures are more awkward and subject to inaccuracies.

It would appear that this unified graph makes the analysis of the individual tradeoffs inconsequential. This is not so. An understanding of the influences of the block size, set size and cache size on performance has two benefits: first, it facilitates an early pruning of the design space, so that only caches likely to be competitive are fleshed out for more detailed analysis; second, it builds an awareness of the underlying processes that is the foundation on which designers' intuitions and predictions of future trends are based.

The tradeoffs exposed in Chapter 4 imply that efficient CPU/cache pairs with short cycle times are not good design points and that there is an upper bound to the performance attainable with a single-level hierarchy. Specifically, the slopes of the lines of constant performance are very large for small caches. That means that it is likely that a larger, slower cache could be built that performs better overall. Also, because the slopes of the lines of constant performance tend towards zero for large cache sizes, at any given point in time there is a cache at which the performance is maximized. A larger cache cannot be built without excessively degrading the cycle time, and all smaller caches have too high a miss ratio. The same applies to the set associativity and block size. At any particular moment, there is a single-level cache organization that cannot be improved upon: the best organization shifts with changes in the available implementation technologies. Chapter 5 explores the possibilities of breaking this performance barrier and of improving the optimality of short cycle time machines through the use of multi-level cache hierarchies. Basically, short cycle times become optimal if small caches are optimal. Small caches are better than large caches if and only if the cache miss penalty is small: on the order of a few cycles total. By introducing one or more levels of cache between the primary cache and main memory, the optimality of a short cycle time machine with a small cache is improved. The machine's maximum performance is improved both because the optimal cycle time is reduced and because the total cycle count is reduced.

One of the most significant results presented in Chapter 5 is that a cache's global miss ratio can be approximated by its solo miss ratio if the immediate upstream cache is at least four to eight times smaller. In this case, the smaller cache does not have much influence on the data resident in the larger one, and as a result, the reference stream below the larger cache is independent of the existence of the smaller cache. In other words, the presence of the upstream cache reduces the number of references reaching the cache. In doing so, it reduces the number of hits in a cache without significantly affecting the number of misses. These observations allow for an important decomposition and compaction of the general memory hierarchy design problem. Once the execution time is phrased in terms of the global cache miss ratios, and the appropriate approximations are made, we can apply all of our intuition and knowledge about the behaviour of the solo cache miss ratio to multi-level hierarchies.

The design of a cache as part of a multi-level system is then attacked in the same way as the single-level problem before it: the problem of designing a cache as part of a larger hierarchy is explored one organizational parameter at a time. Section 5.3.2 begins by showing that the presence of an upstream cache dramatically shifts the lines of constant performance to the right, noticeably increasing the optimal cache size. Specifically, the slope of the lines of constant performance are multiplied by the inverse of the upstream cache's global miss ratio. Linear dependence on the cache miss penalty and the weak dependency of the optimal cache size on the workload remain from the single-level case.

The presence of an upstream cache has a more significant impact on the viability of set associativity. The break-even implementation times are also multiplied by the inverse of the upstream cache's global miss ratio. For a small to moderate sized upstream cache, this easily produces break-even implementation times greater than 10ns. The greater the depth in the hierarchy, the greater the viability of set associativity as a mechanism for improving performance. Since the upstream caches handle most references that would have hit in a cache, further down in the hierarchy, there is a greater emphasis on a low cache miss rate over a short cache hit time.

The selection of the block and fetch sizes are basically unaffected by the presence of an upstream cache. As in the single-level case, the optimal fetch size is to first order still solely dependent on the product latency and transfer rates from the next level in the hierarchy.

Section 5.4 then shows how dynamic programming can be used to select the performance-optimal hierarchy from a pool of potential caches without having to evaluate a large number of possible combinations. Again, the knowledge gained about the individual tradeoffs is useful in pruning the number of potential caches to reduce the effort involved in finding the optimal hierarchy. With suitable constraints, the same modified dynamic programming algorithm can be used to find the best single-level hierarchy and, consequently, the maximum performance improvement that can be attained by investing more hardware in the memory hierarchy. In a detailed example in Section 5.5, a three-level hierarchy is found from a group of 14 candidates; the performance level attained is twice that possible with a single-level cache. The first-level cache size is only 2KB because its miss penalty was only three cycles. The final level is four-way set-associative.

Chapter 5 concludes with an exploration of a power function model of the miss ratio as a function of the cache cycle time. The optimal number of levels in the hierarchy increases slowly as the main memory access time increases with respect to the minimum CPU cycle time. Depths of four and five are predicted when the ratio of the two is about 50. For a single-level cache, the degradation between the minimum and optimum CPU cycle time increases alarmingly with the relative main memory speed. However, for depths greater than or equal to two, the CPU cycle time remains less than 2.5 times the minimum specified in the model. Most of the performance advantage of multi-level hierarchies is obtained by increasing the depth from one to two. The additional performance improvement gained with depths greater than three is very small.

6.2. The Implications of Performance-Directed Cache Design

6.2.1. Real-Life Cache Design

A great many of the issues facing a designer of a machine destined for the marketplace are rarely mentioned in papers about cache design. Performance is only one of several goals and constraints that machine designers must deal with on a routine basis. This book focuses on execution time because it is easily quantifiable, and it is the metric most commonly used to judge final designs. More often than not, however, the optimization of performance is limited by immutable constraints in several of the other primary factors: cost, power, size, marketability, design time and the availability of parts. Alternatively, the mandate can be for a machine with a fixed cost and with a given cost performance ratio. Missing either specification, by being either high or low, could either hurt the sales of other products or leave too large a gap in the product line.

Possible inflexible constraints on the design include the maximum power dissipation rating of an IC package or cabinet, the maximum total power dissipation tolerable in the target environment, the largest manufacturable die or PC board, and the need to conform to a particular form factor.[37] These factors all limit the amount of hardware that can be applied to the CPU and the cache hierarchy.

Maximizing the performance of a system given a constraint on the number of transistors in the CPU and first-level caches is a difficult problem. This is the problem currently facing microprocessor designers. It is complicated by the division of resources between the CPU and cache subsystems. Allocating more area to the caches may improve the miss rate, but only at the expense of the base CPI. High performance floating point in particular can consume a great deal of hardware that may or may not be better off allocated to the memory subsystem.

Power dissipation is a crucial aspect of high performance system design. Many technologies used to build VLSI circuits, and ECL in particular, have the

---

[37] PC board size and shape.

interesting characteristic that increasing the power level decreases the gate delays. Since the power budget of most large integrated circuits will not permit running all the gates at a power level necessary to approach the minimum gate delay, the allocation of power is an integral part of determining the cycle time of the system. This applies to the caches as well as to the CPU and FPU.

Manufacturing frequently imposes cost-oriented constraints on the design. Aside from the cost of the parts, how they are to be assembled can dramatically affect the assembly yield, test time and maintenance costs. All of these can adversely affect a highly cost sensitive or high volume product. One way in which manufacturability is generally improved is by limiting as much as possible the total of number of different parts in a design. Ensuring the availability of parts is equally important. A requirement that all possible parts be second sourced[38] can be one of the most frustrating constraints for a designer intent on maximizing performance.

But cost is by far the most common constraint that computer system designers have to deal with. At a time when the cost of processing power is falling at an unprecedented rate, even apparently insignificant costs can be important, depending on the nature of the product and the marketplace into which it is going to be thrust. Lifetime product costs are strongly influenced by field service costs. Design for serviceability, like design for testability, is an important, yet often ignored, indirect means for improving the competitiveness of a product.

Chapters 4 and 5 ignored possible limitations on the amount of hardware available for the implementation of the caches, instead focusing on the unrealistic problem of maximizing performance regardless of implementation cost. Assuming that each of the candidate caches is individually implementable within all the real design constraints, specific aggregate constraints on the amount of hardware would disallow certain combinations of candidate caches or limit the depth of the hierarchy. Unfortunately, the one-pass hierarchy selection algorithm of Section 5.4 cannot properly deal with this sort of cumulative constraint. The search for the optimal implementable hierarchy must consist of continually evaluating and discarding hierarchies until a hierarchy is found that satisfies all such constraints.

Marketing and engineering organizations frequently have an adversarial relationship. They are often at odds over the goals, constraints, and schedules of a project. As a machine designer, it is frustrating to be told that a machine must incorporate some feature to improve a single benchmark, or worse, because some competitor's machine has either the feature or its inverse. These arguments

---

[38]Be available from more than one vendor.

have long been applied to set associativity, and soon they will be applied to other aspects of memory hierarchy design. Hierarchy depth parity, irrespective of the optimality of the performance or efficiency of the design, may become a sales and marketing tool, just as scoreboarding was in 1988 [Hinton 88, Manuel 88, Tomasulo 67].

There is another important dimension of cache design that has been ignored in most academic treatises, including, for the most part, this book: the need to provide operations other than read and write [Cho 86]. Many of these operations invariably come with a significant cycle time penalty. The most significant of the secondary, yet indispensable, operations is the cache flush. Regardless of the virtual or physical nature of the cache, some or all of the cache entries need to be flushed on a context switch, a change of the memory map or a recycling of a process identifier. A wide variety of implementation options are available, depending on the size and organization of the cache. The extreme with the minimum hardware impact forces the CPU to flush the cache by successively accessing all the sets that need to be invalidated. One common technique near the other extreme is to use special RAM chips with a bulk clear for the tags or valid bits. Unfortunately, there is usually a speed or size penalty associated with such parts, when compared with the most recent regular SRAMs.

There is also a need to have some references, especially data references, bypass the cache. This can be specified either on a per-page basis, via a processor mode bit, or it can be encoded into the physical address. The requirement for uncached references stems from I/O devices and the need to access their registers unambiguously. Caching of I/O device registers, particularly in a write-back environment, forces device driver writers to perform the equivalent of figure skating's quadruple axle jump: the very best can do it, but they would much rather not try in competition. Cache flushing and uncached references often together play a role in the solution to the boot problem: how the machine begins executing when its cache is uninitialized.

Parity checking has become the norm for large caches built of SRAMs. Error detection is becoming increasingly common in integrated caches as well. If done carelessly, incorporation of parity generation and checking logic into the data paths can add significantly to the cycle time. The control problem that comes with a detected parity error is even more delicate. Depending on the intended end uses of the machine, valid behaviour varies from a machine check [DEC 80], to an automatic retry and a switch to a duplicate copy of the cache or CPU. The performance-directed tradeoff is the balance between the system cycle time and the performance hit associated with either a soft or hard failure in a single word or large portion of the cache, coupled with the presumed frequency of such events.

For I/O to be handled properly and efficiently, the cache designer must interact with the virtual memory architect and the operating system designer. There are two basic approaches to the problem of ensuring a consistent view of main memory in the presence of I/O activity: 1) designing an I/O consistent cache and 2) managing the movement of I/O data through the cache in the operating system. With the first approach, all I/O operations query the cache as well as main memory. If the cache contains old data that is being overwritten by fresh data, the old data is invalidated or replaced. On an output operation, if a write-back cache contains a more recent value than the main memory does, the cache must preempt main memory and deliver the most recent value to the output device. With the second approach – software enforced I/O consistency – the operating system must ensure that on an input operation, no stale values remain in the cache after they are overwritten in main memory. On an output operation, the operating system must make certain that main memory contains the most recent values of all written locations being sent to the output device. This can be accomplished either through the use of special cache flush and invalidate instructions,[39] or strictly through the use of read and write operations. Software management of direct-mapped caches is simplified by the observation that using cached writes to zero out a page in memory removes from the cache all data from pages with the same cache tag bits.

The ability to test a cache can also be critically important. The data paths necessary to arbitrarily and unambiguously stimulate and query the data, tag, valid, dirty and parity bits can be quite awkward to incorporate into the design. The difficulty can arise particularly in integrated environments from the apparent need to provide a dedicated bus joining the data and address portions of the cache control so that the tag array can be exercised. The addition of a single additional multiplexor to the read access path can take a substantial bite out of the overall cycle time. Some processors provide mechanisms to allow the CPU to test the caches under program control, while others include special counters, pattern generators and checkers to exercise the cache bits automatically.

Large integrated caches on the same chip as the CPU frequently have the same redundancy options as standard SRAMs. At wafer sort, prior to the silicon wafer being cut up into individual chips for assembly, each die is tested. In particular, the RAM arrays are exercised. If there are a few small portions of an array that are bad, a redundant portion can take the place of the bad portion by having a few fuses blown. This, too, requires extra paths and control logic. Care must be taken to ensure that the read and write timing for the replaced section is the same as for the rest of the RAM.

---

[39]An invalidate instruction or cache operation marks as invalid all blocks in the cache that match a given address or address range. A flush instruction is an invalidate instruction that also writes to main memory any dirty words before they are invalidated.

Split I/D organizations aggravate many of these complications. Testing and flushing the instruction cache may be particularly painful since some of the useful data paths that are needed to handle writes are not normally present on that side of the CPU. In addition, in a multi-level cache hierarchy, each of these secondary requirements extends to each of the layers, regardless of their sizes and configurations.

High-speed caches made out of discrete SRAMs are constrained by a unique set of concerns. The width of available RAMs determines the loading on the address lines. The size of the cache and the size of the SRAMs determine the number of chips needed to implement it, which in turn determines its physical dimensions. As the number of chips involved increases, the loading on the address lines increases, as does any time-of-flight delays on data and tag busses. The loading on the various busses and the time-of-flight delays can play important roles in determining the difference between the access time of the SRAMs, as specified on their datasheet, and real minimum cycle time of the cache. As noted in Section 4.2, multiplexors and latches are particularly expensive in a discrete cache.

CPU chip designers have always worried about pin counts. Limits in the number of pins can restrict the organization of any off-chip caches or the transfer rate into any on-chip caches. The limitation in the total chip bandwidth is one of the primary motivations for migrating caches on-chip as cycle times decrease and performance goals increase.

All of these various effects combine to seriously degrade the cache cycle time from the basic RAM access time. Though there are some exceptions [Freitas 88, Garner 88, Tanksalvala 90, Roberts 90], typically, the access times of the cache RAMs take up about half of the machine cycle time [Clark 87, Wilhelm 87].

6.2.2. Rules of Thumb for Cache Designers

This section summarizes the results for single- and multi-level caches into a succinct list of rules based on the results presented in Section 6.1 that may help machine designers probe the design space and make some early global decisions.

Guideline 1:
Cache size dominates the other organizational parameters in determining performance just as it does in determining miss rates.

Block size and set associativity are relatively minor factors compared with the cache size. In situations of limited area or power, concentrate on data bits over tag bits by increasing the block size.

> **Guideline 2:**
> **For a single-level cache hierarchy, optimal cache sizes are likely to be in the 32KB to 128KB range, depending on the relationship between cache size and cycle time. Also, after any cycle time penalty is accounted for, set-associative caches seldom perform better then their direct-mapped counterparts.**

As the cache size drops below 32KB, the slope of the lines of constant performance increases dramatically. Much below this level, it is inevitable that slowing the machine down in order to achieve a larger cache size will be warranted. Similarly, cache sizes above 128KB total do not make much sense if there is any cycle time penalty. If your processor can cycle faster than a 32KB cache, consider a multi-level hierarchy to reduce the optimal cache size and the performance-optimal cycle time.

The set-associativity break-even implementation times are often too small to warrant the implementation of set-associative caches for performance reasons. For anything other than very small caches or very long cache miss penalties, the break-even implementation times are consistently less than the cycle time penalty associated with a MSI implementation of large sets. Even with on-chip caches, where the cycle time penalty is generally less, set-associative caches are not necessarily better than the direct-mapped caches of the same size.

> **Guideline 3:**
> **Focus on the fetch size rather than the block size. Typically, fetch sizes of 4, 8 or occasionally 16 words are best, depending on the memory characteristics. Simple fetch strategies with the right fetch size make very good use of the available memory bandwidth.**

Most of the traditional performance improvement due to increases in the block size really stems from the accompanying increase in the fetch size. The best fetch size is a function of the memory characteristics. The block size is more appropriately selected in conjunction with the write-strategy. Since cache misses are very tightly clustered in time and across reference streams, complicated fetch strategies have difficulty doing better than a simple fetch strategy with the appropriately selected fetch size.

Guideline 4:
> **To clarify design tradeoffs, translate prospective changes in the associativity and block size into equivalent changes in the cycle time or cache size.**

This idea is the basis behind the cache comparison chart, Figure 4-35. It allows the straightforward performance evaluation of widely differing cache organizations.

Guideline 5:
> **To increase the performance beyond that possible with a single-level cache, or to decrease the size and cycle time of the optimal first-level cache, investigate multi-level cache hierarchies.**

Single-level cache hierarchies have an upper limit to their performance. They also have a discouragingly large optimal size (greater than 32KB). As CPU cycle times improve with respect to main memory access times, multi-level cache hierarchies present a route to higher levels of performance and optimal hierarchies involving small caches with short cycle times.

Guideline 6:
> **The final cache in a multi-level cache hierarchy is likely to be somewhat bigger and more set-associative then the optimal single-level cache for the same memory system.**

This rule derives from the analysis of Section 5.3. The block size remains unaffected by any upstream caches; there is a moderate pull to increasing cache sizes as the upstream cache becomes more effective; and the set associativity break-even times are multiplied by the inverse of the previous cache's global miss rate.

Guideline 7:
> **First-level caches smaller than 8KB, with a short cycle time, are viable only if a second-level cache can be built that has a significantly lower miss rate and an access time that is no more than two or three times the CPU cycle time.**

Without cache miss penalties of two or three cycles, the curves of constant performance do not shift enough to make these small caches good designs. To accomplish this, the second-level cache may have to be in the same basic technology as the primary cache and the CPU. Even with such short miss penalties, caches below 1KB are a very dubious choice, regardless of their cycle time.

Guideline 8:
Design the memory hierarchy in tandem with the CPU.

It is an easy trap to fall into: design the CPU, shrink its cycle time as much as possible, then design the best cache possible that can cycle at the same rate. If either the cache or CPU must be designed first, it should be the cache. Look at the resources available to it and determine what attainable cycle time and size pair yield the highest performance. Then build the CPU with whatever resources are left. Better yet, consider the whole problem: the system design. Partition the resources among the various functional units so that they are all matched in cycle time and together they yield the best overall system-level performance.

Guideline 9:
Mistrust broad, sweeping, guidelines.

The empirical results presented in this book are fine for pruning the design space and selecting a few caches or cache hierarchies for detailed simulation and analysis, but the best choice is very dependent on the workload and a wide variety of organizational and competitive factors mentioned briefly in the previous section. The specific numerical results of Chapters 4 and 5 are based on a single set of eight traces and a small set of hardware configurations. Variations due to workload, fetch strategy, write policy and the location of address translation can significantly affect the results. Verify all results for your particular environment and assumptions.

6.3. Suggestions for Further Research

As has been noted several times, this book explores only a small portion of the overall cache design space. Several regions of the design space have yet to be explored from the perspective of performance-directed hierarchy design.

The most significant variable that has been fixed in all of the experiments and analyses throughout this book has been the write strategy. Investigation of the performance impact of variants of write-through and write-back caches is definitely warranted. The experiments with multi-level cache hierarchies indicate that the need for write buffering varies with the cache depth and characteristics. There are also some tantalizing hints regarding the flow of dirty data through the hierarchy towards main memory. Tracking and analyzing this movement will lead to a better understanding of write strategy design.

Another major variable that has not been discussed at all is the location of address translation. Particularly for large direct-mapped caches, the miss rate differences between a virtual and physical cache can be significant. This difference needs to be balanced with the cycle time implications of serial or parallel address translation before the performance implications can be properly attributed. Memory management in general is one of several system issues, such as I/O traffic, process scheduling, and code and data sharing, that can subtly affect the memory system.

The interaction between cache layers needs to be carefully examined. It would be interesting to know precisely how and why the miss rate of a downstream cache is affected by the presence of an upstream cache; measures of the spatial and temporal localities as a function of upstream cache size would probably be illuminating.

Another interesting tradeoff exists between the CPU and cache hierarchy: given limited overall resources, what is the appropriate balance between hardware spent on the two portions of the system's design? As mentioned in the previous section, this is a difficult problem worthy of further study.

If the cache design is properly influencing the cycle time decision, CPU designers are now potentially confronted with an additional resource: more cycle time. If CPUs are generally too fast for their caches, computer implementors should reconsider what architectural and organizational changes will allow effective use of time to increase overall performance.

Naturally, the faction of the research community actively investigating cache coherent multiprocessors should also adopt performance as their primary metric. A detailed comparison of the various protocols on the basis of expected cycle time penalty and of effectiveness at reducing the miss and traffic ratios would be significant. This might stop the trend towards ever more complicated cache consistency protocols.

One major concern regarding the empirical data presented throughout this book is distinct from all these cache design issues. Computer usage today is very different from that of ten years ago: programs and the problems they solve have grown immensely. Operating system and multiprocessing characteristics have also changed dramatically. Though the traces used to generate the graphs are sizable and representative of contemporary applications, it is impossible to tell how long they will remain relevant. Though this issue is addressed in Appendix A, it remains unclear whether the tradeoffs in memory hierarchy design will shift enough over the course of time to invalidate the empirical results in Chapters 4 and 5. There is a pressing need to quantify the likely changes to long- and short-term spatial and temporal localities of reference of programs so that we can predict the evolution of the cache design and its optimal solution.

Appendix A

Validation of the
Empirical Results

A man's most valuable trait is a judicious sense of
what not to believe.

— Euripides

This appendix discusses the validity of the empirical results presented in
Chapters 4 and 5. Confidence in the numerical results depends on the credibility
of the traces used to generate them: this appendix focuses on the traces as the
main source of uncertainty in the conclusions of those chapters. The two sets of
traces were used as stimulus to the simulation models: the four VAX
architecture traces and four R2000 architecture traces are briefly described in
Section 3.2. Following a description of how these traces were generated and
their individual strong points and shortcomings, the appendix concludes with a
discussion of the wisdom of combining all eight traces to form a single basis for
evaluation of caches and memory hierarchies. Part of that discussion is an
exploration of the relationship between code density and instruction miss ratio.

A.1. The VAX Traces

The VAX traces were generated using ATUM [Agarwal 86], a technique for
capturing address traces applicable to some microcoded machines. Agarwal

altered the microcode of a VAX 8200 to write to memory the virtual addresses of all data and instruction references. Periodically, tracing is halted while the memory reserved for the trace data is dumped to disk. Since only a finite amount of memory is reserved for the trace data, each snapshot of system execution is limited to 400,000 contiguous references before a disk transfer is necessary. In his thesis, Agarwal developed a measure of the similarity of different snapshots based on the working set sizes. This similarity measure is used to decide the validity of concatenating those shorter trace fragments to form larger ones [Agarwal 87b]. Each of the four VAX traces, *mu3sp0* through *savecsp0*, is comprised of three or four individual snapshots taken within a short time of one another.

The numerical results presented primarily in Chapters 4 and 5 are based on warm-start measurements. The first portion of the trace, prior to the warm-start boundary, is used to initialize and fill the cache. The miss rate and execution time statistics are reported for the second portion of the trace, from the warm-start boundary until the end of the trace. The selection of the warm-start boundary between the initialization phase and the measurement period balanced the conflicting desires to have confidence that steady state behaviour has been reached before data collection is begun and the importance of accumulating data over as many references as possible. Agarwal noted that the number of references needed to reach steady state in the miss rate increases with cache size. As the cache size increases and the number of non-stationary or compulsory misses[40] becomes a larger proportion of the total, the number of references needed to reach steady state becomes dependent on the frequency of references to new blocks – blocks not previously referenced in the trace. Figures A-1 and A-2 plot the cumulative distribution of references to new blocks for a block size of one word. The absence of any distinct knee to these curves indicates that the exact placement of the warm-start boundary is not important, provided that it is sufficiently large to ensure that steady state is achieved in the intrinsic and extrinsic components of the miss ratio for small and medium sized caches. Based on these requirements, the warm-start boundaries were chosen to be 450,000 references. The horizontal lines through the graphs of Figures A-1 and A-2 show the number of unique blocks or addresses touched prior to the warm-start boundary. The tick marks along this line indicate context switches.

---

[40] See Section 3.4 for a description of Agarwal's breakdown of misses into three categories: non-stationary, intrinsic and extrinsic. In his thesis, Hill classifies misses as either compulsory (those due to first reference), capacity related (a miss encountered by a fully associative cache of a specified size) or conflict (a miss in a set-associative or direct-mapped cache not experienced by its fully associative counterpart) [Hill 87].

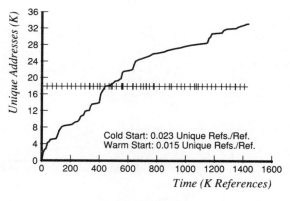

mu3sp0

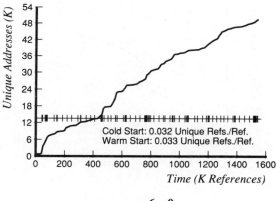

mu6sp0

Unique References as a Function of Time: VAX Traces

Figure A-1

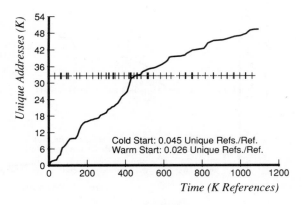

mu10sp0

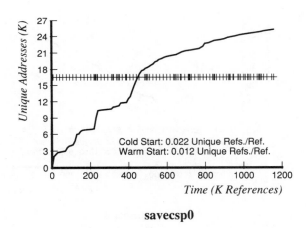

savecsp0

Unique References as a Function of Time: VAX Traces (cont.)

Figure A-2

A.2. The R2000 Traces

The original four VAX traces were augmented with four RISC machine traces for two main reasons. First, these four traces alone are too small to be sure that the observed measurements were not the result of peculiarities of these particular traces and the programs that they represent. Second, by introducing additional traces generated on a different computer, it was possible to look for and possibly factor out architectural effects. In addition to increasing the validity and general confidence level, the applicability of the results as a whole was increased. The final section of this appendix examines some of those architectural differences reflected in the traces and their effects on the various tradeoffs exposed in Chapters 4 and 5.

The four R2000 traces were derived from address traces of the user references of six programs. The uniprocess address traces were obtained by adding code to each basic block to emit the effective address of each load or store and the start of each basic block [Killian 86]. By unwinding the basic blocks into streams of instruction references and appropriately interleaving the data references, the reference stream seen by the cache and memory subsystems was reproduced.

The six programs used to generate these traces were chosen as representative of the activity on personal engineering workstations: a mixture of unix utilities, text processing and CAD programs. An edit session (*emacs*), a C compile (*ccom*), a text search (*grep* and *egrep*), and text formatting (*troff*) each had realistic input characteristic of typical daily usage of the author's MicroVAX in 1987. The two CAD tools were a MOS switch-level simulator (*irsim*) and a program that analyzes address traces (*analyzer*). Again, both were solving real problems while tracing was enabled. Execution times varied from 1.1 million instructions (*grep*) to 801 million references (*analyzer*). Figures A-3 through A-5 display the total of the instruction and data spaces as a function of execution time of these programs. The curves expose two important characteristics: first, programs commonly touch most of their total instruction and data space shortly after beginning execution, and second, the ratio of unique addresses to references is quite small overall. It is not uncommon for a program to touch the vast majority of its instruction and data spacing within the first few percent of its execution time.

For each of the programs, a tracing start point was randomly selected. For all but the *grep* and *egrep* programs, the starting points were beyond the initial start-up period. Seven uniprocess traces were generated by capturing the one million references following the start point for each program. After measuring the distribution of context switch intervals in the VAX traces, the RISC traces were synthesized by multiplexing between the selected uniprocess traces so that

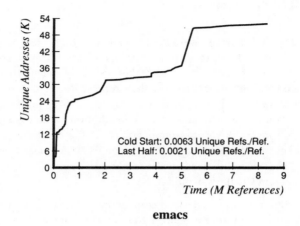

emacs

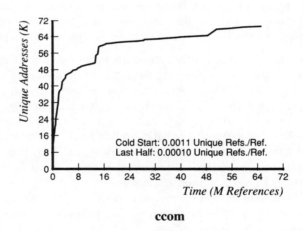

ccom

Unique References as a Function of Time: Entire Programs

Figure A-3

the distribution was duplicated. For two of the traces, *rd2n4* and *rd2n7*, the average time slice was kept the same as that of the VAX traces (16,000 references), and for the other two, *rd1n3* and *rd1n5*, the average interval between context switches was doubled to 32,000 references. The number of active processes was varied from three through seven according to Table 3-1 on

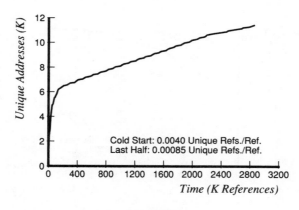

egrep

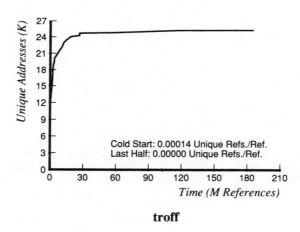

troff

Unique References as a Function of Time: Entire Programs (cont.)

Figure A-4

page 34. Unfortunately, there was no mechanism by which operating system references could be gathered on the M/1000 machine used to generate the uniprocess address traces.

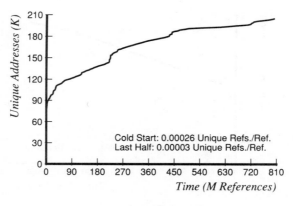

analyzer

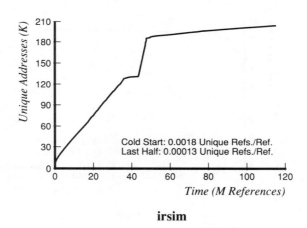

irsim

Unique References as a Function of Time: Entire Programs (cont.)

Figure A-5

For some time, cache designers have struggled with nagging doubts regarding the validity of trace-driven simulations of large caches [Thiebaut 88]. As cache sizes have increased with improvements in implementation technologies, the traces used to stimulate the models have increased as well. But as seen in Figures A-1 and A-2, there is a severe problem of diminishing returns with increasing trace length. For the VAX traces, each of which is over a million references, the total size of the instruction and data spaces ranges between 100KB and 200KB. It is difficult to believe that the miss rates for these traces will be realistic for caches greater than 128KB. For a 1MB cache, at most 20% of the sets will have been used by the end of the trace. Since the number of unique addresses in a trace is a slowly growing function of the trace length, even if statically larger programs are simulated, impractically long traces would have to be used to ensure credible miss rates for large caches.

However, one can construct traces for a given application that have demonstrably realistic miss rates for all cache sizes. If the contents of the cache at the warm-start boundary of the simulation are identical to the cache contents in a real system, then the measured miss ratio for the remainder of the simulation run will be the same as the real miss ratio that would be observed in a running system for that same reference stream. The problem with most trace generation techniques is that the cache contents at the warm-start boundary are just an approximation of the actual cache contents at any particular time. While that approximation is accurate for small caches, its faithfulness declines as the cache size increases. For a uniprocess simulation, the correct cache residency can be obtained by keeping track of all addresses that the program has touched up to the point that trace generation begins. If references to all those addresses are added to the front of the address trace, then the contents of the cache will be correct regardless of its size and regardless of the depth of the cache hierarchy. To ensure that at the start of the trace proper each set has the correct memory block resident, the prepended references must start with the least recently used addresses and conclude with the most recently used. Since the number of unique addresses is small compared with the number of references prior to the start of tracing, the number of references that need to be prepended to accurately initialize that cache is tolerably small. Finally, if reads and writes to the same address are treated separately, then the correct blocks and sub-blocks will be dirty at the start of the real address trace, regardless of the write strategy and cache organization.

This idea of prepending initialization references can be extended to multiprocess traces by multiplexing the initialization references of each of the processes in the final trace. If the individual trace prefixes are interleaved according to the same distribution of context switch intervals used for the trace proper, the desired context switch behaviour can be simulated right back to the beginning of each program's execution. This is possible since the time of the most recent access to each memory location is maintained for all locations touched by each program between the start of execution and the start of trace generation.

Figures A-6 and A-7 show the unique reference activity for the resulting four R2000 traces. The bilinear nature of the traces differentiates the cache initialization phase, before the warm-start boundary, and the actual address trace, with its much lower rate of growth in the address space. Notice that this rate of growth in the address space for the four R2000 traces, which corresponds to the miss rate for an infinite sized cache with a block size of one word, is comparable to the growth rate of whole program executions (Figures A-3 through A-5); the growth rates of the VAX traces are much higher. This indicates that for large caches, the miss rates for VAX traces would be significantly higher than are seen in a real system.

A.3. Combining the R2000 and the VAX Results

As mentioned in Chapter 3, the numerical results presented in this book are based on the geometric mean of results of the four VAX traces and the four R2000 traces. This section examines the propriety of combining those two sets of results, and some of the differences between them. The two groups of traces will be compared on the basis of both their miss ratios as a function of cache and block size, and the cache comparison chart that they yield individually. It is safe to conclude that the quality of the empirical results is improved by using both sets of traces together.

Figure A-8 displays the miss rates for the two sets of traces and the combined miss rate for all eight. The block size is fixed at one word as a reference, and the caches are direct-mapped and split I/D. For each cache size there are two range bars that indicate the range of miss rates within the two sets of traces: just to the left of each data point is the range for the R2000 traces for that size, and the bar on the right indicates the maximum and minimum with the four VAX traces. The number indicated by each name in the key is the absolute minimum miss rate, based on the number of new blocks touched while statistics are being gathered. Where this compulsory miss rate is within the range of this and the following graphs, it is indicated by a faint horizontal line. The slight difference between the two sets for cache sizes less than 132KB total stems from the instruction stream, since the data miss rates are essentially identical across the entire range of cache sizes.

Each of the two sets of traces has a significant flaw: the miss rates for the VAX traces are unrealistic for large caches, and the RISC traces suffer from a lack of operating system references. We expect the miss rates for the VAX traces to be artificially high for large caches, while the miss rates for the R2000 traces would be worse if system references were included [Agarwal 87b]. The strength of each of these two factors can be observed in other set of traces.

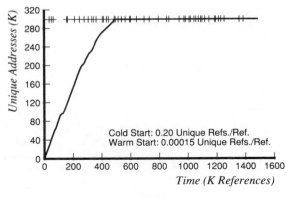

rd1n3

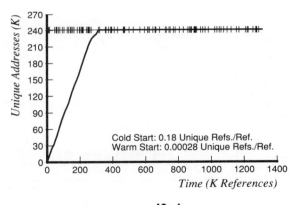

rd2n4

Unique References as a Function of Time: R2000 Traces

Figure A-6

Figure A-9 shows the overall read miss ratio for the four R2000 traces with and without the accurate initialization of the cache contents prior to data gathering. For the dashed line, the first half of the trace is used to initialize the cache, and data is gathered over the second. Again, error bars indicate the ranges encountered: the leftmost being with the initialization references prepended, the

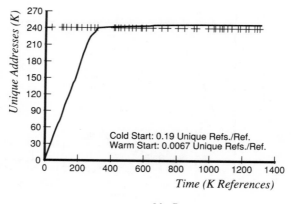

rd1n5

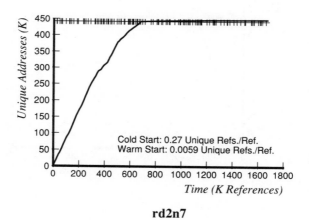

rd2n7

Unique References as a Function of Time: R2000 Traces (cont.)

Figure A-7

rightmost being without them. It is apparent that there is a difference for cache sizes less than 64KB total. However, as the cache size approaches a megabyte and beyond, the percentage difference between the actual and approximate miss rates becomes significant, even though the magnitude of the difference is quite

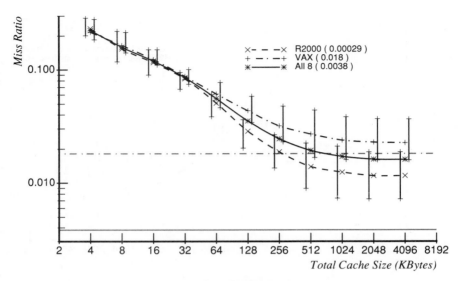

VAX and R2000 Miss Ratios

Figure A-8

small in this portion of the design space. The cache initialization affects the instruction and data streams similarly.

Figure A-10 shows the miss rates for the VAX traces with and without the system references. Since the proportion of the system to user references is almost the same as the ratio of the system to user unique references, the compulsory miss rate is essentially unaffected. Thus the relative difference between the two decreases as the cache size gets very large and a larger proportion of the miss rate is due to compulsory misses.

The R2000 traces without the initialization references and the VAX traces with system references are comparable: only architectural and workload differences remain. Figure A-11 plots those two sets of traces and their geometric mean. Below 64KB the architectural difference dominates, indicating consistently higher miss rates for the RISC machine. This is consistent with the results of some earlier studies of instruction traffic ratios [Mitchell 86]. For the large caches, though, differences between the workloads are more substantial. The significantly lower compulsory miss rates for the R2000 traces indicates that the programs represented in the VAX traces touch a greater number of unique instruction and data locations per reference. The difference in the

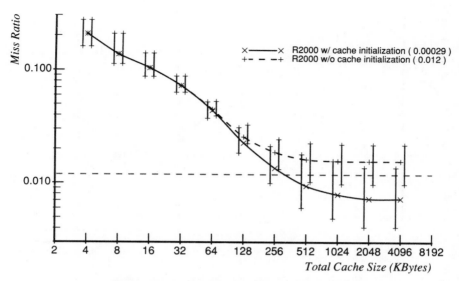

R2000 Miss Ratios with and without Cache Initialization

Figure A-9

compulsory rates accounts for all of the difference between their overall read[41] miss rates for large caches.

Interestingly, as the block size increases, the R2000 traces improve relative to the VAX traces so that for block sizes greater than two words, the RISC machine exhibits lower miss ratios. Figure A-12 shows the equalized miss rates for a block size of four words. Below 128KB, the mean of the miss ratios for the R2000 traces is between 10% and 23% lower than that of the VAX traces. Though this may seem counter-intuitive – it has been argued that machines with tighter instruction encodings should always have better miss ratios – application of the techniques used in Chapter 4 illustrates the reason for the flip.

Steenkiste has shown that given a uniform expansion in the code by a factor of ρ between two architectures, M_1 and M_2, the number of misses experienced by two caches $C_1(C,A,B)$ and $C_2(\rho C,A,\rho B)$ will be the same [Steenkiste 88]. He assumes that both the dynamic and static code sizes increase identically in the transition from M_1 to M_2. Since the number of word instruction references is ρ times larger for the second architecture, its miss rate is also ρ times smaller:

---

[41] Recall that a read is defined to be either a load or an instruction fetch.

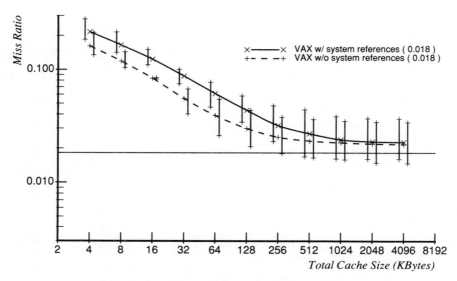

VAX Miss Ratios with and without System References

Figure A-10

$$m(\ \mathbf{C}_1(C,A,B)\ ) \ = \ m(\ \mathbf{C}_2(\rho C,A,\rho B)\ )\times\rho \qquad\qquad [A.1]$$

We have seen in Section 4.1 that a change in cache size results in a fairly constant proportional decrease in the miss ratio over a reasonably large range of cache sizes. If we denote K to be the proportional decrease due to a doubling of the cache size,[42] then the ratio of rates across a non-binary increase in cache size is K raised to the fractional increase in size:

$$\frac{m(\ \mathbf{C}(\rho C,A,B)\ )}{m(\ \mathbf{C}(C,A,B)\ )} \ = \ K(B)^{\rho-1}$$

Similarly, the characteristics of the relative change in the miss ratio due to a doubling of the block size, $R(B)$, are exposed in Figure 4-15 and Equation 4.6.

---

[42] Figures 4-1, A-8 and A-11 show K to be independent of the cache initialization and system reference issues. K is a weak function of the block size, varying from 0.69 for a block size of one word to 0.63 for a block size of 32 words.

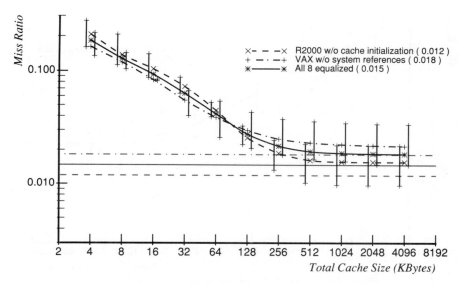

Equalized VAX and R2000 Miss Ratios: Block Size = 1 Word

Figure A-11

We can postulate the continuous equivalent, $R'(\rho,B)$, to be the miss ratio ratio across a non-binary change in the block size. Since $R'(\rho{=}1,B)=1$, and $R'(\rho{=}2,B)=R(B)$, the continuous miss ratio ratio, R', is $R(B)$ again raised to the fractional increase in program size:

$$R'(\rho,B) = R(B)^{\rho-1}$$

Equation A.1 combines the cache and block size effects to predict the ratio of the miss ratios for the two caches and architectures:

$$\frac{m(\ \mathbf{C}_1(C,A,B)\ )}{m(\ \mathbf{C}_2(\rho C,A,\rho B)\ )} = \rho \times K(B)^{\rho-1} \times R(\rho C,B)^{\rho-1}$$

Figure A-13 plots this ratio of miss ratios for a variety of block sizes and code expansion factors for a unified 2KB cache. The solid lines are the miss ratio ratios as computed using the above formula, while the dotted line is the observed

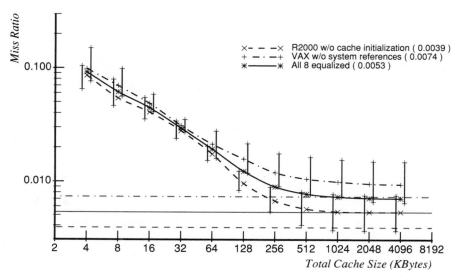

Equalized VAX and R2000 Miss Ratios: Four Word Block Size

Figure A-12

ratio of the mean VAX miss ratio to the mean R2000 miss ratio, for a 2KB total split I/D cache. The dynamic code size expansion between these two architectures is about 2.0, depending on the program [MIPS 87]. The differences between the calculated and measured values stem from a variety of factors: non-uniform expansion between the two architectures due to radically different instruction sets and the use of optimizing compilers, variation in behaviour between unified and split caches, and differing workload dependencies on block size.

Contrary to popular belief, this graph shows that RISC machines do have lower miss ratios than CISC machines. Though the total amount of memory traffic may be lower for the CISC machine, the fact that it is making fewer instruction references means that its miss ratio can be higher. RISC machines, with their longer basic blocks, derive greater benefit from larger block sizes, reducing and eventually eliminating the difference in miss ratios. It is important to remember that since the number of instruction references is different, the instruction miss ratio alone is not a particularly meaningful architectural metric for the evaluation of different instruction encodings.

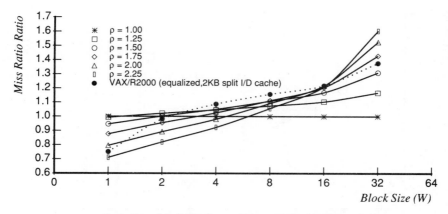

Code Density Miss Ratio Ratio (2KB Unified Cache)

Figure A-13

For very large caches, the architectural miss ratio ratio stops being dependent on the block size. In this region of the design space, architectural characteristics are overshadowed by trace characteristics. The VAX traces are "larger" in the sense that they touch more unique user-level instruction addresses per reference than the RISC traces. This larger active instruction address space is reflected in the larger compulsory miss rate, which is indicated by the faint lines in Figure A-11.

Both sets of traces reach plateaus in their miss ratios for caches above 1MB. Other researchers have argued that as the cache size increases, the miss rate continues to decline and ultimately reaches zero for infinitely large caches [Stone 90, Singh 88]. They have concluded that very long traces, in excess of 100M references, are needed to accurately and reliably measure caches over about 512KB [Borg 89]. There are several important considerations for the simulation of large caches that warrant discussion. First of all, in this domain, the virtual or physical nature of the cache plays a large role in number of extrinsic conflict misses. The similarity in the usage patterns of the virtual address space across processes means that unhashed virtual direct-mapped caches, such as those simulated for Chapters 4 and 5, experience many more misses than their hashed or physically-indexed cousins [Agarwal 88]. This also explains the increase in the benefit due to set associativity for large caches that is apparent in Figure 4-5. Furthermore, the system model inherently assumed that the caches are not I/O coherent, so that processes not sharing any code or data pages begin their lives resident only in main memory. The validity of this assumption when applied to a real system depends primarily on a couple of factors: whether I/O affects the cache as well as main memory, and how physical pages are cleared between their use by different processes. In systems in which processes do not have an opportuntity to migrate into the cache before they begin to execute, the miss rate cannot be zero because the number of compulsory misses needed to bring the code and initial data into the cache is not zero.

Another important concern is the statistical significance of the observed miss ratio. Since the conficence interval about the mean of a set of observations is related to the sample size, it is important to simulate enough references so that the desired confidence interval is significantly smaller than the measured miss rate [Lapin 83]. The calculation is complicated by the fact that misses are highly correlated between sets and that the distribution of refences among sets is highly skewed. In very large virtually-addressed caches, most of the references, and most of the misses involve a very small proportion of all of the sets. This helps increase the confidence level for the observed miss ratio within the sets and for the cache as a whole.

Though it has been demonstrated that these miss rates are representative for this mix of applications on these virtually addressed caches, the questions that have yet to be answered are whether this is a reasonable set of programs and whether this is a useful class of caches. If the applications are too small or if the caches are unrealistic, then the question becomes how would larger applications behave differently on other caches, and how would that behaviour affect the cache design tradeoffs. Let us consider those questions separately.

The applications in both the VAX and R2000 traces are a mix of small utilities, such as *grep* and a directory search, larger system programs, such as compilers and text formatters, and a few large CAD applications, such as *rsim* and *spice*, solving real problems. These programs and their input decks are typical of current workstation usage. However, the major trend over the last few years in programs being run by this class of machines is the rapid increase in the size and complexity of the application programs. Much more dramatic than the increase in their object files is the ongoing explosion in their data space sizes. As this class of applications continues to grow with machine capacity, this one component of the eight traces will become unrepresentative. The rate of change of this class of programs and their relative importance to computer systems design will determine how quickly the specific empirical results presented in this book will become suspect.

Assume then that the application programs represented in the traces are too small. The question then is how would the overall miss ratios and performance differ if larger problems were traced, perhaps for a longer period of time. Miss ratios are determined by small and large scale program characteristics. An example of local behaviour is the distribution of the instruction run length between taken branches, whereas the amount of code encompassed by the program's largest loop is a global attribute. The local characteristics of the instruction and data streams are not likely to change much unless a radically different programming paradigm becomes widely used. The more global characteristics, such as total data size, will change much more. The miss rates for small caches are more affected by the shorter term characteristics, and so the miss rates for this region of the design space should not change too much over the long term. Poorer large-scale locality should decrease the incremental improvement with increases in the cache size because an increase in the overall working set size will mean that each increment in size will be able to capture a smaller portion of the outstanding working set. For very large caches, the compulsory miss rate will eventually be reached, though presumably at a larger cache size than before. Increasing algorithmic complexity translates to an increase in the amount of computation per datum. This in turn should decrease the data stream compulsory miss rate because more instructions will be executed between each increase in the data size. The instruction stream compulsory miss rate should remain unchanged, depending on whether the increased code size is matched by the increase in the mean interaction count per loop caused by a general increase in the problem size. The combined effects will be that as working sets increase, a moderately lower compulsory miss rate will be reached at a larger cache size.

The net result of this trend will be to flatten the lines of constant performance and to move the knee of the curves out to larger caches. Small slopes would, in some cases, reduce the optimal single-level cache size. More slope for the largest cache sizes would increase the viability of caches above 1MB in multi-level hierarchies. In general, larger program sizes will have the effect of speeding the introduction of three- and four-level memory systems. As is discussed in Section 5.6, decreasing the rate of change in the miss rate as a function of cycle time or cache size increases the relative merits of a multi-level hierarchy over a single-level cache.

We concluded above that the plateau in the miss rate observed for very large cache sizes was primarily the result of the virtual, unhashed nature of the caches and the particulars of the system model. Other systems, running different programs could easily reach their plateau at lower miss ratios – conceivably as low as zero, given the right set of hardware. However, it is important to realize that none of the major conclusions of Chapters 4 and 5 are significantly altered for such systems. The slope of the lines of performance flatten out to zero slope regardless of whether it is because the miss rate stops changing or because the change stops having an effect on the performance. At most, the curves could retain a nominal slope for another binary order of magnitude or two before becoming effectively flat. The set-associativity break-even times are related to the ratio of miss ratios across the changes of associativity, regardless of whether or not the miss ratios are still declining with further increases in cache size. Finally, the web of points that define the optimal block/fetch size stops edging to the right when the miss ratio stops declining with increasing cache sizes. If the miss ratio didn't stop declining, the web would shift a small additional amount, but not sufficiently to cause a noticeable change in the best binary-sized block size for those very large caches. The same lines of reasoning apply to caches within a multi-level cache hierarchy. Fundamentally, whether or not the miss ratio continues to decline for extremely large caches does not consequentially influence any of the primary design tradeoffs.

The theme of this book is performance-directed cache evaluation. Thus far, however, the two sets of traces have been compared from the perspective of miss ratios alone. The ultimate test of their similarity is their effect on the Cache Comparison Chart of Section 4.4 (Figure 4-35). Figures A-14 and A-15 are the charts derived from the four VAX and R2000 traces, respectively. The two are remarkably similar. The lines of constant performance are virtually identical in shape and vertical position. In Figure A-14, based on the VAX traces, the lines of constant performance are shifted by about three-quarters of a binary order of magnitude to the right compared to the lines in Figure A-15. This shift indicates that a VAX implementation needs a cache almost twice as large to obtain the same fraction of its best-case performance at a given cycle time. However, the best-case performance improves with increasing code density because fewer instruction references are needed to complete a program. At any given combination of cache size and cycle time, the slope of the line of constant performance is greater for the VAX traces, and thus the regions of slope are shifted towards larger cache sizes. Because the miss rate is lower, for a direct-mapped cache with a block size of four words, the optimal cache size will be slightly smaller for the RISC machine. For the smaller block sizes, where the VAX has smaller miss rates, the R2000's optimal cache size would be the larger of the two, given identical cycle times and speed-size choices.

The two sets of traces also react differently to changes in associativity. These differences manifest themselves as a slight warping of the various horizontal axes across the two figures. Increases in set associativity only cause a noticeable difference for the largest cache sizes. This is because the R2000 traces have a much more significant improvement in miss ratio for increases in associativity for large cache sizes. This is a result of the virtual nature of the caches and the common virtual address reference patterns among the different processes.

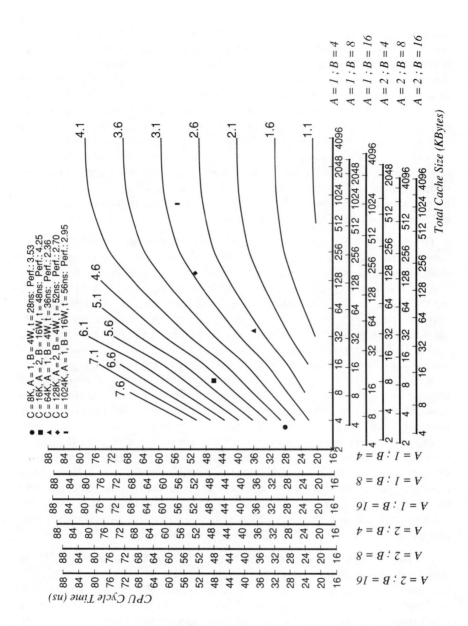

Cache Comparison Chart: VAX Architecture

Figure A-14

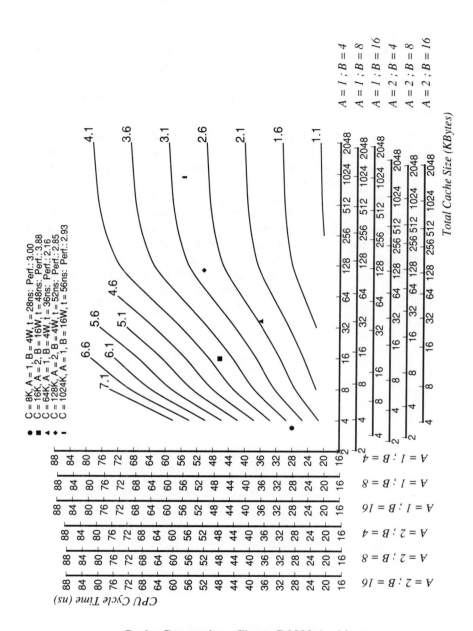

Cache Comparison Chart: R2000 Architecture

Figure A-15

A more intuitive way to view this shift is that at a given cache size or cycle time, the lines of constant performance are closer together for the VAX architecture. This means that a doubling of the cache size is equivalent to a smaller change in cycle time, and it is easier to obtain the same percentage improvement in performance by improving the cycle time as compared to the cache size.

The fact that the two sets of traces produce similar cache comparison charts validates combining them. Using the mean of all eight traces as the basis for the numerical results presented in the body of the book has two advantages. First, by using a larger number of traces, the results are less dependent on the peculiarities of any one trace. The results are thus more likely to be applicable to a variety of general purpose environments. The weaknesses that exist in either set are compensated for by the other, resulting in a data set that is reliably applicable to a wide region of the cache design space. Second, by combining traces from two different architectures, some of the architectural effects are factored out. Those architectural differences are individually exposed in Figures A-14 and A-15, where they can be examined separately from the organizational issues central to memory hierarchy design.

Appendix B

Modelling Write
Strategy Effects

True ease in writing comes from art, not chance.

– Alexander Pope

At first glance, the model used throughout this book to analytically predict the performance of a multi-level hierarchy is naive in its treatment of writes. This appendix justifies the treatment of writes in the first and subsequent levels of the cache hierarchy by showing that the simple model described in Section 3.4 is adequately accurate.

The multi-level performance model was introduced as Equations 3.4 and 3.10. Together, they equate the total execution time to the product of the CPU cycle time and total cycle count, which in turn is equal to the total number of cycles doing reads, plus the number of cycles doing writes into the first level of the hierarchy. On the other hand, the time to do reads has a component for each level of the hierarchy: being the product of the level's read access time and the previous level's global miss ratio.

$$T_{Total} = N_{Read}\left(t_{L1} + M_{L1}(C_{L1}) \times t_{L2} + M_{L2}(C_{L2}) \times t_{L3}\right.$$

$$\left. + \cdots + M_{Ln}(C_{Ln}) \times t_{MMread}\right) + N_{Write} \times t_{L1} \times \bar{n}_{L1write}$$

The contribution due to writes is equal to the number of writes multiplied by CPU or L1 cycle time (t_{L1}) and the average number of CPU cycles needed to satisfy a write request into the L1 cache, $\bar{n}_{L1write}$. There is no accommodation for variations in total cycle count as a result of variations in the write policy at any but the first level of the hierarchy.

This model adequately accounts for the writes for the class of machines under consideration in this book. The class of machines under study was explicitly limited in Section 3.2 to those with one particular aggressive write strategy: all the caches are write-back, with write buffering between all caches and main memory. Each buffer has a depth of four and a width equal to the block size of the upstream cache. The delay through the write buffer is such that a read miss is handled at the next level before the write-back that it generates. A write into a cache is assumed to take twice as long as a read, since the tags must be checked before the data array is written.

With this write policy, there are only two ways in which writes anywhere in the hierarchy can affect the total cycle count. The primary contribution is in the form of writes into the L1 cache. A particular write's contribution to the total execution time depends on both the basic organization and the state of the machine when the write is issued. If the machine has a unified first-level cache, then both write cycles must always be accounted for in the total cycle count. If, on the other hand, the machine has a split I/D L1 cache, a write's contribution can be two, one or zero cycles, depending on whether there is a simultaneous instruction fetch issued, and if so, whether the instrcution fetch hits or misses in its cache. If the write missed in the cache and caused a write-back, then at least one additional cycle is needed to put the old dirty data into the write buffer before the issued write can complete. This write-miss penalty would be substantially greater if a fetch-on-write policy were used. These write cycles, which are accounted for in the model, can constitute a significant proportion of the total execution time.

Beyond the first level of the hierarchy, all write operations are write-backs, so the second mechanism by which write operations can affect the total execution time occurs if a write-back in progress causes a read to be delayed because the cache is busy. It is this effect, this delaying of read requests by writes in progress, that is not modelled in the above equation. However, given the aggressive write strategy used, this delay constitutes a small fraction of the total execution time and so can safely be ignored.

To illustrate the accuracy of the model with respect to writes, Figure B-1 dissects the cycle count for the default two-level system (see Figure 3-6) stimulated with the *rd2n4* trace. The solid bars classify all cycles into one of three categories: execute cycles, exposed write cycles in the L1 cache, and L1 cache miss cycles. Recall that the CPU model used, described in Section 3.3.2, mimics a pipelined RISC machine capable of issuing simultaneous instruction and data references on each execute cycle. The execute cycles are those during which the CPU is not waiting on the memory hierarchy. In this situation, the only writes that contribute to the total execution time are those that are paired with an instruction fetch that hits in the instruction cache. For these writes, only the second write cycle and any write-back cycles contribute to the execution time. With the relatively small 4KB L1 size used in this scenario, the number of write cycles is substantially smaller than the number of cache miss cycles. The L1 write cycles are of two varieties, indicated by the third and fourth bars from the bottom on the histogram. The vast majority are the second cycles of the writes themselves. The cycles due to write-backs caused by the writes constitute less than 0.2% of all the cycles. So the average number of cycles per L1 write cycle, $\overline{n}_{L1write}$ of the model above, is almost the number of cycles per write minus one, multiplied by the instruction cache *hit* ratio. Finally, the contribution of write references to the total cycle count can be accurately calculated by multiplying this quantity by the CPU cycle time:

$$N_{Write} \times t_{L1} \times \overline{n}_{L1write} = N_{Write} \times t_{L1} \times (n_{L1write} - 1) \times (1 - M_{L1I})$$

To investigate the validity of ignoring the contribution of write-backs deeper in the hierarchy, the L1 cache miss cycles must be further broken down into subcomponents: the cycles spent interrogating the second-level cache, the time spent waiting for an L2 write to complete before an L1 read miss can be processed, and the time spent fetching data from main memory when there is an L2 read miss. Figure B-1 shows that the delays due to writes are less than a tenth of either of the other components of the L1 cache miss cycles, and about 4% of all the L2 cycles. These are precisely the delays omitted in the analytical model.

Similarly, the L2 miss cycles can be further decomposed into two types of delays in the main memory: time to actually fetch the needed data and time waiting for main memory to complete a write. These are shown as the top two bars in the Figure B-1. In this case, the write delays make up 20% of the main memory time. The relative increase in the proportion of the total delay that is attributable to writes compared with the other layers in the hierarchy results from two separate effects. First of all, the overall percentage of busy cycles due to writes increased. Smaller write-back caches are relatively better at reducing the write traffic ratio than the read miss ratio. Thus, with increasing depth, the number of read requests drops faster than the number of write requests, increasing the ratio of the two. Figures B-2 and B-3 are the cycle breakdowns

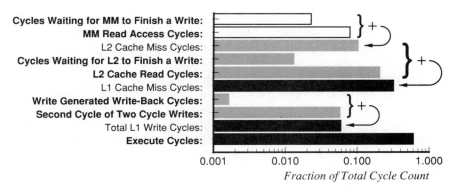

CPU Cycle Breakdown

Figure B-1

for the last two levels of the hierarchy. The sum of the solid bars is the total execution time, while the components whose titles are boldly printed contribute directly to the overall cycle count.

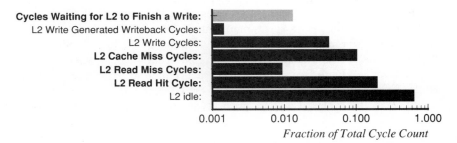

L2 Cache Cycle Breakdown

Figure B-2

The second and more significant reason for the greater contribution of the main memory's write delay to the execution time is that the ratio of its access time to its successor's access time is larger. In this scenario, the L2 read access time is three times that of the L1 cache's; when the recovery time is included, the main memory access time is more than 12 times the L2 access time. The

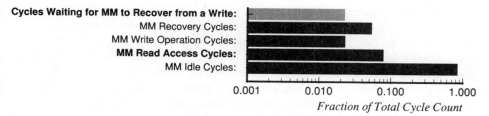

Main Memory Cycle Breakdown

Figure B-3

temporal clustering of cache misses exposed in Section 4.3.3 propagates down the hierarchy; this means that in times of heavy main memory use, it is more difficult to interleave the main memory writes between the L2 read misses. Despite the write buffering between memory and the L2 cache, a much higher proportion, 58%, of the main memory write and write recovery cycles end up displacing a read access and, consequently, increase the overall execution time. In contrast, 30% of the L2 write and write-back cycles show up in the final cycle count as read-delaying cycles. Fortunately, though, the main memory write delay cycles are only 2.2% of the total.

An alternative way of accounting for the cycles resulting from writes below the first level of the hierarchy is to equate their contributions to the execution time with changes in the appropriate miss ratios and cycle times. For instance, if writes into L2 writes took no time, then the execution time would decrease by 1.3%. This same reduction can be achieved by decreasing the L1 miss ratio by 6%. Even the 2.2% contribution of main memory writes can be equated to a relatively small 22% change in the L2 global miss ratio. The important observation is that these effective changes in miss ratio are much smaller than the differences in miss ratios observed among the eight traces used for the empirical results.

The question at issue is whether the lack of proper accounting of writes invalidates the analytical results. Since the range of miss rates and, consequently, the range of performance levels is much greater than the variation with and without the write cycles, any model that was otherwise accurate, but which failed to account for these write cycles, should still yield predictions within the range of empirical observations.

In conclusion, the analytical model of the performance attained by a multi-level memory hierarchy is adequate with respect to its treatment of writes because it accurately accounts for the write cycles at the first level of the hierarchy and because the write cycles at subsequent levels – that is, those that are not modelled – are inconsequential. They are inconsequential for two reasons: they represent a small percent of the total number of cycles for the class of systems considered in Chapters 4 and 5, and the uncertainty in the read miss rate resulting from variation in the workload is much greater than the error due to the omission of these cycles.

References

[Agarwal 86]   Agarwal, A., Sites, R., Horowitz, M.   ATUM: A New Technique for Capturing Address Traces Using Microcode. In *Proceedings of the 13th Annual International Symposium on Computer Architecture*, pages 119-129, Tokyo, Japan, June, 1986.

[Agarwal 87a]   Agarwal, A., Chow, P., Horowitz, M., Acken, J., Salz, A., Hennessy, J.   On-Chip Instruction Caches for High Performance Processors. In *Advanced Research in VLSI*, pages 1-24, Stanford University, Stanford, CA, March, 1987.

[Agarwal 87b]   Agarwal, A. *Analysis of Cache Performance for Operating Systems and Multiprogramming*. Ph.D. Thesis, Stanford University, May, 1987. Available as Technical Report CSL-TR-87-332.

[Agarwal 88]   Agarwal, A., Hennessy, J., Horowitz, M. Cache Performance of Operating System and Multiprogramming Workloads. *ACM Transactions on Computer Systems* 6(4):393-431, November, 1988.

[Agarwal 89]   Agarwal, A., Horowitz, M., Hennessy, J. An Analytical Cache Model. *ACM Transactions on Computer Systems* 7(2), May, 1989.

[Akeley 89]   Akeley, K.   The   Silicon   Graphics   4D/240GTX Superworkstation.   *IEEE Computer Graphics and Applications* 9(4):71-84, July, 1989.

[Alexander 86]   Alexander, C., Keshlear, W., Cooper, F., Briggs, F. Cache Memory Performance in a Unix Environment. *SigArch News* 14(3):41-70, June, 1986.

[Alpert 83]   Alpert, D. *Performance Tradeoffs for Microprocessor Cache Memories*. Technical Report CSL-TR-83-239, Computer Systems Lab., Stanford University, December, 1983.

[Alpert 84]   Alpert, D. *Memory Hierarchies for Directly Executed Language Microprocessors.* Ph.D. Thesis, Stanford University, 1984. Available as Technical Report CSL-TR-84-260.

[Alpert 88]   Alpert, D., Flynn, M. Performance Tradeoffs for Microprocessor Cache Memories. *IEEE Micro* 8(4):44-55, August, 1988.

[AMD 87]   *Am29000 User's Manual.* Advanced Micro Devices, Inc., Sunnyvale, CA, 1987.

[Archer 87]   Archer, D.W., Deverek, D.R., Fox, T.F., Gronowski, P.E., Jain, A.K., Leary, M., Miner, D.G., Olesin, A., Persels, S.D., Rubinfeld, P.I., Supnik, R.M. A CMOS VAX Microprocessor with On-Chip Cache and Memory Management. *Journal Solid State Circuits* SC-22(5):849-852, October, 1987.

[Archibald 86]   Archibald, J., Baer J.-L. Cache Coherence Protocols: Evaluation Using a Multiprocessor Simulation Model. *ACM Transactions on Computer Systems* 4(4):273-298, November, 1986.

[Atkinson 87]   Atkinson, R.R., McCreight, E.M. The Dragon Processor. In *Proceedings of Second International Conference on Architectural Support for Programming Languages and Operating Systems (ASPLOS-II)*, pages 65-71, October, 1987.

[Baer 87a]   Baer, J.-L., Wang, W.-H. *Architectural Choices for Multi-Level Cache Hierarchies.* Technical Report TR-87-01-04, Department of Computer Science, University of Washington, January, 1987.

[Baer 87b]   Baer, J.-L., Wang, W.-H. *On the Inclusion Properties for Multi-Level Cache Hierarchies.* Technical Report TR-87-11-08, Department of Computer Science, University of Washington, November, 1987.

[Bellman 57]   Bellman, R. *Dynamic Programming.* Princeton University Press, Princeton, NJ, 1957.

[Bennett 82]   Bennett, B.T., Pomerene, J.H., Puzak, T.R., Rechtschaffen, R.N. Prefetching in a Multilevel Hierarchy. *IBM Technical Disclosure Bulletin* 25(1):88-89, June, 1982.

[Berenbaum 87]   Berenbaum, A.D., Colbry, B.W., Ditzel, D.R., Freeman, H.R., McLellan, H.R., O'Connor, K.J., Shoji, M. CRISP: A Pipelined 32-Bit Microprocessor with 13-Kbit of Cache Memory. *Journal Solid State Circuits* SC-22(5):776-782, October, 1987.

[Borg 89]   Borg, A., Kessler, R.E., Lazana, G., Wall, D.W. *Long Address Traces From RISC Machines: Generation And Analysis.* WRL Research Report 89/14, Western Research Laboratory, Digital Equipment Corp., 1989.

[Cho 86]   Cho, J., Smith, A.J., Sachs, H. *The Memory Architecture and the Cache and Memory Management Unit for the Fairchild CLIPPER Processor.* Technical Report UCB/CSD 86/289, Computer Science Division, University of California, Berkeley, April, 1986.

[Chow 75]   Chow, C. K. Determining the Optimum Capacity of a Cache Memory. *IBM Technical Disclosure Bulletin* 17(10):3163-3166, March, 1975.

[Chow 76]   Chow, C. K. Determination of Cache's Capacity and its Matching Storage Hierarchy. *IEEE Transactions on Computers* C-25(2):157-164, February, 1976.

[Clark 83]   Clark, D.W. Cache Performance in the VAX-11/780. *ACM Transactions on Computer Systems* 1(1):24-37, February, 1983.

[Clark 87]   Clark, D.W. Pipelining and Performance of the VAX 8800 Processor. In *Proceedings of Second International Conference on Architectural Support for Programming Languages and Operating Systems (ASPLOS-II),* pages 173-178, IEEE, October, 1987.

[Cohen 89]   Cohen, E.I., King, G.M., Brady J.T. Storage Hierarchies. *IBM Systems Journal* 28(1):62-76, 1989.

[Cole 88]   Cole, C.B. Advanced Cache Chips Make the 32-Bit Microprocessors Fly. *Electronics* 60(13):78-79, June 11, 1988.

[Colglazier 84]   Colglazier, D.J. *A Performance Analysis of Multiprocessors Using Two-Level Caches.* Technical Report CSG-36, Computer Systems Group, University of Illinois, Urbana – Champaign, August, 1984.

[DEC 80]   *VAX Hardware Handbook.* Digital Equipment Corp., Maynard, MA, 1980.

[Denning 68]   Denning, P.J.   The Working Set Model for Program Behavior. *Communications of the ACM* 11(5):323-333, May, 1968.

[Duncombe 86]   Duncombe, R.R. *The SPUR Instruction Unit: An On-Chip Instruction Cache Memory for a High Performance VLSI Multiprocessor.*   Technical Report UCB/CSD 87/307, Computer Science Division, University of California, Berkeley, August, 1986.

[Easton 78]   Easton, M., Fagin, R. Cold Start vs. Warm Start Miss Ratios. *Communications of the ACM* 21(10):866-872, October, 1978.

[Edenfield 90]   Edenfield, R.W., Gallup, M.G., Ledbetter, W.B., Jr., Mcgarity, R.C., Qunitana, E.E., Reininger, R.A. The 68040 Processor: Part 1, Design and Implementation. *IEEE Micro* 10(1):66-79, February, 1990.

[Eggers 88]   Eggers, S., Katz, R. Characterization of Sharing in Parallel Programs and Its Application to Coherency Protocol Evaluation. In *Proceedings of the 15th Annual International Symposium on Computer Architecture,* pages 373-383, June, 1988.

[Freitas 88]   Freitas, D. 32-Bit Processor Achieves Sustained Performance of 20 MIPS. In *Proceedings of Northcon,* October, 1988.

[Fu 87]   Fu, J., Keller, J.B., Haduch, K.J. Aspects of the VAX 8800 C Box Design. *Digital Technical Journal* 1(4):41-51, February, 1987.

[Garner 88]   Garner, R., Agarwal, A., Briggs, E.W., Brown, D., Joy, W.N., Klienman, S., Muchnick, S., Namjoo, M., Patterson, D., Pendleton, J., Tan, K.G., Tuck, R. The Scalable Processor Architecture (SPARC). In *Digest of Papers, COMPCON 88,* pages 2-14, February, 1988.

[Gecsei 74]   Gecsei, J. Determining Hit Ratios for Multilevel Hierarchies. *IBM Journal of Research and Development* 18(4):316-327, July, 1974.

[Gindele 77]   Gindele, B.S.   Buffer Block Prefetching Method.   *IBM Technical Disclosure Bulletin* 20(2):696-697, July, 1977.

[Goodman 85]   Goodman, J.R. *Cache Memory Optimization to Reduce Processor/Memory Traffic.*   Department of Computer Sciences 580, Computer Sciences Department, University of Wisconsin – Madison, 1985.

[Goodman 87]   Goodman, J.R.   Coherency for Multiprocessor Virtual Address Caches. In *Proceedings of Second International Conference on Architectural Support for Programming Languages and Operating Systems (ASPLOS-II)*, pages 72-81, October, 1987.

[Gygax 78]   Gygax, G.   *Advance Dungeons and Dragons Players Handbook.* TSR Games, Inc., Lake Geneva, WI, 1978. Page 96.

[Haikala 84a] Haikala, I.J. Cache Hit Ratios with Geometric Task Switch Intervals. In *Proceedings of the 11th Annual International Symposium on Computer Architecture,* pages 364-371, June, 1984.

[Haikala 84b] Haikala, I.J., Kutvonen, P.H. Split Cache Organizations. In *Performance '84,* pages 459-472, 1984.

[Haikala 86]   Haikala, I.J. *Program Behaviour in Memory Hierarchies.* Ph.D. Thesis, University of Helsinki, 1986. Available as Technical Report A-1986-2.

[Hamacher 78] Hamacher, V.C., Vranesic, Z.G., Zaky, S.G. *Computer Organization.* McGraw Hill, New York, NY, 1978.

[Hattori 83]   Hattori, A., Koshino, M., Kamimoto, S.   Three-level Hierarchical Storage System for the FACOM M-380/382. In *Proceedings Information Processing IFIP,* pages 693-697, 1983.

[Hennessy 90] Hennessy, J.L., Patterson, D.A. *Computer Architecture: A Quantitative Approach.* Morgan Kaufmann, San Mateo, CA, 1990.

[Hill 84]   Hill, M.D., Smith, A.J. Experimental Evaluation of On-Chip Microprocessor Cache Memories. In *Proceedings of the 11th Annual International Symposium on Computer Architecture,* pages 158-166, June, 1984.

[Hill 85]   Hill, M.D., Eggers, S.J., Larus, J.R., Taylor, G.S., Adams, G., Bose, B.K., Gibson, G.A., Hansen, P.M., Keller, J., Kong, S.I., Lee, C.G., Lee, D., Pendleton, J.M., Ritchie, S.A., Wood, D.A. *SPUR: A VLSI Multiprocessor Workstation.* Technical Report UCB/CSD 86/273, Computer Science Division, University of California, Berkeley, December, 1985.

[Hill 86]   Hill, M.D., Eggers, S.J., Larus, J.R., Taylor, G.S., Adams, G., Bose, B.K., Gibson, G.A., Hansen, P.M., Keller, J., Kong, S.I., Lee, C.G., Lee, D., Pendleton, J.M., Ritchie, S.A., Wood, D.A., Zorn, B.G., Hilfinger, P.N., Hodges, D., Katz, R.H., Ousterhout, J., Patterson, D.A. Design Decisions in SPUR. *IEEE Computer* 19(11):8-24, November, 1986.

[Hill 87]   Hill, M.D. *Aspects of Cache Memory and Instruction Buffer Performance.* Ph.D. Thesis, University of California, Berkeley, November, 1987. Available as Technical Report UCB/CSD 87/381.

[Hill 88]   Hill, M.D. The Case for Direct-Mapped Caches. *IEEE Computer* 21(12):25-41, December, 1988.

[Hill 89]   Hill, M.D., Smith, A.J. Evaluating Associativity in CPU Caches. *IEEE Transactions on Computers* 38(12):1612-1630, December, 1989.

[Hinton 88]   Hinton, G., Riches, R., Jasper, C., Lai, K. A Register Scoreboarding Mechanism. In *IEEE International Solid-State Circuits Conference, Digest of Technical Papers,* pages 270-271, February, 1988.

[Horowitz 87]   Horowitz, M., Chow, P., Stark, D., Simoni, R., Salz, A., Przybylski, S., Hennessy, J., Gulak, G., Agarwal, A., Acken, J. MIPS-X: A 20 MIPS Peak, 32-Bit Microprocessor with On-Chip Cache. *Journal Solid State Circuits* SC-22(5):790-799, October, 1987.

[Jog 88]   Jog, R., Sohi, G.S., Vernon, M.K. *The TREEBus Architecture and Its Analysis.* Technical Report CS 747, Computer Sciences Department, University of Wisconsin – Madison, February, 1988.

[Jouppi 88]   Jouppi, N., Dion, J., Boggs, D., Nielsen, M.J.K. *MultiTitan: Four Architecture Papers.* WRL Research Report 87/8, Western Research Laboratory, Digital Equipment Corp., April, 1988.

[Jouppi 89]   Jouppi, N.P. Architectural and Organizational Tradeoffs in the Design of the MultiTitan CPU. In *Proceedings of the 14th Annual International Symposium on Computer Architecture,* pages 281-290, May, 1989.

[Karlovsky 89]   Karlovsky, S.R. *Automatic Management of Programmable Caches: Algorithms and Experience.* CSRD Report 892, Center for Supercomputing Research and Development, University of Illinois, Urbana – Champaign, July, 1989.

[Katz 85]   Katz, R.H., Eggers, S.J., Gibson, G.A., Hansen, P.M., Hill, M.D., Pendleton, J.M., Ritchie, S.A., Taylor, G.S., Wood, D.A., Patterson, D.A. *Memory Hierarchy Aspects of a Multiprocessor RISC: Cache and Bus Analyses.* Technical Report UCB/CSD 85/221, Computer Science Division, University of California, Berkeley, January, 1985.

[Killian 86]   Killian, E. pixie(1). UMIPS Man Page, MIPS Computer Systems, Sunnyvale, CA, 1986.

[Killian 88]   Killian, E. Miss Ratio Data as a Function of Cache and Block Sizes. Personal Communication, MIPS Computer Systems, Sunnyvale, CA, January, 1988.

[Kobayashi 89] Kobayashi, M., MacDougall, M.H.   The Stack Growth Function: Cache Line Reference Models. *IEEE Transactions on Computers* 38(6):798-805, June, 1989.

[Kohn 89]   Kohn, L., Fu, S.-W. A 1,000,000 Transistor Microprocessor. In *IEEE International Solid-State Circuits Conference, Digest of Technical Papers,* pages 54-55, February, 1989.

[Laha 88]   Laha, S., Patel, J.H., Iyer, R.K. Accurate Low-Cost Methods for Performance Evaluation of Cache Memory Systems. *IEEE Transactions on Computers* 37(11):1325-1336, November, 1988.

[Lapin 83]   Lapin, L.L.   *Probability and Statistics for Modern Engineering.* PWS Publishers, Boston, MA, 1983.

[Larson 78]   Larson, R.E., Casti, J.L.   *Principles of Dynamic Programming.* Marcel Dekker, Inc., New York, NY, 1978.

[Lee 87]   Lee, R.L., Yew, P.-C., Lawrie, D.H. *Data Prefetching in Shared Memory Multiprocessors.* CSRD Report 639, Center for Supercomputing Research and Development, University of Illinois, Urbana – Champaign, January, 1987.

[Liptay 68]   J. S. Liptay. Structural Aspects of the System/360 Model 85, Part II: The Cache. *IBM Systems Journal* 7(1):15-21, 1968.

[MacDonald 75] MacDonald, J.E., Sigworth, K.L.   Storage Hierarchy Optimization Procedure. *IBM Journal of Research and Development* 19(2):164-170, March, 1975.

[MacGregor 84] MacGregor, D., Mothersole, D., Moyer, B. The Motorola MC68020. *IEEE Micro* 4(8):101-118, August, 1984.

[Mahon 86]   Mahon, M.J., Lee, R.B.-L., Huck, J.C., Bryg, W.R. Hewlett-Packard Precision Architecture: The Processor. *Hewlett-Packard Journal* 37(8):4-22, August, 1986.

[Manuel 88]   Manuel, T. Taking a Close Look at the Motorola 88000. *Electronics* 61(9):75-78, April 11, 1988.

[Mashey 86]   Mashey, J.R. MIPS and the Motion of Complexity. In *Uniform Conference Proceedings,* , 1986.

[Matick 77]   Matick, R.E. *Computer Storage Systems and Technology.* John Wiley and Sons, New York, NY, 1977.

[Mattson 70]   Mattson, R.L., Gecsei, J., Slutz, D.R., Traiger, I.L. Evaluation Techniques for Storage Hierarchies. *IBM Systems Journal* 9(2):78-117, 1970.

[McCrosky 86]   McCrosky, C. *An Analytical Model of Cache Memories.* Technical Report 86-7, Department of Computational Science, Univeristy of Saskatchewan, 1986.

[McFarling 89]   McFarling, S. Program Optimization for Instruction Caches. In *Proceedings of Third International Conference on Architectural Support for Programming Languages and Operating Systems (ASPLOS-III),* pages 183-191, IEEE, April, 1989.

[MIPS 87]   MIPS Performance Brief. MIPS Computer Systems, Sunnyvale, CA, October, 1987.

[Mitchell 86]   Mitchell, C. *Architecture and Cache Simulation Results for Individual Benchmarks.* Ph.D. Thesis, Stanford University, 1986. Available as Technical Report CSL-TR-86-296.

[Miya 85]   Miya, E.N. Multiprocessor/Distributed Processing Bibliography. *SigArch News* 13(1):27-29, March, 1985.

[Moussouris 86]   Moussouris, J., Crudele, L., Freitas, D., Hansen, C., Hudson, E., March, R., Przybylski, S., Riordan, T., Rowen, C., Van't Hof, D. A CMOS RISC Processor with Integrated System Functions. In *Digest of Papers, COMPCON 86,* pages 126-131, March, 1986.

[Mulder 87]   Mulder, J.M. *Tradeoffs in Processor-Architecture and Data-Buffer Design.* Ph.D. Thesis, Stanford University, December, 1987. Available as Technical Report CSL-TR-87-345.

[Peng 89]   Peng, C.-J., Sohi, G.S. *Cache Memory Design Considerations to Support Languages with Dynamic Heapo Allocation.* Technical Report 860, Computer Sciences Department, University of Wisconsin – Madison, July, 1989.

[Pohm 83]   A. V. Pohm and O. P. Agrawal. *High-Speed Memory Systems.* Reston Publishing Company, 1983.

[Przybylski 88] Przybylski, S. *Performance-Directed Memory Hierarchy Design.* Ph.D. Thesis, Stanford University, September, 1988. Available as Technical Report CSL-TR-88-366.

[Puzak 85]   Puzak, T.R. *Analysis of Cache Replacement Algorithms.* Ph.D. Thesis, University of Massachusetts, February, 1985.

[Rao 78]   Rao, G. S. Performance Analysis of Cache Memories. *Journal of the ACM* 25(3):378-395, July, 1978.

[Rau 77a]   Rau, B.R., Rossman, G. The Effect of Instruction Fetch Strategies Upon the Performance of Pipelined Instruction Units. In *Proceedings of the 4th Annual International Symposium on Computer Architecture,* pages 80-89, June, 1977.

[Rau 77b]   Rau, B.R. *Program Behaviour and the Performance of Memory Systems.* Ph.D. Thesis, Stanford University, 1977.

[Rau 77c]   Rau, B.R. *Sequential Prefetch Strategies for Instructions and Data.* Technical Report CSL-TR-77-131, Digital Systems Laboratory, Stanford University, January, 1977.

[Roberts 90]   Roberts, D., Layman, T., Taylor, G. An ECL RISC Microprocessor Designed for Two Level Cache. In *Digest of Papers, COMPCON 90,* pages 228-231, February, 1990.

[Short 87]   Short, R.T. *A Simulation Study of Multilevel Cache Memories.* Master's Thesis, Department of Computer Science, University of Washington, January, 1987.

[Short 88]   Short, R.T., Levy, H.M. A Simulation Study of Two-Level Caches. In *Proceedings of the 15th Annual International Symposium on Computer Architecture,* pages 81-89, June, 1988.

[Sieworek 82]   Sieworek, R.R., Bell, C.G., Newell A. *Computer Structures: Principles and Examples.* McGraw Hill, New York, NY, 1982.

[Singh 88]   Singh, J.P., Stone, H.S., Thiebaut, D.F. *An Analytical Model for Fully Associative Cache Memories.* Research Report RC 14232 (#63678), IBM, November, 1988.

[Smith 77]   Smith, A.J. Two Methods for the Efficient Analysis of Memory Address Trace Data. *IEEE Transactions on Software Engineering* SE-3(1), January, 1977.

[Smith 78a]   Smith, A.J. A Comparative Study of Set Associative Memory Mapping Algorithms and Their Use for Cache and Main Memory. *IEEE Transactions on Software Engineering* SE-4(2):121-130, March, 1978.

[Smith 78b]   Smith, A.J. Sequential Program Prefetching in Memory Hierarchies. *IEEE Computer* 11(12):7-21, December, 1978.

[Smith 78c]   Smith, A.J. Sequentiality and Prefetching in Database Systems. *ACM Transactions on Database Systems* 3(3):223-247, September, 1978.

[Smith 79]   Smith, A.J. Characterizing the Storage Process and Its Effects on Main Memory Update. *Journal of the ACM* 26(1):6-27, January, 1979.

[Smith 82]   Smith, A.J. Cache Memories. *ACM Computing Surveys* 14(3):473-530, September, 1982.

[Smith 83]   Smith, J.E., Goodman, J.R. A Study of Instruction Cache Organizations and Replacement Policies. In *Proceedings of the 10th Annual International Symposium on Computer Architecture,* pages 132-137, June, 1983.

[Smith 85a]   Smith, A.J. Cache Evaluation and the Impact of Workload Choice. In *Proceedings of the 12th Annual International Symposium on Computer Architecture,* pages 64-73, June, 1985.

[Smith 85b]   Smith, J.E., Goodman, J.R. Instruction Cache Replacement Policies and Organizations. *IEEE Transactions on Computers* C-34(3):234-241, March, 1985.

[Smith 85c]   Smith, A.J. Problems, Directions and Issues in Memory Hierarchies. In *Proceedings of the 18th Annual Hawaii Conference on System Sciences,* pages 468-476, 1985.

[Smith 86]   Smith, A.J. Bibliography and Readings on CPU Cache Memories and Related Topics. *Computer Architecture News* 14(1):22-42, January, 1986.

[Smith 87a]   Smith, A.J.   Line (Block) Size Choice for CPU Cache
                 Memories.   *IEEE   Transaction   on   Computers*
                 C-36(9):1063-1075, September, 1987.

[Smith 87b]   Smith, A.J. *Design of CPU Cache Memories.* Technical
                 Report UCB/CSD 87/357, Computer Science Division,
                 University of California, Berkeley, June, 1987.

[So 88]   So, K., Rechtschaffen, R.N.   Cache Operations by MRU
                 Change. *IEEE Transactions on Computers* 37(6):700-709,
                 June, 1988.

[Sohi 87]   Sohi, G.S., Chiang, M.-C.   *Memory Organization for
                 Multiprocessors with Onchip Cache Memories.* Unpublished
                 Memo, Computer Sciences Department, University of
                 Wisconsin – Madison, January, 1987.

[Sparacio 78]   Sparacio, F.J.   Data Processing System with Second Level
                 Cache. *IBM Technical Disclosure Bulletin* 21(6):2468-2469,
                 November, 1978.

[Steenkiste 88] Steenkiste, P. The Impact of Code Density on Cache
                 Performance. 1988. In Preparation.

[Stone 90]   Stone, H.S.   *High Performance Computer Architecture.*
                 Addison-Wesley, Reading, MA, 1990. Second Edition.

[Strecker 83]   Strecker, W.D.   Transient Behavior of Cache Memories.
                 ACM Transactions on Computer Systems 1(4):281-293,
                 November, 1983.

[Tanksalvala 90] Tanksalvala, D., Lamb, J., Buckley, M., Long, B., Chapin, S.,
                 Lotz, J., Delano, E., Luebs, R., Erskine, K., McMullen, S.,
                 Forsyth, M., Novak, R., Gaddis, T., Quarnstrom, D., Gleason,
                 C., Rashid, E., Halperin, D., Sigal, L., Hill, H., Simpson, C.,
                 Hollenbeck, D., Spencer, J., Horning, R., Tran, H., Hotchkiss,
                 T., Weir, D., Kipp, D., Wheeler, J., Knebel, P., Yeter, J.,
                 Kohlhardt, C. A 90MHz CMOS RISC CPU Designed for
                 Sustained Performance. In *IEEE International Solid-State
                 Circuits Conference, Digest of Technical Papers,* pages
                 52-53, February, 1990.

[Thacker 86]   Thacker, C.P.   Cache Strategies for Shared-Memory
                 Multiprocessors. In *New Frontiers in Computer Architecture,*
                 pages 51-62, March, 1986.

[Thacker 87]   Thacker, C.P., Stewart, L.C.   Firefly: A Multiprocessor
                  Workstation.   In *Proceedings of Second International
                  Conference on Architectural Support for Programming
                  Languages and Operating Systems (ASPLOS-II)*, pages
                  164-172, October, 1987.

[Thiebaut 87a]   Thiebaut, D.F., Stone, H.S. Footprints in the Cache. *ACM
                  Transactions on Computer Systems* 5(4):305-329, November,
                  1987.

[Thiebaut 87b]   Thiebaut, D.F., Stone, H.S., Wolf, J.L. *A Theory of Cache
                  Behavior*.   Research Report RC 13309, IBM, November,
                  1987.

[Thiebaut 88]   Thiebaut, D.F., Stone, H.S., Wolf, J.L. *Synthetic Traces for
                  Trace-Driven Simulation of Cache Memories*.   Research
                  Report RC 14268 (#63748), IBM, December, 1988.

[Thiebaut 89]   Thiebaut, D.F.   On the Fractal Dimension of Computer
                  Programs and Its Application to the Prediction of the Cache
                  Miss   Ratio.   *IEEE   Transactions   on   Computers*
                  38(7):1012-1027, July, 1989.

[Thompson 87]   Thompson, J.G.   *Efficient Analysis of Caching Systems*.
                  Technical Report UCB/CSD 87/374, Computer Science
                  Division, University of California, Berkeley, October, 1987.

[Thompson 89]   Thompson, J.G., Smith, A.J. Efficient (Stack) Algorithms for
                  Analysis of Write-Back and Sector Memories.   *ACM
                  Transactions on Computer Systems* 7(1):78-116, February,
                  1989.

[TI 86]   *ALS/AS Logic Data Book*. Texas Instruments, Dallas, TX,
                  1986.

[Tomasulo 67]   Tomasulo, R.M.   An Efficient Algorithm for Exploiting
                  Multiple Arithmetic Units. *IBM Journal of Research and
                  Development* 11(1):25-33, January, 1967.

[Tucker 86]   Tucker, S.G. The IBM 3090 System: An Overview. *IBM
                  Systems Journal* 25(1):4-19, 1986.

[Vernon 89]   Vernon, M.K., Jog, R., Sohi, G.S. Performance Analysis of
                  Hierarchical   Cache-Consistent   Multiprocessors.
                  Performance Evaluation 9(4):287-302, August, 1989.

[Wang 88]   Wang, W.-H., Baer, J.-L., Levy, H.M. *Organization and
                  Performance of a Two-Level Virtual-Real Cache Hierarchy*.
                  Technical Report 88-11-02, Department of Computer
                  Science, University of Washington, November, 1988.

[Welch 78]   Welch, T.A.   Memory Hierarchy Configuration Analysis.
                  IEEE Transactions on Computers C-27(5):408-413, May,
                  1978.

[Wilhelm 87]   Wilhelm, N. Cache Design for the Titan Processor. Personal
                  Communication, Western Research Laboratory, Digital
                  Equipment Corp., October, 1987.

[Wilkes 65]   Wilkes, J.M.   Slave Memories and Dynamic Storage
                  Allocation.   *IEEE Transactions on Electronic Computers*
                  EC-14(2):270-271, April, 1965.

[Wilson 87]   Wilson, A.W., Jr.   Hierarchical Cache/Bus Architecture for
                  Shared Memory Multiprocessors. In *Proceedings of the 14th
                  Annual International Symposium on Computer Architecture*,
                  pages 244-252, June, 1987.

[Wong 88]   Wong, W.S., Morris, R.J.T.   Benchmark Synthesis Using
                  LRU Cache Hit Function. *IEEE Transactions on Computers*
                  37(6):637-645, June, 1988.

Index

Address traces 14
adwf 91
Agarwal, A. 17, 33, 41, 52, 126, 177
Analytical modelling 14, 26, 36, 52, 64,
   73, 80, 123, 151, 191, 201
Architectural differences 189
Associativity, degree of 11, 13
   (*see also* Set associativity)
ATUM 177
Average access time 15, 16

Background material 9
Balancing equation 36, 52, 124
Base scenario 29, 30, 69, 115, 202
Bibliography 13
Block size 10, 13, 22, 67, 130
   implementation 68, 132
   optimal size 68, 130, 163
   ratio of cache miss ratios 74, 191
Buddha 9
Bus utilization 94

Cache 9
Cache comparison chart 104, 197
Cache contents 185
Cache design problem 21, 159
Cache flush 170
Cache initialization 34, 185, 188
Cache miss 11
   temporal clustering 204
   temporal distribution 95
Cache miss ratio 13, 22, 46, 59, 69

compulsory miss ratio 189
global cache miss ratio 12, 115, 166
joint condition probability 96
local cache miss ratio 12, 26, 115
minimum miss ratio 186
solo cache miss ratio 12, 115
steady state 178
Cache selection algorithm 137
Cache size 10, 13, 22, 47
Candidate caches 135, 169
Capacity misses 178
Chow, C.K. 151
Clustering of cache misses 95, 117
Code density 33, 190, 197
Compulsory misses 178
Conflict misses 178
Context switch interval distribution 181
CPU cycle time 21, 47, 78, 137, 149
   minimum cycle time 55, 135, 152
   optimal cycle time 153
Cycle count 23, 37, 123, 137
Cycle time degradation 78, 113, 131,
   143, 163
Cycles Per Instruction (CPI) 3

Data stream 186
Decomposition of cache hierarchies 115
Design for testability 171
Direct-mapped cache 11, 57, 178
Dirty bit 11
Downstream cache 10, 26, 115
Dynamic programming 134

Dynamic RAMs 113

Effective cache size 104
Execution time 2, 21, 25, 36, 149, 201
    breakdown by cache level 119
Experimental limitations 175, 183, 195
Experimental method 21, 27, 160, 177
Extrinsic cache miss 41, 60, 178

Fetch size 11
    optimal size 163
Fetch strategy 12, 13, 90, 164
    early continuation 90
    fetch always 91, 98
    fetch on fault 91, 98
    prefetching 95
    wrapping fetch 90
First-level Cache 10
Fully associative cache 11, 178

Global cache miss ratio (*see* Cache
    miss ratio)
Guidelines for cache design 172

Hardware limitations 169
Harvard organization (*see* Split
    instruction/data cache)
Hierarchical independence 115, 130
Hierarchy depth parity 170
Hill, M.D. 17, 18, 59, 65, 66, 178

I/O considerations 170
Implementation constraints 168
Input traces 33, 177
Instruction stream 186
Intermediate cache design 115, 117
Intrinsic cache miss 41, 178

Killian, E. 78

L1, L1I, L1D, L2 10
Latency 23, 30, 38, 68
Levy, H.M. 17
Limits to performance 144
Line size (*see* Block size)
Lines of constant performance 49, 103,
    122, 133, 196
Local cache miss ratio (*see* Cache miss
    ratio)

Locality of reference 2
    (*see also* Temporal locality; Spatial
    locality)

Main memory 10, 30
    access time 38, 40, 51, 68, 113, 126,
    153
    interleaved writes 204
Main memory latency (*see* Latency)
Marketing issues 169
Maximum performance level 148, 149,
    151
Memory block 10
Memory hierarchy 10
    design space 136
Memory speed product 71
Method 21
Minkowski, H. 1
MIPS R2000 33, 181
Miss rate (*see* Cache miss ratio)
Miss ratio spread 59, 65
Miss ratio versus access time 150
MM 10
Multi-level cache hierarchy 10, 26, 111,
    154
Multiprocess traces 185
Multiprogramming 33

nbdwf 91
Non-stationary cache miss 41, 178

Open questions 175
Operating system references 186
Optimal cache organization 26, 36, 101,
    112, 165
Optimal cycle time (*see* CPU cycle
    time)
Optimal design procedure 137
Optimal memory hierarchy 15, 134, 146,
    149, 166
Optimal single-level hierarchy 154

Parity checking 170
Path length 2
Performance improvement 143
Performance-directed cache design 45,
    161, 176
Performance-optimal hierarchy
    (*see* Optimal memory hierarchy)

Physically addressed caches 57, 58, 175
Pixie 181
Pope, A. 201
Power function model 151, 167
Predecessor cache 10, 115
Prefetching (*see* Fetch strategy)
Primary cache 10

Ratio of cache miss ratios 65
Read miss (*see* Cache miss)
Read request 11
Real-life cache design 168
Regions of slope 50, 119
Replacement policy (*see* Replacement
  strategy)
Replacement strategy 12
  Least Recently Used (LRU) 12
  Random 12, 59
RISC versus CISC 193
Rules of thumb 172

Second-level cache 10
Secondary cache 10
Set 11
Set associativity 11, 17, 22, 57, 197
  break-even implementation time 127,
    134, 59, 62, 64
  implementation 57, 129
  (*see also* Associativity, degree of)
Set size 11
  (*see also* Associativity, degree of)
Sets, number of 22
Shakespeare, W. 21, 111
Short, R.T. 17
Simulator 27
Singh, J.P. 15, 54
Single-level performance limit 149, 166
Smith, A.J. 13, 16, 65, 66, 68, 75
Solo cache miss ratio 12
Spatial locality 2, 67
Speed – set size tradeoff 57, 127, 162
Speed – size tradeoff 47, 113, 118, 161
Split instruction/data cache 10, 144, 172
Steenkiste, P. 190
Stone, H.S. 15
Sub-block size 11
Successor cache 10, 115

Tag 10

Temporal locality 2
Terminology 9
Thiebaut, D.F. 15
Trace-driven simulation 26
Traffic ratio, read 12
Traffic ratio, write 12, 46
Transfer period 38
Transfer rate 23, 30, 68
Transfer size (*see* Fetch size)
Two-level caches 17, 30, 115, 203

Unified instruction/data cache 39, 144
Unique references 178
  per reference 181
  versus time 185
Upstream cache 10, 26, 115

VAX 33, 177
Virtual memory 57

Warm-start boundary 28, 33, 34, 178,
  185
Warm-start cache miss 41
Word 13
Working set 14, 184
Workload 14, 33, 160, 176, 194
Write buffers 30, 202
Write policy (*see* Write strategy)
Write request 11
Write strategy 30, 175
  fetch on write 202
  motivation 13
  performance effects 201
  write-back 12
  write-through 12
Write traffic ratio (*see* Traffic ratio,
  write)

DATE DUE

DEC 17			
NOV 9 REC'D			

Demco, Inc. 38-293